HYPNOTHERAPY
A PRACTICAL HAN

HYPNOTHERAPY
A PRACTICAL HANDBOOK

HELLMUT W.A. KARLE

JENNIFER H. BOYS

FREE ASSOCIATION BOOKS / LONDON

First published in Great Britain in 1987 by
FREE ASSOCIATION BOOKS
57 Warren Street, London W1T 5NR

A CIP catalogue record for this book is available
from the British Library

ISBN 0 946960 79 8 pbk

10 09 08 07 06 05 04 03 02 01
10   9   8   7   6   5

Printed in the European Union by
The Athenaeum Press, Gateshead, England

CONTENTS

Part I: Basic Techniques

1	Introduction	1
2	Nature of hypnosis	9
3	Induction	22
4	Deepening	44
5	Self-hypnosis	56
6	The first interview	66

Part II: Treatment Strategies with Adults

7	Habit disorders	83
8	Physical and psychosomatic disorders	101
9	Anxiety	116
10	Pain	131

Part III: Treatment Strategies with Children

11	Basic techniques	149
12	Habit and behaviour disorders	166
13	Physical disorders and pain	179
14	Anxiety and disorders of mood	188

Part IV: Hypnosis in Analytic Psychotherapy

15	Basic concepts	199
16	Uncovering techniques	216
17	Treatment strategies	232
18	Dissociation, multiple personality and ego state therapy	242
19	Other uses of hypnosis	257

20	Epilogue	271

Notes	277
Bibliography	290
Index of scripts	293
Index	296

HYPNOTHERAPY
A PRACTICAL HANDBOOK

PART I

BASIC TECHNIQUES

1

INTRODUCTION

This book, as its title indicates, is designed to be a practical guide to the use of hypnosis in therapy. It emerged from the first few years of the Hypnotherapy Workshops at the Bloomfield Clinic, Guy's Hospital, London, which were run by the authors, and the similar workshops they presented to psychiatrists in training at that hospital. The participants at these workshops found themselves presented with a fairly long list of expensive books, from which they would need to draw selectively. Over and again, they asked for scripts they could consult in the early stages of using hypnosis in their own clinical settings before developing the confidence and fluency that would enable them to work more spontaneously. They also expressed the need for a more direct and succinct account of treatment methods and strategies than they found in existing books.

The authors therefore put together the material they used in the workshops, adding to it substantially since the span of a book allows for more material than that of a series of workshops, and incorporating also much of the material that arose in the informal discussion sessions of those meetings. The approach is therefore very much on the lines of 'How to do it', although it is hoped always with a vivid awareness of the theory underpinning the approach. As a necessary consequence, it is assumed that the reader is familiar with the basic concepts of behaviour modification and of personality theory, and therefore rather less space is given to theoretical issues than is common in textbooks on psychotherapeutic techniques. This is even more the case in this book, since hypnosis or hypnotherapy is not a system of therapy but a technique or procedure by means of which therapy is delivered. Thus the theoretical aspects that are crucial, concern the ways in which hypnosis can be used therapeutically within the framework of whatever theory and practice of therapy the reader espouses, from behaviour modification to analytic psychotherapy. It is not intended to present the principles of any specific model of therapy, but to indicate ways in which hypnosis may be subsumed within any individual practitioner's current practices.

However, an exception had to be made to this general approach in chapter 15. Here, the authors endeavour to outline a formulation of the fundamental principles common to the analytic therapies, in order to ensure as far as possible that the terms and language used are understood as intended: all psychologists tend to resemble Humpty Dumpty, who Alice met in her adventures, whose determination that any word should mean what he meant it to mean was unshakeable. We have tried to avoid the pitfalls of misunderstanding that the idiosyncratic use of words and jargon presents by attempting the formidable task of outlining a general theory or model of analytic psychotherapy. Naturally, to do so in a single chapter means that it is incomplete, skeletal and in many ways unsatisfactory, but we hope it will ensure that what follows is clear. This theoretical discussion is placed late in the book, since it does not apply to the treatment strategies discussed in Parts I and II.

As is made clear in the text, the formulae and scripts presented are not intended to be used as they stand except in the earliest stages of the reader's using the techniques involved. Even the most experienced hypnotherapist will occasionally find himself suddenly struck dumb in mid-flow and will either have recourse to some script he has not used for years or, if more confident, will 'vamp' until his amnesia fades. The beginner will generally find it necessary to have the words put into his mouth. Other books have similarly provided word-for-word scripts for induction, deepening and so on, but all suffer from the same defects and undergo the same fate as the present volume: another person's words sound ill, stilted and impersonal, however well-written, compared with one's own verbal style. Even the best, most lucid and fluent script will sound dated and awkward after a few years as colloquial usage alters. Sadly, if one could write like a Shakespeare, one would be unlikely to write textbooks on hypnosis.

Many people find it helpful to read one or more of these scripts aloud into a tape-recorder and then listen to the recording in order to adjust and refine their delivery, diction, pitch and tone of voice and all the other characteristics that contribute to the attention-holding quality and pleasant character of the induction. Practising in this way will reveal uneven delivery, hesitations, inappropriate stresses and many other features in the most experienced practitioner as well as in the beginner, and it is not only helpful to the latter but salutary for the former to repeat this exercise from time to time.

The scripts presented for various aspects of hypnotherapy and various stages and tasks in a typical session are therefore intended to be used rather like the ingredients in a recipe and not as the speeches in a classic play. Many of our workshop participants found that the verbatim scripts served as a vehicle that carried them through their first exercises in using hypnosis, and that they followed the scripts word for word for only a short time and very quickly found themselves modifying and editing them so that progressively these became adapted to their own individual styles. This is the intention in presenting as many and as detailed verbatim scripts as have been included.

The same is true of the treatment strategies presented. These reflect, as clearly as do the scripts for preparation, induction, deepening and so on, the therapeutic styles, orientation and experience of the authors. Experienced therapists will be able to incorporate hypnotic techniques into the treatment strategies with which they are familiar without much, if any, recourse to the specific suggestions given here, but the less experienced may find it helpful to use what is provided here with such adaptations as will make them feel comfortable and bring the technique involved into closer accord with their personal style.

It is unlikely that we have much to say that is truly original. There is very little indeed to be found anywhere 'under the sun' that is entirely original and new, and in general, textbooks are full of quotations and references from which the book at hand has in part been constructed. The present volume has grown from two main sources: the authors' own clinical use of hypnosis and their learning through teaching in workshops. Inevitably, the authors have learned from others, through books, papers, workshops, conferences, personal meetings: all the ways in which professionals communicate and share experiences. Wherever really appropriate and necessary, material coming directly from others is quoted and the source acknowledged, but the number of references is perhaps very much smaller than is common in books such as this. Implicitly, of course, the extensive bibliographies given in those books mentioned here can be subsumed as included in this book.

In addition, this volume cannot be looked on as any kind of attempt to survey and summarize the academic field of clinical hypnotherapy: this is not intended. Nor is it intended to give an account of the history of hypnosis in clinical use. One of the irritating aspects of so many textbooks is the fact that the first third or so of each is given over to much the same survey of the history published in every other book on the same subject. The history of hypnosis has been repeatedly surveyed by various authors, and enough is enough. The reader interested in this aspect is advised to read one or more of the books listed. History changes little, but written histories differ markedly sometimes, the historian's interests and quirks shaping his account. The interested student should therefore read several accounts rather than one only, and will find nothing in the present volume to feed his appetite.

Hypnotic techniques can be taught, learned and used very easily indeed, and it is not necessary to have any prior training in anything at all in order to use them. To use them ethically, professionally, and scientifically is another matter altogether. At the time of writing, the only statutory control over the use of hypnosis in Britain is the ban on its use in theatrical shows in the form of the Hypnosis Act of 1952. Currently, members of the two professional bodies concerned, The British Society of Medical and Dental Hypnosis and the British Society of Experimental and Clinical Hypnosis, are restricted by the terms of their membership to the use of hypnosis only within their professional boundaries. That is to say, the members of these bodies are under an obligation not to use hypnotic techniques in treatments or procedures for which they are not qualified quite independently of any training in hypnosis. Unfortunately, these ethical restraints apply only to members.

Furthermore, at present there are no officially recognized or validated training courses or qualifications. Unfortunately, a growing number of unofficial and unregulated commercial organizations exist in Britain (and no doubt elsewhere) which are capitalizing on the absence of formal regulations and the growing public demand for alternative approaches to conventional medicine by providing self-styled training and qualification.

The irony is therefore that a hypnotherapist calling himself such, and claiming to be so qualified, is unlikely to be qualified in any officially recognized way: anyone quoting a qualification in hypnotherapy will not be a member of a profession such as medicine, clinical or educational psychology, dentistry, etc., and will not have any recognized or validated professional training. On the other hand, the most highly qualified psychiatrist, anaesthetist, clinical psychologist, etc., will neither hold nor claim any qualification in hypnosis, however well trained and experienced he may be in that field, since no acceptable qualification in hypnosis alone exists in the UK. The absence of any statutory definition and regulation of the practice of hypnosis therefore allows *anyone* to call him- or herself a hypnotherapist, and means that the consumer has no protection.

Members of the British Society of Experimental and Clinical Hypnosis are under an obligation not to teach hypnotic techniques to persons lacking the qualifications and status necessary for membership of the Society. The publication of this book could be taken as a breach of that obligation by the authors (who are members of that Society), since it quite explicitly and directly teaches hypnotic techniques to anyone with the price of the book available.

Hypnosis is a very powerful tool in therapy, and like all powerful techniques has as much power for harm as for good. A drug that cannot harm when used improperly is highly unlikely to do any good either. Hypnosis can be as easily and as dangerously misused as any technique or drug. Its dangers are twofold: those which arise from its use in the wrong circumstances, and those which stem from its application in the absence of the knowledge and skills necessary for the safe use of the treatment conveyed through hypnosis.

For example, hypnotic techniques for the control of pain are powerful and easy to use. It is possible to mask the symptom of pain that signals the development of a disease or the presence of damage. It is essential to conduct a thorough and technically competent examination to establish the source of and reason for the pain. If this is not done, and hypnosis is used to diminish or eliminate the pain, one runs the risk of ignoring a highly significant indication that a serious problem exists and should be attended to. Damping down such an 'alarm signal' may well result in postponement of proper investigation to such a point that the disease responsible for the pain has reached very damaging proportions.

With psychological problems, techniques for the recovery of distressing and therefore often repressed memories can release powerful emotional reactions which may have a seriously damaging effect if the process is not handled with the necessary knowledge, understanding and skill. Severe disturbances can result from such experiences. There are indeed some people for whom hypnosis presents dangers, and the professional (whether a doctor, psychologist or psychotherapist) will know when its use is indicated as appropriate and safe, while the amateur will not.

At the same time, it must be acknowledged that there always have been and presumably always will be sensible, wise and helpful individuals whose lack of any formal training makes no difference to the fact that they provide a genuinely therapeutic service. If such informal healers use hypnosis, it is likely to be beneficial to many people. Indeed, some States of Australia that have legislated in such a way as to restrict the use of hypnosis to medical practitioners, psychologists and related professionals generally include a 'Grandfather Clause': people who can bring satisfactory evidence that, despite their lack of qualifications, they possess and exercise satisfactory skills, can be registered as practitioners and licensed to use hypnotic techniques.

In the days when hypnotic demonstrations were given in theatres, music halls and the like, it was not unusual for some members of the audience to be brought to doctors next day to be 'de-hypnotized'. Amateur practice carries such dangers. It is, as said before, very easy to learn how to hypnotize someone. It is much less easy to know how to 'de-hypnotize' someone who does not come out of the trance in the usual way, or what to do if something goes wrong; and it requires specific skills to deal effectively with many of the results of hypnotic techniques, the reactions of the patient to suggestion, the material recovered from the unconscious, and so on.

It is therefore earnestly emphasized that the techniques described in this book should be used only within the boundaries of an already acquired professional competence. It would be as wrong for a dental surgeon to attempt to treat a psychological disorder as for a psychologist to apply his hypnotic skills in the practice of dentistry. The 'practice of medicine without a licence' is very properly a criminal offence. Sadly, the practice of psychotherapy 'without a licence' is currently not so regarded by the law, but is as dangerous. It is hoped that before much longer, Britain will follow the example set by some other countries in regulating all such techniques and practices, including hypnosis and hypnotherapy.

Hypnotic techniques are used by many people quite unconsciously. Suggestion, distraction, relaxation, imagery and confusion are employed by medical practitioners, psychologists, midwives, street-market salesmen, insurance agents, advertisement designers, conjurors, usually without the person concerned or their patients or victims being aware that their practices could be so labelled. The use of hypnotic techniques and the ways in which hypnotic processes are utilized in various forms of psychotherapy, including analysis, are discussed elsewhere (chapter 2), as is the spontaneous occurrence of hypnotic states and phenomena in the everyday lives of many people. The present book is intended to provide health-care professionals with explicit, consciously designed and applied ways of employing the natural capabilities of their clients and patients for the constructive and therapeutic application of mental processes, cognitive, affective, conative, and above all imaginative, in the service of mental and physical health.

The authors envisage that this book will serve as a basic introduction to the use of hypnotic processes in therapy, both of physical conditions and psychological difficulties. As suggested above, the newcomer to this field may find that he needs to use the scripts provided as they stand, either discreetly reading them as he works with a patient or learning them by heart, but before long will find himself amending and then re-writing them completely. With the passage of time and the accumulation of experience he will use the book less and less until at last he has outgrown it, as indeed we all outgrew the primers we used at school, and the book begins to gather dust. At that point, the authors' purpose will have been fulfilled.

The range of conditions, treatment strategies and programmes covered is relatively limited. No attempt has been made to provide a comprehensive manual of treatments. It is hoped that the techniques and models presented will enable any skilled and experienced physician, surgeon, clinical or educational psychologist, psychotherapist or other health-care practitioner to apply the principles outlined to those conditions or therapies that have been omitted.

The books noted in the bibliography contain many treatment strategies that have not been provided here or provide those that have been briefly sketched in greater detail, but the essential principle remains: the individual therapist should aim at designing his own treatment programmes, models and imagery, and above all meet the individual patient's needs, personality and characteristics in a wholly creative way. A parrot-like reproduction of standard treatments is at best ineffective, and is never the hallmark of the professional. Truly professional practice is characterized by the creation of a unique and original approach to each new patient, even though this will always be based upon and informed by validated theoretical models and principles.

From time to time in the text considerable emphasis is laid on the importance of accurate and detailed diagnosis. Diagnosis is, quite obviously, a vital precursor of any treatment, whether by medication, surgery, psychotherapy or indeed hypnotic techniques. It would be both inappropriate and impracticable to attempt to include diagnostic techniques in this book. As is repeatedly emphasized, hypnotic techniques should be employed only within the range of the practitioner's already acquired professional skills, which include diagnostic knowledge and skills, and these are therefore taken for granted.

Finally, a remark concerning the style of this book. There is much demand currently for texts to avoid the use of gender-linked pronouns. It is very difficult to meet this demand without becoming clumsy and verbose or otherwise imprecise. For simplicity's sake, the authors have plumped for the use of masculine pronouns except when a specific (female) patient is being discussed.

2

NATURE OF HYPNOSIS

In view of the practical emphasis intended for this book, it is not proposed to enter in much detail or at great length into the more abstract and theoretical aspects of the hypnotic state or trance. In academic circles, research, both in the laboratory and in the armchair, proceeds on whether hypnosis is 'an altered state of consciousness' or constitutes a different kind of cognitive processing. It is convenient here to speak of the 'hypnotic state', or of 'the trance', and such terms seem appropriate in describing the experiences of people undergoing hypnosis. In all that follows these two terms will be used interchangeably, without commitment to any particular position in the academic dispute, simply because one or other fits the experience of both patient and therapist and is a simple and direct way of communicating about the practicalities of hypnotherapy.

The public in general, both lay and professionally involved in psychology and psychiatry, tend to regard the experience of hypnosis and the behaviour manifest in that state as different from everyday waking experience and behaviour. It is pretty generally believed to be a different frame of mind, a different kind of awareness, from normal waking life; perhaps akin in some ways to dreaming sleep, yet different from that in its continuing consciousness. Hypnotic states and experiences are, in fact, commonplace in ordinary life and often occur without recognition as such. An adolescent whom one of the authors introduced to hypnosis to help her with anxiety and depression of mood remarked after her first hypnotic session: 'Oh, that was just like what I do when the other girls really get at me. I go inside myself and then I don't get so badly hurt by what they say.' On another occasion, a professional musician from whom one of the authors had an occasional lesson, when he had had his first formal experience of hypnosis, said: 'That was what I told you to do when you first sit at the keyboard.'

Most car drivers experience periods of abstraction when, as some put it, they 'go into auto-pilot mode'. While driving down a familiar road (less often in unfamiliar territory), one may 'come to' quite suddenly and realize that one has travelled several miles without any memory of having done so, detached from the outside world, in a 'brown study'. During that period driving has proceeded normally, with due attention to road conditions, other traffic and so on, apparently without any conscious attention or control. It could be argued that the driver was perfectly conscious throughout this period and then suffered an amnesia for the relevant time span, and then became amnesic of the content of consciousness during the period of 'abstraction', but this seems out of keeping with the subjective experience and with similar experiences. For example, while absorbed in a book or film, a piece of music or some activity demanding close attention, one may simultaneously hold a conversation without, again, later having any memory of having done so.

Skilled behaviour and behaviour requiring choices and decisions can be performed while the central awareness of the individual is abstracted and turned elsewhere. Absent-mindedness, 'woolgathering', day-dreaming are among the expressions commonly used to describe the overt manifestation of such a state.

During such a period of abstraction, detailed experiences may occur that may have considerable affective components. A 'day-dream' can arouse anger, anxiety, joy, erotic responses and so on as vividly, and to the subject as actually, as if the experience had been real. This is indistinguishable, both subjectively and from the observations of an onlooker, from experiences under hypnosis.

Barber (1969) suggested that suggestions made to an individual in such a way as to carry conviction had much the same effect as suggestions made to someone who had been given an hypnotic induction. On the basis of considerable experimental evidence to this effect, he suggested that hypnosis *per se* was no different from normal waking experience. This standpoint assumes in effect that hypnosis is that which follows an induction. An equally tenable interpretation of the same data can be made on the lines that hypnosis may occur without any formalities or rituals and that if an individual responds positively to suggestions that he would more usually discount or refuse, then his current mode of experience is somehow altered or modified so as to suspend constraints normally acting upon him. It seems legitimate to include such events within the field of hypnosis.

Hypnotic phenomena and experiences are even more clearly paralleled in sleep. The borderline between dreams during sleep and hypnotic hallucinations is defined by little more than the difference between sleep and waking states. In the hypnotic state, no matter how absorbing or compelling the images filling the awareness of the subject, he remains alert to the outside world (even if at some remove) and can extract himself instantaneously from the hypnotic experience at will. Here too, the distinction is very thin: for example, the mother of a young child will, while asleep and dreaming, waken instantly to full awareness the moment her baby cries. Until that moment of arousal, however, she has accepted the reality of her dream-world in the same way that the hypnotic subject accepts the reality of the images he is holding in his mind until he chooses to reject them and return to the 'reality' of his sensory inputs.

A story is told of a young child returning from a day at school who related, as is common, the events of the day to her mother. She explained that the class had studied the bumblebee that day, and the teacher had explained that the bumblebee is actually too heavy to fly: its wings are neither large nor strong enough to lift its weight, but that 'luckily bumblebees don't know that and so they *can* fly'.

Similar to this is the science fiction novel describing how a group of scientists ranging from nuclear physicists to archaeologists had been assembled by a government agency in a remote farmhouse to study the workshops, laboratories and library accumulated by an eccentric who had lived there. They were then shown a hand-held film of the eccentric carrying a small box on his back, on which he made a few adjustments before rising slowly into the air, without sign of any system of propulsion. Once he was well up, an explosion occurred and the man was killed. The scientists were informed that this man had clearly invented 'anti-gravity' but had left no systematic notes of his discovery. Their task, they were told, was to replicate his work by studying his equipment, library and so on. In a few years' time, they succeeded in building an 'anti-gravity generator', previously, of course, believed to be impossible. At that point, they were told that the whole episode had been stage-managed and the 'inventor' was a fiction, designed solely to convince them of the *possibility* of 'anti-gravity'.

In an experiment on hypnosis, a subject may be told things that are contrary to his beliefs about the world and he will then act on the basis of these new 'beliefs'. For instance, he may be told that there is no such number as 6, and if he accepts this suggestion will find, to his no small confusion, that he now has eleven fingers. Similarly, the patient in hypnosis, believing himself to have returned to an incident that had occurred when he was five years old having just been admitted to hospital in pain and distress, will react overtly, and subjectively experience this as though this were really happening. Hypnosis is very like the early-morning state of the Red Queen.

In everyday life, human behaviour is determined in part by the beliefs, both conscious and less so, of the individual. If an important belief is altered by suggestion or otherwise the behaviour of the individual, both overt and covert or internal, will change to accommodate the shift.

It is probably more useful to describe hypnosis than attempt to define it. Features of the hypnotic state include the following:

1.   acceptance of imaginary phenomena in place of sensory experience, and detachment from the sensorium;

2.   suspension of reality testing, suspension of everyday cognitive logic and secondary-process thinking;

3.   narrowing of attention (a sort of mental tunnel vision) to the content of the focus of the hypnotic exercise: suggested by the therapist or created by the subject's own imagination or memory;

4.   'splitting' of consciousness into separate channels that communicate in only one direction (i.e. the subject's normal consciousness, attitudes, reality testing and so on continue and

are aware of the content of the hypnotized self,
but the latter is unaware of the former);

5.   a rather regressed or developmentally immature
frame of mind (closely akin to some transference
phenomena in analysis or analytic therapy);

6.   commitment to a substitute reality described by
the therapist or the patient's own imagination
and memory.

In all these features, the similarity between hypnosis on the one
hand and a wide range of experiences including day-dreaming,
absorption in a work of fiction, experiences while in psychoanalytic sessions, dreaming during sleep, religious excitement and so
on, is very clear.

    In a seminar at the 10th International Conference of the
International Society for Hypnosis (Toronto, 1985), Graham
Wicks, drawing on the writings of several authors but putting
various concepts together in an original form, described hypnosis
as a 'multistate phenomenon'. The hypnotic state is characterized, he suggested, by a number of features. These comprise five
special states, in which input is processed differently from the
non-hypnotic state. The five states are as follows:

1.   de-automatization: normally automatic or self-
regulating mental and physical processes are
given over to the control of another person;

2.   role play: the subject commits himself to the role
described for him, and subjectively experiences
himself in that role rather than acts it;

3.   atavistic regression: the subject regresses to a
primitive mode of functioning in which he
responds to the therapist as though the latter
were an important person in a much earlier
phase of his life;

4.   cognitive regression: the subject reverts to
primary-process thinking, since he regresses
cognitively as well as emotionally;

5.   autonomic changed state: the muscular
relaxation produced by the trance state triggers
off parasympathetic activity so that all
physiological processes slow to a baseline level,
while at the same time one or more autonomic

functions come under voluntary control.

There is considerable overlap between these two lists of characteristics, as there is between any two or more attempts to describe this state. Authorities differ more in terms of emphasis than content, and most texts will contain the observations noted here. Descriptions such as these allow one to suggest why and how hypnosis can be useful and indeed powerful in various forms of psychotherapy and in the treatment of various physical and psycho-somatic conditions.

For instance, if a patient is suffering from a condition relating to and perhaps expressing a traumatic episode much earlier in his life, the dual (cognitive and emotional) regression that occurs in hypnosis permits him to re-experience, rather than simply recall, a childhood event in the form in which it was originally experienced without this original event being interpreted and modified by his ontologically later secondary-process thinking. At the same time, the splitting of awareness permits the patient's mature self to observe and learn from the experience, or, in another form of treatment ('ego state therapy') may be invited to intervene in such a way as to make the experience more manageable for the regressed part of the patient or to modify the traumatizing aftermath of emotion resulting from the experience.

The vividness and feeling of reality of the experiences undergone in hypnosis make it possible to carry out behaviour modification programmes with greater impact than one otherwise achieves in *in vitro* procedures. In a willing subject, who enters trance in such a way as to exhibit the features listed above, the suggestions made will be experienced more vividly and with greater impact than in a non-hypnotic state. The usual limitation of inadequate generalization from *in vitro* practice to *in vivo* experience, often reported in the literature, appears to be less evident when treatment is carried out in hypnosis. Further, one finds in practice that it takes less time to work through one rehearsal of, say, a desensitization schedule using hypnosis than without; one is therefore able to carry out more as well as more vivid rehearsals in a given time.

It could well be argued that hypnosis plays a part in all behaviour modification programmes employing imagination, where the patient accepts, for the purposes of treatment, that which he knows not to be true as true for the time being: for example in an attempt to desensitize a patient to feathers, he knows there are no feathers in the room but pretends for the moment that there are. All *in vitro* behavioural programmes demand that the patient regard the treatment as the proverbial schoolboy regarded religion, who replied to Dr Arnold's question as to the nature of faith: 'Believing something you know is not true'. In so far as suspension of reality testing and disbelief are set up in such a programme, one could reasonably regard the latter as using hypnotic processes. At the same time, however, the formal establishment of an hypnotic state enhances the patient's commitment to the process and heightens his acceptance of the conventions and subjective reality of the treatment experience.

The establishment of control over the autonomic system features in both the lists of characteristics of hypnosis given above. This has obvious applications in a wide range of psychological, psychosomatic and physical disorders. Most physical and psychological disorders are accompanied by anxiety and are generally exacerbated by it; its management is therefore crucially important. In some cases the anxiety may be seen as primary and therefore responsible for the establishment, and usually maintenance, of the condition, while in others it may be understood to be generated by the experience of illness or trauma, that is, to be secondary to it. Most commonly, however, one is able to discern both primary and secondary anxiety in the condition of the patient. It is always the case that anxiety and its physical manifestations exacerbate the related condition and delay recovery and their management is therefore crucial to all treatment.

Anxiety, with its associated physical manifestations, can be brought under voluntary control first in response to the suggestions made by the therapist and then by the patient's own volition. Post-hypnotic suggestions to this effect, based on the experience of establishing control over anxiety symptoms and feelings in the therapy session, can subsequently give the patient genuine control over such reactions. The establishment of voluntary control over normally automatic or self-regulating processes which may not even be perceived consciously in the ordinary way (such as peristalsis of the gut, gastric secretions, raised blood pressure, etc.) allows intervention in a wide variety of pathological processes.

Similarly, if it is possible to change perceptual processes

and substitute chosen stimuli for those naturally present, the application of hypnosis to the management of pain becomes obvious. Current theories of pain perception indicate clearly that in general pain is the result of an interpretative process rather than a direct perception, at least in so far as its noxious quality is concerned. Pain can be experienced without distress and can even be pleasurable, as in some sexual perversions. A specific sensation may not be perceived as pain until it is associated cognitively with anticipated or actual bodily damage or threat. Thus the possibility of modifying first the content of the sensorium and secondly the cognitive response to sensation points to a major role for hypnosis in the treatment and management of pain, whether chronic or acute and whether inherent or produced in, for example, surgery.

It is now well established that bleeding after dental extraction is substantially less, sometimes even absent, in the hypnotized patient. Similarly, bleeding from trauma of any kind can be reduced and abbreviated by hypnosis, a phenomenon exploited by *fakirs* for centuries. It has been well demonstrated in clinical trials that hypnosis reduces the effects on tissue of severe and extensive burns.

Conditions such as eczema take a middle ground between the wholly psychological and the wholly physical. Hypnosis can readily control and even totally inhibit the experience of itching, with obvious benefits, and will additionally improve the condition of the skin. With hindsight, this is really quite obvious: we take for granted that distress, anxiety and so on exacerbate all skin disorders, yet until quite recently, the obverse of this observation, that ameliorating the patient's state of mind will improve the condition of his skin, was not applied. In all such psychosomatic conditions, as well as in primarily physical trauma, hypnotherapy is the application of simple well-known principles in a systematic way. We know that anxiety, embarrassment and so on produce vasodilation in the skin of the face and thorax; vasoconstriction in the viscera with vasodilation to the skeletal musculature appears in fear, the reverse pattern occurring in relaxation; physical sexual arousal and responses occur in response to imagery. Similarly, picturing a burned limb being bathed in cool water reduces the actual damage done by the trauma and the consequent physiological changes such as inflammation, etc., *as long as* the imagery is vivid; a condition much more easily achieved with hypnosis than without.

Ever since Freud first remarked on the frequency with which his female patients described sexual experiences in childhood (nowadays much more accepted as probably genuine rather than fantasized), we have witnessed controversy as to the truth (that is, the historical accuracy) of childhood memories, especially of a distasteful kind, emerging in psychoanalysis or therapy. Similar controversy occurs around the topic of experiences during hypnosis that purport to be re-enactments of childhood episodes, especially traumatic episodes. Experiments on 'Age Regression' have at times demonstrated the re-emergence of childlike mannerisms, voice, even appearance, to match the age to which the subject has regressed. In extreme cases it is claimed that the Moro, Babinski and other infantile reflexes reappear.

A demonstration commonly carried out is as follows. The subject is asked to feel that he is going back to an earlier time in his life, to feel himself gradually getting younger and younger, and at various points is asked to write his name. Generally this 'succeeds' in demonstrating, to the observers' and to the subject's satisfaction, that age regression really does work. The subject's handwriting grows progressively less mature and eventually becomes a childish scrawl; the name is wrongly spelled, changes to a nickname and finally the subject denies being able to write.

The fact that the subject usually reports appropriate and vivid memories makes the whole episode convincing, yet does not provide solid evidence of the reality of the process. The 'recovery' of previously inaccessible memories which plays a large part in some forms of psychotherapy, especially if these memories are of birth or even intra-uterine experience, is generally not possible to validate, yet can be wholly convincing to both therapist and patient and is not infrequently followed by major changes in personality, reactions, mood and so on.

With Freud's patients, it seemed to make little difference whether their accounts of incestuous experiences in childhood were historically valid or stemmed from fantasy. In age regression in hypnotherapy it similarly seems to make little difference whether the 'recovered memories' are of real or fantasized events. While the treatment of such material is considered in detail in Part IV of this book, it should be noted here that as far as the patient is concerned, the same controversy or uncertainty may persist: many patients are themselves unconvinced of the historical truth of their memories. Others, however, are utterly convinced, while the majority remain between these extremes. Yet all three groups will express awareness of beneficial changes following therapy based on age regression, quite independently of their stand on this question.

The question then arises as to why the hypnotic state facilitates such events or experiences. The suspension of reality testing, the detachment of critical functions and the dual regression that occurs in hypnosis enable the subject to modify or alter his adult experiential mode and thus be open to experiences that would normally be blocked by, for example, secondary process logic. Further, the regressed posture of the hypnotized subject predisposes him to the immature ego state aimed at. In addition, the splitting of awareness which allows two or more ego states to co-exist in consciousness makes it possible for the patient, while fully participating at one level, to remain at another level detached from the experience, and this apparently creates the conditions wherein repressed material can enter consciousness without alerting the ego-defences. In some instances, the hypnotic state makes it possible to separate the affect of the experience from its content, again thereby evading the 'censor' and making the memory thus recalled tolerable, which originally it was not.

In other forms of hypnoanalysis, the patient may retrieve a repressed memory in a 'second-hand' way: by, for example, observing himself as a child undergoing some traumatic experience rather than experiencing it directly. This is illustrated by a female patient 'regressed' to the age of three, at which time she witnessed her father beating up her mother. By observing this as though present at the event in her adult self, she was able to *feel for* the child rather than feel the child's terror and to employ her adult warmth and strength in comforting the 'child', thereby neutralizing the effects of the experience and showing, in her subsequent behaviour and mood, changes of a major and beneficial nature. This apparent capacity for simultaneous processing at several developmental levels is the basis of much of the dynamically or psychoanalytically orientated application of hypnosis in psychotherapy.

Hypnotizability is another area of conflict. It is generally accepted that some individuals are markedly resistant to hypnotic induction and score low on tests designed to measure hypnotic response, while others score maximally on such ratings and appear to have an especial talent or facility for producing hypnotic phenomena. It has been shown experimentally that response to hypnotic suggestions is both consistent for any given individual and is normally distributed in the population (Weitzenhoffer and Hilgard, 1959 and 1962), yet estimates vary as to the proportion of the population that can use hypnosis effectively. Edelstien (1981, p.33) reports that the induction procedure he uses for preference will induce a satisfactory trance in 90 to 95 per cent of patients in the hands of any practitioner and many other writers claim comparable results.

In Britain, it seems that the same procedures are less effective. The authors and those practitioners with whom they have discussed this find that two out of three adult patients respond satisfactorily, although a substantial proportion of them reach only a very shallow trance. No major study of cultural differences appears to have been carried out as yet, although such research would be of considerable interest. Suggestions that virtually any patient who is willing will respond successfully are somewhat misleading, and wholly discouraging to anyone practising in the UK. There is no doubt that some individuals are simply unable to detach themselves from sensory inputs and the immediate real environment and immerse themselves in an inner world of imagination; or to concentrate their attention enough to enter a recognizable hypnotic state and respond effectively to suggestion and therefore rating scales.

Most writers agree that hypnotizability varies with age. Children below the age of four are often, though by no means always, unwilling or unable to attend to an induction or to suggestions for long enough to become wholly absorbed, although if the induction is cast in the form of a story, they may be successfully taken into hypnosis. Response to hypnotic induction and suggestions seems to reach a peak around the ages of ten to twelve, and then reduces progressively through the adult years. Some individuals retain a high capacity for hypnosis through to their latter years, although generally this capacity does seem to fall off with aging.

It is sometimes argued with considerable truth that Freud himself, despite his beliefs and statements, never gave up using hypnosis in therapy, but rather that he began to use it effectively at precisely the point where he thought he had found a better alternative. S.L. Mitchell (1914) suggested that Freud unconsciously induced an hypnotic state in his patients through the technique of 'free association' (much more effectively than he had been able to do by the explicit induction methods he had tried and abandoned), and that it was the hypnoidal state so achieved that was responsible for the effects of the analytic process. The patient in analysis demonstrates many of the characteristics of the hypnotic state, and the phenomena of the transference in particular suggest the presence of hypnotic regression as well as the substitution of internally generated perceptions for perception of the actual environment.

Hypnotherapy by direct suggestion of symptom removal or by precipitating abreaction does indeed work with some patients but, as Freud found, improvement is short-lived, and in consequence such techniques are unpopular except outside professional circles. The process of free association, however, and the whole format of the psychoanalytic session is very like hypnotherapy, and the patient in analysis demonstrates many of the features of the hypnotic state. In both conditions, material that is normally inaccessible to consciousness re-emerges and can be re-processed by secondary-process thinking, with or without the aid of interpretations from the therapist. Abreaction may occur, often with great benefit to the patient through the reunion of split affect with its content, in all forms of analytic psychotherapy, and in a way no different from that shown in hypnoanalysis.

The argument still raging in academic circles as to whether hypnosis is defined as something that follows an hypnotic induction, is highlighted here. We would argue, as was made clear in discussing the spontaneous establishment of hypnotic states in everyday life, that most if not all forms of psychotherapy precipitate and employ clearly hypnotic phenomena, and that techniques that enhance hypnotic skills and characteristics can be used with substantial benefit in perhaps all therapies. The difference is largely one of recognition and explicit application; that is to say, any therapist will find himself at times using hypnotic phenomena in the course of therapy and will do so the more effectively if he is aware of the fact and is equipped with overt and conscious understanding of the possibilities available in this field, consequently applying such skills deliberately and with the backing of experience and familiarity.

One of the most commonly accepted axioms of hypnotherapy is that nothing can be done with hypnosis that cannot be done without. Barber, as previously noted, offered considerable experimental evidence for 'Anything you can do I can do ...'. At the same time, since hypnosis occurs spontaneously in therapy as well as in ordinary life, it seems inefficient if not actually negligent to ignore the part played by hypnosis in therapy and to fail to take deliberate and purposeful control of these phenomena in the service of the patient. Subsequent chapters of this book detail specific applications in various forms of therapy and with different groups of conditions in a very practical way, with illustrative cases and where appropriate, research findings. The main thrust, however, is towards practical applications rather than theoretical issues – 'How to do it' – the rationale of each application or model being adumbrated. For more theoretical discussion or for clinical studies and formal research, readers should consult some of the books listed in the bibliography.

3

INDUCTION

INTRODUCTION

It was argued in the previous chapter that the hypnotic state is by
no means confined to events occurring after some specific and
formal process. To recapitulate: it was noted that hypnotic
experiences occur spontaneously in everyday life, are frequently
encountered in various forms of psychotherapy and can be
established by very informal, not to say casual, means. However,
if the therapist wishes to use hypnosis in the course of treatment
and has agreed with the patient to do so, some specific action is
generally called for to produce the required state. The patient
expects it, and with such a 'set' is less likely to enter a trance
without some special procedure. Even when the therapist is
confident that in the course of the interview, if properly managed, the patient will enter the hypnotic state, this may not occur
until after a considerable lapse of time so that in the interests of
economy as well as effectiveness, a specific procedure is desirable.
Such a procedure we call an 'induction'.

     Many patients at this point expect the therapist to produce
a gold half-hunter and dangle it beguilingly before their eyes.
There is no doubt that this gesture would produce the desired
result in many patients, but more commonly would be likely to
elicit giggles rather than trance. This 'classical' technique (if
B-feature films are to be believed) exploits, however, several of the
basic principles of hypnotic induction: catching and holding the
patient's visual attention and producing oculo-motor fatigue;
speaking slowly, rhythmically and compellingly, so holding the
patient's attention; and repeatedly suggesting increasing fatigue
and sleepiness as the patient begins to experience these very
phenomena, thus convincing him that he is indeed being hyp-

notized. This belief is probably the most important ingredient in any induction.

 PREPARATION OF THE PATIENT

Most patients approach their first experience of hypnosis with a variety of expectations that owe more to fiction than to reality, and commonly also with feelings of apprehension and anxiety. It is usually necessary to correct the patient's expectations and beliefs and to allay fears, since any misapprehensions or anxiety will interfere with the entire experience and may possibly even prevent him from entering the hypnotic state. In addition, it is important that he should be able to recognize the hypnotic state and not become disappointed or lose faith in the therapist through a mismatch between his expectations and the actual experience. However, even if a detailed account of what it is like to be hypnotized has been given, patients are commonly still surprised that they remained alert, able to speak and fully aware.

One common belief is that in hypnosis you are 'put out', i.e. become unconscious, and that the contents of the session, from the moment of entering the trance onwards, will not be remembered after the session is over. Another belief often encountered is that the patient will be unable to carry out any voluntary action, including speech; another, that he will be unable to exert any choice or will about what happens. It is important to ensure that the patient understands that he will be conscious and in control throughout the session; he will be as capable of voluntary action as at any other time; he, and not the therapist, is in charge of what happens; he will remember all that happened while he was in the trance, and the usefulness of the trance depends entirely upon his willingness to participate and continue to maintain the process.

Patients also frequently believe that they will have no control over what they say during hypnosis, and may be very afraid of some self-exposure: 'I may say things while I am unconscious that I would not normally say, and I won't know about it.' If, as is often the case, the patient has already developed some degree of relationship with the therapist through previous sessions, fears of shocking the therapist or otherwise disturbing the relationship by disappointing him or letting him down may be in evidence. There may also be fears about what would happen if the therapist failed to end the trance.

Most patients experience considerable anxiety and doubt about their first experience of hypnosis. Naturally, anything unknown makes one anxious, and fear of failure compounds this. Hypnosis is, after all, very commonly specifically sought only as a last resort, when every other form of treatment has failed. This further heightens the anxieties felt by many patients, and such anxiety needs to be resolved as far as possible if the patient is to be able to involve himself effectively in the work to be done. Such anxieties are often shown by no more than giggles and uncontrollable impulses to laugh or, occasionally, by the patient repeatedly interrupting and pointing out that he has not yet become hypnotized.

These and many other points need to be discussed with the patient before an induction is attempted. Our practice is to ask a number of questions to elicit his existing beliefs and ideas of hypnosis and then offer some answers and explanation on the following lines. Naturally, this has to be edited to match what the patient says about his understanding of hypnosis.

████████   Script 3.1

Most people know little about hypnosis except from what they have read in novels or seen in films. I wonder what picture you have of what it is like to be hypnotized and what happens?

You have probably actually been in an hypnotic state many times without realizing it. Do you drive a car? *[If the patient says: 'Yes', continue as follows; if he does not drive, go on to speak about reading, watching television, etc., – see below.]*

I expect, then, that you have had the experience of driving along a familiar road and suddenly realizing that you have driven several miles without apparently seeing anything or being aware of what you were doing? Yet during that time you drove perfectly normally, avoided dogs and children, stopped at red lights, changed gear and so on. Or perhaps you have got so engrossed in a book or in what you were thinking that you did not notice having a conversation with someone else and afterwards did not remember it at all? At those times, when you were abstracted or absorbed, you were actually in a spontaneous hypnotic state.

All hypnosis is like that, a state of abstraction from the outside world and absorption in your own thoughts and images, and like the experiences you have had before, can come about only through you. I cannot hypnotize you nor can anyone else: only you can hypnotize yourself, and all I can do is to show you how to do it deliberately and then how you can use it to solve your problems.

Many people think that they will not know or have any control over what they do or say while they are hypnotized. if you did not know or remember afterwards what happened in the session, it really would not do you much good! Also, you are in control of the experience, not I. I was working with a colleague some time ago who wanted to learn to use hypnosis. I led him into the trance state and then we carried out some experiments. I suggested he should imagine his hands to feel like two pieces of steel, welded together, and then try to pull them apart. He sat, straining hard to pull his hands apart, then suddenly opened his eyes, said 'What the hell!' and separated his hands quite normally. At any moment in the trance, if you do not like what I suggest, you can ignore what I say or change it to suit what you want, and if you want to end the experience you can do so simply by deciding to do so.

You will remember everything that happens while you are in the hypnotic state, with the exception of anything you do not want to remember. For instance, if we explore some of the feelings and memories that underlie your difficulties, and come across something you are not ready yet to deal with and which you find distressing, you may simply choose not to remember it when you leave the trance. If this were to happen, you would probably find that the memories concerned gradually emerge again during the days or weeks that follow

the session, as and when you are ready to cope with them, so
that you do not get distressed or disturbed by them.

You will be conscious and in control the whole time. You will
be able to move about; for instance if you find yourself
becoming uncomfortable, you can change your position. You
will be able to speak, although sometimes you may find it is
just too much of an effort.

Going into hypnosis is something that has to be learned. It is a
knack, rather like learning to ride a bicycle or to swim. It
needs practice, and it cannot be forced. You have to let it
happen, just like when you learned to ride a bicycle. Just let
yourself go along with the suggestions I make and you will
soon learn how to get into that state and find out just how
pleasant, as well as helpful, it really is.

If you agree, then, we will try out one or two of the many
different ways there are of getting into the trance. If the first
does not suit you, we will try another until we find a way that
suits you and you find congenial. When you have reached a
really detached and comfortable state, I will then describe a
self-hypnosis exercise for you to use and practise on your own,
and we shall probably try it out immediately to make sure you
are comfortable with it and that it works for you. To make
sure you are not bothered about coming out of the trance
again, I will describe several ways for you to bring yourself
out. In fact this is not really important, since if you need to
come out of the trance if something cropped up that needed
your attention, you would in any case come out and back into
normal alertness immediately, and without actually having to
do anything special.

Additional material would be added and some elements omitted,
depending on the replies the patient gives before and during this
discussion. On occasion it may be helpful to suggest that the
patient should read a leaflet or an appropriate book on the
subject. The British Society of Experimental and Clinical Hypnosis
provides such a leaflet for use by members. Alternatively, for

those patients who wish to read in more detail, books such as Karle (1987a) may be recommended.

The final stage in preparation consists of discovering any fears that may be relevant to the imagery to be used during the induction and the deepening process that follows. For example, if a patient is phobic of lifts, one would not use such an image. While it is useful to check in this way, use of such an uncongenial image need not interfere with the process. In the course of a research programme in which, for obvious reasons, the induction and so on was standardized, an image used was that of a lift. One elderly lady told one of the authors after the session that when she had been asked to see the lift doors open ready for her to get in, she had decided to go down the stairs instead. However, patients who suffer from hay fever may find themselves reacting physically (as though actually exposed to an allergen) to images of walking in a meadow on a summer day, and this would be unnecessarily uncomfortable.

In addition, it is useful at this point to ask the patient about a memory that would make a good experience to revisit, a place and time that he would find especially pleasurable, relaxing and calming, his 'Favourite Private Place'. This image can be used whenever necessary to reduce tension, anxiety, distress, etc. This technique is discussed in detail in chapter 6.

Finally, one tries generally to make the patient as comfortable as possible and to ensure freedom from interruption. It is obviously useful, if the patient is to relax, that his body should be at rest and comfortable. Physical relaxation is one of the most common suggestions made in the induction (since it is one of the principal characteristics of the hypnotic state), so that ideally one would place the patient in a really comfortable chair or on a couch, with good support, including support for his head. Freedom from interruption by the telephone or from people entering the room should be arranged, and both the therapist and the patient should be satisfied that they need not empty their bladders during the anticipated period of the planned session.

However, very satisfactory hypnotherapy can be carried out without any of these precautions. One of the authors was travelling across the Channel one night when one of his companions began to feel seasick. Fortunately, she had worked with hypnosis previously so was readily taken into trance while sitting on a rigid bench in the middle of a gang of drunk and rowdy young people. She was able to control her nausea quickly, and then spent the remainder of the trip blissfully subjectively engaged in her favourite hobby and unaware of the noise, discomfort and stress of the real crossing.

PRINCIPLES OF INDUCTION

The nature of the hypnotic state as discussed so far implies a number of principles to be observed and applied in induction. First, an induction should be designed to facilitate the process whereby the patient progressively detaches himself from awareness of his surroundings and the sense data he is receiving and absorbs himself in the images and thoughts suggested to him by the therapist or drawn from his own memory or imagination. This is most readily done by asking the patient to focus with increasing exclusiveness on as few and as simple stimuli as possible and to reduce his attention progressively further, with the exception of continuing and uninterrupted attention to what the therapist says to him.

Secondly, the patient must believe in what is happening. The therapist will therefore include in his suggestions those sensations and other experiences that are about to occur or are just occurring in such a way as to appear to produce those experiences through suggestion. This not only enhances the patient's belief in what is happening but also reassures him that he is playing his part correctly and is co-operating successfully with the therapist, whose competence is also confirmed by what the patient experiences.

For instance, when employing an eye-fixation process (see Script 3.2 below), the patient will necessarily experience some fatigue and even strain around the eyes, and will begin to blink from time to time. Therefore one makes suggestions, in advance of the event, that the patient will feel increasing fatigue and strain around his eyes and that he will find himself blinking. When this occurs, it is then re-inforced and further suggestions added for the next stage, increasing desire to close the eyes and heaviness of the eyelids. The patient, noting that the first suggestions have indeed come true, is more ready to accept further suggestions and so implement them (unconsciously), thus being carried gently into the desired state. The therapist will watch carefully for other small items of behaviour such as movements, changes in breathing and so on, and incorporate these into what he says.

Monotony of delivery is helpful in producing a detached and relaxed state; this will be familiar to anyone who has sat through a lecture delivered in this way. Similarly, repetition of particular words and phrases adds to the delivery's seductive character as well as emphasizing gently and discreetly the key ideas involved. The principle held by the Bellman on the trail of the Snark applies: 'If I say a thing three times, then it is true'! The 'hypnotic' character of the induction script is enhanced by rhythm, especially if linked to the patient's respiratory rhythm, so generally one will deliver the induction in a monotonous but rhythmic style, with much repetition of key words and phrases, with especial emphasis timed to coincide with the patient's exhalations. However, monotony, quiet and soothing tones and repetitiveness are not always necessary: very effective inductions can be carried out in the most casual tone of voice and with minimal repetition, as Script 3.6 below.

Matching the rhythm of delivery to the patient's respiration ('pacing') is helpful. If the therapist matches his own breathing to that of the patient and then gradually slows both this and his delivery, the patient will be drawn to slow his own respiration in sympathy, and feel himself fulfilling the suggestion made that his breathing is gradually slowing and deepening.

The patient's experience during the induction will include elements that are not openly visible to the therapist, such as finding his thoughts wandering. Such things, since they are known to occur frequently, can be included in the induction: 'You may find your thoughts wandering from time to time, or ideas and images coming into your mind. When that happens, just let the thoughts come and go and pay no particular attention to them.' Similarly, one includes suggestions about any noises from outside the room, and so on.

The scripts that follow may seem rather lengthy for regular use. Some patients do take quite a long time, especially the first time, to reach even a shallow trance. It may well seem that if one is to go through such a lengthy introduction to trance, most of the time available for the treatment session will be consumed in the preparatory stage alone. After the first or first few experiences of hypnosis, most patients can be trained to enter as deep a trance as they need through an abbreviated induction, sometimes of only a few words. Suggested procedures for this training are included below.

Inductions, when seen in cold print, appear excessively repetitious and boring and one may find it difficult to imagine oneself reading them at such length. When delivered with a patient listening, and gradually responding, the length seems less and the repetition and monotony more appropriate. In part this is due to the fact that the patient needs *time* to respond to the suggestions made. The first few scripts are given *in toto*, while later ones are curtailed to give only the major ingredients.

In using these scripts, the newcomer is advised to modify them as he reads so that if, for example, a patient's eyes close before that part of the script is reached, the therapist moves on to the appropriate point in the script. Similarly, if the patient's eyes have not closed when expected, the previous passages are repeated until eye-closure occurs. It is clear from this that the therapist must pay close and particular attention to the behaviour and responses of the patient and adapt the induction to his observations.

Inductions differ in style and manner. They can be authoritative ('You are becoming more and more relaxed and you will feel yourself ...', or 'I want you to imagine yourself ...') or they can be more permissive ('Perhaps you would like to ...' or 'You may find that ...'). Such differences are likely to be shown equally in the tone of voice, style of delivery, and so on. Each practitioner will find or choose a style that he finds congenial and that suits the particular patient of the moment. Generally, it is helpful to use a quiet, steady and even articulation.

In the course of carrying out an induction, the practitioner may find himself drifting into a somewhat trance-like state himself. Some therapists have suggested that this can actually be very helpful, and that in 'sharing' the patient's trance the therapist will be more aware of what the patient is experiencing and able to use this awareness in guiding the therapy.

It is, however, possible to become so remote and detached oneself that one loses track of what is happening to the patient, and one may become lost for words, or even thoughts. The story is told of the medical school lecturer who was asked by a student how to deal with the possibility of responding in this way to one's own suggestions. The lecturer is reported to have replied: 'Oh, that is no problem; just say to yourself repeatedly: "This is all b — s." ' Obviously, one needs to remain alert to what the patient is doing and to remain aware of the treatment programme to be pursued, and if one's attention is firmly on the patient and the process, one will be safe from entering so deep a trance as to lose contact.

Many people taking their first steps in hypnotherapy find themselves stuck for words at some crucial point or fear that they will 'dry up'. It is perfectly satisfactory and practical to use a prepared script, reading from a paper on the desk or one's knee, and many practitioners began in this way, the authors included. With practice and experience and, above all, confidence a more flexible and creative approach becomes possible, enabling the practitioner to adapt the induction both to the personality and temperament of the patient and to the progress being made, thereby achieving a higher 'success rate' than is likely with a standard patter. The inductions given below are drawn from a variety of sources as well as from the authors' own practice and are accompanied, where appropriate, with stage directions. They can be used verbatim or modified as seems appropriate. Notes on the rationale of some points (indicated by the reference numbers) are given at the end of the book.

Script 3.2   Stationary eye-fixation

[In advance of the session, fix a small red disc to the ceiling above the patient's chair so that, with the head resting comfortably and the neck not strained, it can be fixated by turning the eyes upwards in the head. A similar disc should be placed on the wall opposite where the patient will sit. The second is to be used if the patient complains of discomfort in fixating the spot above his head. Remember to use a steady, unhurried delivery.]

Fix your eyes on that little red disc above your head.[1] Keep your head and neck comfortable; do not strain but just turn your eyes upwards in your head. Keep your eyes on that disc and if your eyes stray from it, just bring them back again. Keep your attention on what I say, and your eyes on that disc. Good. Now, relax. Let all the rest of your body relax. Let your arms and legs go heavy and limp, heavy and limp. Relax completely ... relax completely.[2] Let your arms and legs go heavy, heavy and limp, heavy and limp. Good.[3] Quite soon, you will find your eyes becoming tired, tired and strained from staring at the red disc, and you will feel that you want to close your eyes, but I would like you to keep them open as long as possible. You will find after some time that your eyes become so tired and strained from staring at the disc that they will blink more and more,[4] and then they will close as though by themselves,[5] and then you will be able to relax completely. ... In the meantime, just let yourself relax more and more. ... Make sure your shoulders are relaxed. ... Relax the muscles of your neck, ... relax the muscles of your face, ... the muscles in your forehead and cheeks, ... relax the muscles around your mouth. ... Relax completely. ... Relax completely. ... Feeling more and more heavy and limp, ... heavy and limp. ... Your eyes are feeling really strained and tired now, ... strained and tired. Your eyes are blinking more and more, ... blinking more and more, ... more and more. Soon they will close as though by themselves, and then you will be able to relax completely, ... let go completely,[6] ... let go completely. ... Your eyes are blinking ... more and more, ... closing more and more, ... closing, ... closing, ... Close your eyes.[7]

[*When the patient's eyes close and remain closed, continue as follows.*] Good. You can now let go completely, ... let go completely, ... feeling very deeply relaxed, ... relaxed and detached, ... detached and remote, ... detached and remote, ... becoming more and more comfortable and relaxed, ... comfortable and ... relaxed, ... relaxed and detached, ... so comfortable and relaxed. Good.

Script 3.3 Eye-fixation with movement

[*Hold a pen about six inches from the patient's eyes in the midline and slightly above a comfortable forward glance.*[8] *As you speak, move the pen slowly in a circle or ellipse so as to compel the patient to move his eyes continuous to keep the pen fixated.[9]]*

I would like you to fix your eyes on the tip of my pen. Follow it around as I move it by moving only your eyes. At the same time, relax all the rest of your body.[10] Let your arms and legs relax and become heavy and limp, ... heavy and limp. Your eyes will soon become tired and strained from following my pen as I slowly move it around, ... and you will want to close them. ... You will find that the strain in your eyes becomes so great, you would like to rest them, ... but please keep following the pen with your eyes until they become so tired you begin to see double, ... so tired that your eyes will close as though by themselves, ... and then you will be able to relax completely ... and let yourself sink gently and comfortably into the hypnotic state. ... Keep your eyes open and following the pen as long as you can as you relax more and more deeply, ... more and more deeply. ... *[Continue in this vein, perhaps remarking on increasing depth and slowing of breathing, and when appropriate, continue as follows.]* Good; very good. Your eyes are blinking more and more, more and more, and soon they will close altogether. Your eyes are closing, closing, closing.[11] Good.[12] Now just relax and let yourself drift deeper and deeper into trance, ... deeper and deeper. ... You feel yourself sinking deeper ... and deeper ... into the chair as you relax more and more deeply, ... and sinking deeper ... and deeper into trance each time you breathe out. More and more relaxed, ... relaxed and comfortable, ... more and more relaxed and remote, ... remote and detached, ... remote and detached. Good.

Script 3.4   Eye-fixation with intermittent stimulus

[This somewhat pretentious title refers to the use of a metronome fitted with a light that flashes synchronously with its sound. An ordinary metronome can be readily adapted for this use, and instructions on a simple way of

doing it are given in the notes at the end of this book.[13] *Start
the metronome with its light switched on and directed at the
patient's eyes.*[14] *]*

Fix your eyes on the little light on the metronome and watch
it as it flashes on and off in time with the tick ... tock ... tick[15]
of the metronome. Keep your eyes on the little light, and if
they wander off it, just bring them back. Keep your thoughts
on what I say and let yourself relax. Let your arms and legs
relax and become heavy, ... heavy and limp. ... Let your back
relax so you feel yourself sinking into the chair. ... Relax
completely. ... Relax completely. As you stare at that little
light, you will gradually find your eyes becoming tired and
strained. Keep them open as long as you can. Gradually your
eyes will become more and more tired from staring at the little
light, tired and strained and your eyelids will become heavier
and heavier, your eyes will begin to blink more and more,
more and more, and then they will close. And then you will
be able to relax completely. Good. Your eyes are blinking more
and more,[16] ... so tired and strained. Your eyelids feel heavier
and heavier, heavy as lead. Your eyes are closing, ... closing, ...
closing.[17]... Good. Now you can let go and relax completely.

*[Any additions to this script should be added as required to
match the patient's behaviour. This should be easy enough
now. The metronome can be stopped when the patient closes
his eyes, preferably warning the patient a little beforehand:
'In a moment or two, I shall stop the metronome, and as I do
so, as I switch it off, let yourself slip a little deeper still into
a comfortable, deep, state of complete ease.']*

Script 3.5   Loosening of attention

Just relax. If you like, keep your eyes open for the moment, or
if you prefer, let them close. Some people find it easier to relax
and let their imagination run free with their eyes closed. Just
do what feels comfortable and right to you, and gradually
relax more and more. Let yourself begin to feel as though you
were drifting, ... drifting away from the ordinary, everyday

world, ... drifting further and further away. Keep your
thoughts on what I say and let everything else just drift
away.[18] Let everything in the ordinary world become distant,
far away, as you become more and more detached. ...
Detached and distant. ... Bit by bit, you will find yourself
becoming even more relaxed, ... even more comfortable, ...
relaxed and comfortable, ... remote and detached ... *[etc. etc.,
commenting when appropriate on eye-closure if this did not
occur at the start, and ending with a 'Good' or two when it is
clear from posture, muscle tone and breathing that the patient
has entered the first stage of hypnosis].* And as you sink into
the first stage of hypnosis, so comfortable and relaxed, you will
soon be ready to go into the next stage. Good. Just let yourself
sink, ... deeper and deeper, ... deeper and deeper, ... into that
relaxed, comfortable, detached and remote feeling.

██████████   Script 3.6   Early suggestion of phenomena,
                            e.g.'eye-catalepsy'

*[This is a very quick induction that can produce a very deep
trance within moments in some subjects, even without any
'deepening' procedures. The most readily hypnotized subjects
find it congenial and effective, even if they are highly
sceptical of hypnosis; indeed, it often seems as though
scepticism is closely related to aptitude for hypnosis. This
induction is unsuitable for use with subjects whose strong
need to maintain control, especially in the context of
obsessive-compulsive anxiety, makes it inadvisable to make
suggestions of inhibition: of their NOT being able to do
something perfectly ordinary. Suggestions on these lines can
be very disturbing to such people and one runs a major risk
of losing their willingness and co-operation.]*

Just close your eyes, and focus your attention on your eyes
and eyelids. Let them relax and as they relax more and more
completely, you will find that they just will not open; they will
be so firmly closed that it will feel as though you had forgotten
how to open them. And when you reach that stage, when
your eyes are so firmly shut they simply will not open, let me

know, either by telling me or by raising one hand as a signal. So just concentrate on your eyelids, feeling them so firmly closed that they will not open.[19] So firmly closed. I will stop talking for a moment while you concentrate on your eyelids becoming more and more firmly closed, until you let me know you have reached the point where your eyes simply will not open.

[You can then keep silent until the patient indicates that his eyes will not open, or continue, if you prefer, with suggestions of further relaxation and of eye-catalepsy. The most successful use of this technique often occurs with no more than a single statement and a pause of quite brief duration.]

████████████   Script 3.7   Touch, tingle, twitch and arm levitation

[Sit close to one side of the patient. It is helpful to enquire first whether the patient is right- or left-handed, and appear to choose which side you take in response to the answer. There is no evidence at all that this makes the slightest difference except that, by accepting the implicit suggestion, the patient accepts the beginning of a special process and the advent of a special state.]

Relax, let yourself go limp and keep your attention on what I say. Let me pick up your arm; don't help me, just let it go. *[Pick up the patient's arm, supporting it loosely at the wrist on the fingers of one hand.]* In a moment, I am going to run one finger gently up from the tip of one finger to your wrist *[or better, if the patient's lower arm is exposed, to the elbow]*. You will feel a slight tingle,[20] *[begin to run one finger slowly and lightly up the back of the patient's hand from the tip of one finger to the wrist or elbow, barely touching the skin]* and that tingle will go on *[by this time, you are no longer touching the patient with the finger]* after I stop touching you.[21] Good. Now, I am going to do that again, and you will again feel the tingle, but this time you may also feel slight movements in the fingers of that hand,[22] little twitching movements that occur without your will. *[Repeat light touch. As soon as you see any slight movements in the fingers, remark on them approvingly.]* Good. *[If the patient's eyes are still open, you might like to suggest closure at this point, although this is not essential. Note also that the movements will continue until you suggest that they stop. Remember ALWAYS to undo suggested phenomena.]* Now the movements will die away, and that hand will go back completely to normal.[23] Good. Now, I am going to run my finger up that hand *[and arm, if appropriate]* just once more. This time, I would like you to feel that hand and arm are becoming lighter and lighter, becoming as light as a feather, as light as a balloon, and if you can let go of it completely, it will begin to float up off my hand up into the air. *[If nothing much seems to happen, or if you simply feel some reduction in the pressure of the arm on your hand but no actual movement away, try moving the arm gently up and down by slight movements of your own hand. As soon as the arm begins to lift, continue:]* Good. Floating up, light as a feather, light as a balloon; just enjoy the really pleasant feeling of lightness as your arm floats upwards. As it rises up in the air, higher and higher, you can let yourself sink gently and easily into an even more relaxed and comfortable state, as you sink deeper and deeper into trance. *[If the patient's eyes are still open, suggest that he looks at the arm as it floats, apparently without the patient's volition. If the eyes are closed, you may suggest that the patient opens them while remaining completely relaxed, that is, without leaving the trance he has already reached. When the arm has moved appreciably, though not less, perhaps, than two or three inches at the wrist, take hold of the wrist in your hand.]* Now it can stop there and gradually return to its normal feeling of weight so that it slowly begins to sink down again, and *[if the patient's eyes are open]* as it sinks down, your eyes can close again and you can sink down into the next level of trance, even more relaxed, even more comfortable, feeling more and more detached, remote and detached. Good. Now your arm[24] is completely back to normal and you are in a deep, comfortable trance.

Script 3.8   A different eye-catalepsy

[This can be especially useful with the sceptical and
questioning patient who, despite his overt willingness, even
eagerness, to use hypnosis is strongly defended and tense and
really does not believe he can be hypnotized or that hypnosis
is real. It employs the fact that it is virtually impossible to
open one's eyes when the latter are rolled upwards in their
sockets. Be careful, however. One of the authors used this
with an engineer, after trying one or two other approaches
without any gain. It enabled this extremely sceptical
individual to reach a very satisfactory trance very quickly.
The treatment that followed was highly successful: he had
come for help with impotence, having failed to get any
erection at all for some seven years. In the course of the
session, he developed a full erection while picturing himself
getting into bed with his girlfriend. The following week,
however, he arrived for his next [and, as it proved, last]
session, furiously angry with the therapist for having been
tricked, as he saw it. He had done some reading and
discovered that it is physically impossible to open one's eyes
while they are rolled back in the head and asserted that the
therapist had used a music-hall trick on him and that he had
really not been hypnotized at all. He ignored the fact that the
session had been of some benefit and, declaring the therapist
a charlatan, departed.]

I would like you to roll your eyes up in your head as far back
as they will go, without tilting your head. Good. Now allow
your eyelids to come down, so that your eyes are closed, but
still keeping your eyes rolled as far back as they will go. When
you notice that you cannot open your eyes, let me know.
Good. You have reached the first stage of hypnosis. Now just
relax and let your eyes relax too, and let yourself sink deeper
and deeper into relaxation, becoming more and more
comfortable, deeper and deeper into trance. Good.

 Script 3.9   Pacing and leading

*[Carefully match your speech rhythm to the patient's
breathing as you begin, and then, once he appears to be
following your speech with his breathing, begin to slow the
pace and rhythm of your speech slightly more, so that the
patient slows and deepens his respiration.]*

Perhaps you would like to close your eyes, as it does make it
easier to concentrate on what I am saying. Good. Now, just
keep your thoughts on what I say, and if any thoughts or
sounds or anything else intrudes into your mind, just let the
intrusion come and go without paying any particular
attention to it. I would like you to turn your attention to your
breathing. Notice how you can feel the air go down into your
lungs and chest *[N.B. on an INhalation]*, and then flow out
again as your chest relaxes *[N.B. on an EXhalation]*, and then
flow in again ... and out again. And as you concentrate on
feeling the air flowing in ... *[pacing your delivery
appropriately]* and out, ... notice that the air gradually goes
deeper and deeper into your body, ... deeper and deeper in ...
and out. Notice how this makes you feel more and more
relaxed as your breath goes deeper ...[25] and deeper, and so you
can let yourself go deeper ... and deeper ... into the hypnotic
state, more and more relaxed, ... more and more comfortable ...
deeper and deeper. Good.

 Script 3.10   Distraction and confusion; triple instruction

*[Sit close by the patient's side, so that you are in a position
to hold the patient's arm up in the air when the time
comes.[26]]*

In a few moments, I am going to ask you to do a number of
things. When I say One, I would like you to roll your eyes up
in your head as far as they will go and hold them there,
without tilting your head up, because that would make you
uncomfortable. When I say Two, I would like you to close
your eyes and draw a deep breath at the same time. When I

say <u>Three</u>, I will pick up your arm and I would like you to let
your eyes relax, let your breath out and relax all the rest of
you so that you can sink quickly and comfortably into the
first stage of trance. That's quite complicated, so I will go
through it again. *[Repeat the instructions briefly, then take
hold of the patient's arm at the wrist, but do not move it yet.]*
Good. Now: <u>One</u>, roll your eyes up. ... Good. <u>Two</u>, close your
eyes and breathe in. ... Good. <u>Three</u>, let your eyes relax,
breathe out, *[raise the arm at this point until the patient's
elbow is straight and the arm near the vertical, and continue
smoothly]* and let all the rest of you relax. Good.[27] You have
begun to enter the trance state. Good. Now in a moment or
two, I will slowly bring your arm down again and as I do so,
it will gradually go back to normal,[28] and you will feel
yourself sinking deeper and deeper into trance. *[Take hold of
the arm again and gradually ease it downwards until it is
resting on the arm of the chair or the patient's lap, whilst
saying:]* As your arm gradually comes down, let yourself go
deeper and deeper still. Good.

Script 3.11   Contradiction

*[Sit by one side of the patient ready to pick up his arm at the
wrist.]*

Just let me pick up your arm. Don't help me, just let it go
limp. Good. Now, when you were a small child, or as a baby, I
expect your mother used to pick you up and rock you in her
arms to soothe you and help you drift off to sleep. Picture how
that was, how it felt, as she rocked you *[beginning to rock the
patient's arm slightly backwards and forwards in step with
your words]* backwards and forwards, backwards and
forwards. Remember how it felt, as she rocked you backwards
and forwards *[gradually letting your movements get OUT OF
STEP with what you are saying, until you move the arm
FORWARDS when you say 'backwards', etc.]*, backwards and
forwards, making you feel so relaxed and comfortable,
backwards and forwards, so relaxed and comfortable, that you
used to drift off to sleep, gently and comfortably, rocking

backwards and forwards *[by this time, your movements are gradually getting back in phase with your words, only to phase out of step again]* just as you are drifting away now, drifting off far from the everyday world, relaxed and comfortable, drifting off deeper and deeper as you feel yourself rocking backwards and forwards, backwards and forwards. Good. And now, just as your mother used to lay you down when you had drifted off, so I will lay your arm down here, *[suiting actions to words]* so that you can just drift away, enjoying the warm, comfortable, relaxed feelings.

One could add endlessly to these scripts. Further examples can be found in, for example, Hartland (1971), Kroger (1977), Edelstien (1981) Crasilneck and Hall (1985), Erickson *et al.* (1981) and indeed any book on hypnosis. A particularly well-designed induction is given in Edelstien (1981, pp. 32–3), which is especially attractive because of its ease of presentation and for the explanatory notes included. However, it requires rather closer physical contact between therapist and patient than is sometimes either wise or helpful. In any case, with practice based on trying out various scripts, the practitioner will soon develop his own scripts and personal style.

One final example, however, should not be omitted. This is a very brief induction devised by Dr D.B. Ewin of Tulane University Medical School (described in a privately circulated paper) and employed by him in an Accident and Emergency Unit where he practises hypnosis in the management of burns. Naturally, if a patient is in intense distress and pain, and emergency treatments are being applied simultaneously with hypnosis, a lengthy and leisurely approach is not indicated.

Dr Ewin simply explains to the patient in two or three sentences that he can learn to separate himself from the pain and distress by following some simple instructions. Once the patient consents to the procedure he is already, of course, half-way into trance. He is then asked to close his eyes, roll them upwards in his head, draw a deep breath and then, as he breathes out, slowly to allow his eyes to return to their normal position and at the same time to relax and to detach himself. Dr Ewin then says: 'Now, go to your laughing place', having first asked the patient for some happy memory or place to which he will 'go'. This procedure is reported to produce a sufficient trance for pain control to be achieved and for a reduction, through using imagery of coolness, of inflammation, blistering, etc.

Finally, it will be clear that most inductions tend to be somewhat time-consuming, at least with some patients and generally with the first attempt at hypnosis. If hypnosis is to be used regularly with a particular patient, it can be very helpful to set up a 'conditioned response' in the form of a quick transition into trance in response to a simple stimulus. This is best arranged while the patient is still in trance. For example, once the patient is in such a depth of trance as is required for whatever work is to be done, he can be instructed as follows:

Every time, from now on, when you and I agree to use hypnosis, and only then, we will not need to go through the process we used today to help you to enter the trance. I will simply say: 'Close your eyes; go into trance now', and you will be able to let yourself slip easily and smoothly into as deep a trance as you are enjoying at this very moment. I will simply say: 'Close your eyes; go into trance now', and you will go as deeply into trance as you need. This will work only when you want to go into trance, and when you hear my voice say those words.

The patient should then be roused from the trance, agreement should be reached with him to use the abbreviated technique, and then he should be returned to trance in this way. From then on this will be sufficient induction, but when it is used the patient should be allowed a little time to settle into the trance, and it is wise to suggest that he should let the therapist know when he is ready to proceed with whatever treatment has been planned, either with a visible signal or in words.

It was made clear at the beginning of this chapter that inductions should be adapted to the personal style of the therapist and to the personality of the patient being treated. Once the principles of induction have become an automatic part of the therapist's thinking, this adaptation will happen quite naturally.

Most people, when taking their first steps in this method by reading a script word for word, will find themselves amending the script almost involuntarily. This is all to the good. An essential ingredient of the process is comfort: if the therapist is uncomfortable with a phrase or even a whole induction, it will come out awkwardly and disturb both patient and therapist.

The scripts given above represent a fair sample of the techniques used regularly by the authors. There is hardly any limit to the variations possible, and additional inductions quite different from those given here will be found in other books. None has any intrinsic superiority over others, and all have their merits. All psychotherapy demands a degree of creativity on the part of the therapist, and the use of hypnosis does not detract from this; indeed, it gives the therapist an even greater degree of such freedom, not least in the induction, deepening and general management of the trance.

4

DEEPENING

INTRODUCTION

The concept of depth of trance is, like most aspects of hypnosis, the subject of considerable discussion and difference amongst writers on the subject. In practice it is quite self-evident that there are differences in the quality of the hypnotic experience at different times. These are most aptly labelled differences of depth, analogous with that of depth of sleep or of relaxation. In the initial stages of an induction one feels oneself relaxing progressively, becoming 'more deeply' relaxed quite naturally, until a point is reached where the subjective state is felt to change in quality. This can be recognized by most people as entering what we are calling 'the trance' or 'the hypnotic state', and this state is itself experienced to change progressively as further procedures are carried out, or suggestions made by the therapist.

One generally finds that in the early stages of an hypnotic experience some phenomena can be readily elicited, others seem more elusive and may be described by the subject as impossible. For instance, arm levitation (the experience of feeling one's arm seeming to become weightless and floating upwards apparently involuntarily) seems to become possible in a very early phase of hypnosis, and can therefore be used as part of an induction (see Script 3.7 in chapter 3). Suggestions of insensitivity to pain, or even total anaesthesia of some part of the body, require more preparation and more extensive suggestions of increased depth of the hypnotic state. Even more preparation is likely to be required to facilitate the production of amnesia for, say, a particular part of the session, except in the most susceptible of subjects. The term 'depth' seems apt because that is how it feels to the subject, perhaps because of the analogy with sleep (where the term is well established) and finally, and conclusively, because using that word has the effect we seek. That is to say, suggesting to the patient that he should 'sink down, deeper and deeper into trance' is accepted by most subjects and appears to enable them to achieve such a state or condition as they require for the more difficult procedures.

On occasion the patient will reach as deep a trance as is needed for whatever procedure is to follow, simply through an induction of the kind already described. One occasionally meets subjects who enter so profound an hypnotic state with a brief induction, and no further suggestion of depth, that they can produce anaesthesia and even amnesia with no difficulty or delay. Such talent, however, is pretty rare. Most people need time, suggestions, and often imagery of some kind to enable them to become sufficiently established and comfortable in the trance state to begin the work for which the session is intended.

Since the concept of depth is, as suggested above, curiously apt to describe the subject's experiences, images of moving downwards, such as descending in a lift or on an escalator, or walking down a staircase or sloping path and so on, seem to facilitate the desired effect. For the subject, it is as though in picturing, and feeling, oneself descending physically one experiences oneself descending internally to deeper and deeper levels.

As with all suggestions and imagery, it is important first to clarify with the patient that the planned imagery is acceptable and congenial. It is quite obvious that initially suggesting descent in a lift to a patient who is phobic of such things is likely to disturb his attention and concentration. (To be sure, once a good trance has been achieved with such a patient, one may well use imagery of the phobic stimulus very successfully in treatment by either desensitization or implosion.)

Some patients will quite spontaneously and successfully deal with such a situation should it arise, as in the case of the elderly lady mentioned earlier, who said, after her first hypnotic session: 'I hope you don't mind, Doctor, but when you told me the lift doors were opening, I decided I would go down the stairs instead. You see, I *hate* lifts!'. Many patients are likely to be less self-assured and forgiving than this lady and may even break out of the trance with some loss of confidence in the procedure and in the therapist. The effects of inappropriate imagery can be disturbing in other ways: for example, using the image of a summer meadow may precipitate a genuine attack of hay fever in a susceptible patient. Thus part of the introductory discussion should include checking any images that the therapist may have in mind to use for induction and deepening.

Deepening may be carried out without imagery, simply by suggestions of increasing depth of relaxation and trance and increasing detachment from the here and now. Such a procedure would follow most aptly from an induction on the lines of 'Loosening of attention' (Script 3.5).

███████████ Script 4.1

Just let yourself relax more and more deeply as you go on listening to my voice. Let your arms and legs get still heavier, still more limp, more and more heavy and limp, heavy and limp; let your back relax more and more deeply so that you feel yourself sinking deeper and deeper into the chair, and as your neck relaxes more and more deeply, so your head feels heavier and heavier as it rests on the back of the chair. Let the muscles in your cheeks relax more and more deeply so that you feel the weight of your cheeks. Let the muscles of your forehead relax more and more, so that they become soft and loose. Let the muscles around your eyes relax more and more deeply. Let the muscles around your mouth go loose and slack, relaxing more and more deeply. Let yourself sink deeper and deeper, deeper and deeper, relaxing more and more deeply, more and more deeply, and as you relax deeper and deeper you can feel yourself going deeper and deeper inside yourself, deeper and deeper inside yourself.

This, with such embellishments, repetitions and additions as suggest themselves, can be extended until the therapist is satisfied that the patient is sufficiently established in trance and sufficiently detached from all except his voice for the planned work to commence.

More commonly, however, it will be helpful to use imagery of some kind to enhance the feelings of increasing depth and detachment. In addition, since this stage of the session is usually wholly enjoyable, once any initial apprehension and anxiety have faded, the use of pleasant imagery, associated with achievement of the hypnotic state enables the patient to become familiar with and confident about the use of imagery. He will have experienced the subjective reality and power of calling up an image, and so be more ready to respond to suggested imagery that is to be used in the therapeutic strategy to follow.

██████████ Script 4.2

I would like you to imagine that you are standing at the edge of an old terrace. Perhaps there is a house behind you. The terrace is made of flagstones, with plants and flowers growing up between them. Around the terrace is a stone balustrade with climbing plants and flowers growing over it. Perhaps there are some blooms on them, and also on some of the plants that grow here and there between the slabs of the terrace. Opposite where you stand, you can see that there is a gap in the balustrade, and that there are steps going down from the terrace. In a little while,[29] I am going to ask you to walk across to the top of the steps and then slowly down them, and as you go down the steps you can feel yourself leaving the ordinary world far, far behind, and going deep inside yourself. But first, notice that the sun is shining warmly on you. Notice a soft warm breeze gently playing around you, bringing the scents of the flowers to you. Enjoy those feelings, and now walk across to the top of the steps and look down towards the meadow. There are ten steps, again with flowers growing here and there between them. In a moment, I am going to count slowly from one to ten and as I do so, I would like you to go slowly down the steps, one at a time, and let yourself go deeper and deeper into trance as you do so. Good. Now begin to go down the steps. One ... two ... deeper and deeper. Three ... going deeper and deeper into trance. Four ... five. ... Pause there for a moment, halfway down, and notice how you are leaving the ordinary woi.d further and further behind you as you go deeper and deeper into trance. Go on now, deeper still. Six ... seven ... eight ... nearly there now.

Nine ... ten. ... Good. Deep inside yourself, deep in trance, feeling very deeply relaxed and comfortable, relaxed and detached. Deep deep down. Good.

███████   Script 4.3

Picture yourself standing at the top of a long escalator. Look down it as it stretches downwards in front of you, slowly moving down. Notice that there are lights in the roof above it fixed at intervals, ten lights down the length of the escalator. At the bottom, a long way down, you can see that there is a door. In a moment, I am going to ask you to step forward on to the escalator and let yourself be carried down. As you go down deeper and deeper, I will count off the lights as they pass by over your head, and when I reach the tenth, you will reach the bottom of the escalator and step off it in front of that door. As you are carried down, you can let yourself be carried deeper and deeper into trance. Now, step on to the escalator and go down, deeper and deeper. One ... two ... deeper and deeper. ... Three ... four ... leaving the ordinary world further and further behind. ... Five ... six ... deeper and deeper. ... Seven ... deep, deep down, eight ... nine ... nearly there now. ... Ten. Good. You step off the escalator and stand in front of that door. In another moment, I shall ask you to go through that door and find yourself in your favourite place, completely detached from the ordinary world, deep inside yourself, your special private place. Good. Now, open that door, go through it and then close it behind you.

Much the same procedure would be used employing the image of a lift. The picture would begin with the patient standing in front of the lift doors and, when they open, he enters the lift. When the doors close the lift begins to move downwards, the therapist counting the floors being passed, only in this case one would count backwards from, say, ten.

With this image it can be very helpful, having reached the ground floor, to suggest that there are basement floors and so go further down still, rather unexpectedly. This can be helpful to patients who are finding it difficult to 'let go': the unexpected further descent takes them just a little off-guard in such a way as to facilitate their commitment to entering trance. In every case, whether it be stairs, escalator or lift, counting should be in cadence to the patient's exhalations, leading respiration, if necessary, into a slower pace.

Instead of depth, the feeling of distance can be employed. For example, you may ask the patient to picture himself lying comfortably on a raft or in a small boat gently drifting down a river, noting that as he drifts further and further (away from the everyday world) the river is getting wider and wider, so that he is further and further away from the bank on either side, while feeling a gentle rocking motion as he gently drifts towards and into an idyllic inner world.

Any such imagery can be extended if necessary. For example, having descended from the terrace to a meadow, the patient can then be invited to wander through the meadow, enjoying the warmth of the sun, attending to and enjoying the scent of grass and flowers going towards, say, a clump of trees where he can sit and dream, or to the bank of a stream where he can sit and watch the water flowing past. Alternatively, a door is often a useful transitional point at which the patient enters the previously determined 'private place', as suggested in Script 4.3 above.

Another approach is to use hypnotic phenomena in order to give the patient the 'feel' of hypnosis, and thus enable him to enter more and more completely into the hypnotic state, much as is done in those inductions that use this method.

Script 4.4

Turn your attention to your right arm. Notice how relaxed it is, as it lies on the arm of the chair. Feel its weight, and the feel of the material underneath your hand. Let it relax even more, until it feels quite detached from you. Now imagine it becoming lighter and lighter, losing all sensation of weight, lighter and lighter, until it has no weight at all, light as a feather, light as a balloon. If you let it go completely, you will feel it begin to float up into the air, lighter and lighter, floating up into the air quite by itself. Good. Just let it float up by itself, light as a balloon, and as it floats up higher and higher, you can let yourself slip deeper and deeper into trance. Higher and higher, deeper and deeper. Good. Now let it stop there, and you can let it gradually recover its feeling of weight. As it does so, it will slowly sink back down again, and as it comes down, you feel yourself sinking down still deeper, so that when it touches the arm of the chair again you can slip easily and smoothly into as deep a level of trance as you need. Good.

Good. Now it is back completely to normal, and you are in a deep, deep trance.[30]

Readers will be familiar with the phenomenon that psychologists and the like are much given to neologisms and other abuses of the language. Sadly, this cannot be avoided altogether. The technique known as 'fractionating' (which has nothing to do with procedures in differential distillation) can be used with great benefit with patients who find trance difficult and who 'hold on' despite themselves, especially those who are apprehensive and agitated yet at the same time genuinely keen to use hypnosis. It is the term used to describe the process in which repeated changes in depth of trance are sought, with the patient repeatedly being brought nearly or even wholly out of the trance and then led back into it, deeper each time. This creates a sense of some confusion, which loosens the hold the patient is keeping involuntarily on the real world. A very effective way of doing this follows on naturally from the 'eye-catalepsy' induction (Script 3.6 in the previous chapter).

■■■■■■■ Script 4.5

In a moment, I am going to ask you to open your eyes.[31] I would like you to open your eyes just for a moment when I ask you and then immediately close them again. Each time you open and close them when I ask, you will find yourself sinking deeper and deeper into trance. After a few repetitions, you will be so deeply relaxed, your eyes will only open a tiny crack, and that time, when you close them again, you will sink into as deep a trance as you need for the work we are going to do. Good. Now, for the first time, open and close your eyes <u>now</u>... and go deeper, and deeper, and deeper. Good.[32] Now again, open and close your eyes <u>now</u>, and let yourself sink down deeper, and deeper ... and deeper ... and deeper. Good. Now just once more, open and close your eyes <u>now</u>, and let yourself sink right down, ... deep deep down, ... deeper and deeper ... deeper and deeper ... deep, deep down. Good.

A powerful variant on this is to bring the patient quite explicitly out of trance and back in again. It would probably be found helpful for the beginner to practise the delivery and timing of this procedure a number of times into a tape-recorder in order to become fluent and unhesitating as well as getting the pacing right, before applying the technique 'live'.

███████ Script 4.6

In a little while I am going to count backwards, and as I do so, I would like you to let yourself come up out of the trance, back to the ordinary waking state, so that when I reach the count of One, you will open your eyes and be wide awake, and then immediately close them when I ask you to and let yourself sink back into the trance as I count upwards from One again. We will repeat that several times, and each time you will be able to go a little deeper, so that quite soon you will be in a really deep and pleasant trance, totally relaxed and at ease, relaxed and detached. So, now let yourself come back to full wakefulness, five ... four ... three ... two. ... One,[33] eyes open, wide awake, now close your eyes again. One ... two ... three ... four ... five ... six ... seven. Good. Now, again, five ... four ... three ... two ... <u>one</u>, eyes open, wide awake and close your eyes, and go really deep. One, two, three, four ... five ... six ... seven ... eight ... nine. Good. Good. *[Repeat if necessary, using still higher starting and ending numbers. The pace is varied to match the level of alertness of the subject, with increasing speed and urgency as the patient rises out of trance and then slowing progressively with an*

increasingly relaxed tone after an urgent start as the
countdown begins again.]

A young male patient developed an interesting variant of this for himself, when he found both hetero- and self-hypnosis difficult. He was addicted to scuba diving and so imagined himself in his favourite patch of sea, 'sounding' repeatedly to gain greater depth, that is, returning repeatedly to the surface and then diving again, and in this way was able, to his own surprise and pleasure, to use hypnosis very effectively employing this image, both when alone and when working with the therapist.

In all this so far, it has been implied that either the therapist will know in some intuitive way when the patient has entered a sufficiently deep trance to mediate the planned treatment, or that the patient will simply enter trance to the requisite depth judged in some numinous and unspecified way. To some extent both these notions are true, and there is no really objective and easily administered test that can be applied from time to time during induction and deepening to assess depth of trance.

The story is told of Erickson who, when he was asked how one may decide whether a patient's trance is sufficient, replied that he would ask his own unconscious and would observe which finger on his own hand moved 'involuntarily'; if it was the thumb, he would know the trance state of the patient was still very shallow; if it was the little finger, the trance would be as deep as was needed! With experience something of the same sort will be found by the therapist, even if not, perhaps, quite so literally. We find it helpful to suggest to the patient that one (specified) finger should lift when he feels himself to be sufficiently deep to begin work.

At times, despite indications of adequate trance, a treatment strategy or imagery will fail. The patient should be instructed to tell the therapist if this occurs, so that further deepening or more time in the 'private place' can be allowed before proceeding further.

COMMON DIFFICULTIES

A number of things may occur during induction, deepening and the trance period generally which can be alarming to the novice practitioner. For example, some people show various disturbing items of behaviour such as choking or weeping at some point in the descent into trance. Some will produce this every time they go into trance, but always the behaviour diminishes and disappears with further deepening. Naturally, one does not ignore such events but includes them in the induction or deepening by suitable comment, including the reassurance that the behaviour will pass. Such phenomena are not on their own a counter-indication to the use of hypnosis with such patients. Naturally, one would explore the reasons for or meaning of such reactions after the end of the hypnotic session, although generally they appear to be no more than a release of tension.

Also disturbing to the beginner are those patients who open their eyes, sometimes repeatedly, during the induction and further procedures and make comments on what they are experiencing, or worse still, not experiencing. This occurs most commonly with children, who in any case sometimes keep their eyes wide open throughout the session despite the fact that they are deep in trance.

An apt illustration can be taken from a patient who repeatedly returned from deep trance to full consciousness while undergoing an experience of age regression (see chapters 17 and 18). She had re-created in trance an event from early childhood which had been markedly traumatic. The experience was so vividly re-captured that she became alarmed. As she explained subsequently, she had been so astonished at the degree of realism with which she experienced the feeling of being four years old with a four-year-old body, and the event being reviewed, that she felt an intense need to check whether she actually was a grown woman or a small child. Each time she opened her eyes she was readily reassured that all was well and returned to trance again.

The practitioner need not be disturbed by these or other interruptions. Sometimes it is clear that the patient's anxieties about hypnosis, or about therapy, have not been sufficiently allayed or that insufficient explanations have been offered. At other times, one will conclude that hypnotic procedures should be postponed or even abandoned, but more generally calm and confident persistence, perhaps using a different kind of induction altogether, will have the desired effect.

At the other end of the scale is the patient who falls asleep. The very first patient referred to one of the authors in a hospital setting aroused anxiety in this way. The patient had abused alcohol for many years, and was referred for help with controlling this. One of the consequences of her habit was a severe peripheral neuritis, and the attendant pain was one of the targets of therapy. In the course of her first session she was given a pain-management routine, at the end of which she was asked to come back to the waking state. At the moment when she should have opened her eyes she began to snore loudly and continued to do so for some fifteen minutes, during which time the therapist was vividly conscious of the fact that the ward sister kept looking through the window in the door while the patient continued to sleep soundly, despite the therapist's increasingly strenuous (and anxious) efforts to wake her. When at last she did wake, she expressed delight at her freedom from pain and reported that this had been her first experience of normal and spontaneous sleep for some months.

A very few patients will *refuse* to return from trance, and these too can be worrying to the novice. The immediate problem is to end the session, the further being to explore the reasons for this retreat or negativism. If this should occur, it is generally adequate to tell the patient that you are leaving the room to allow him simply to enjoy the experience for a little longer and that he will return to the waking state in his own time. The patient can then be left alone, and will usually put an end to the refusal within a short time.

Kroger (1977) suggests that on occasion this can be handled by encouraging the patient to remain in the trance for as long as he finds it helpful, but to remember that a fee of so much per minute is being charged. Unsurprisingly, the result is that patients acting in this way return out of trance fairly promptly! In National Health Service units this is not, of course, practicable, but we have found that telling this story once the patient is out of trance generally forestalls any repetition.

In instances where exploratory work is carried out, strong emotional reactions are often encountered, occasionally to the point of a major abreaction of some traumatic event and the release of previously dissociated and unconscious affect. It cannot be emphasized too often that no work should be undertaken in hypnosis which the practitioner is not well qualified to carry out independently of hypnosis, and this applies especially to the use of uncovering techniques. The emergence of repressed material *must* be skilfully handled by a therapist who is accustomed to manage such affect-laden experiences and bring them to a satisfactory conclusion.

On occasion patients will abreact spontaneously, that is without any strategies being pursued to uncover traumata. If this should occur to a therapist who does not have appropriate psychoanalytic training and experience, he will find that reassurance of his continued presence and suggestions of gradually discharging the painful affect safely in his presence, or in the safety of the 'private place', without any exploration or questions will serve to minimize the distress and fear and bring the episode to an end. Should this sort of event occur, it would be wise to refer that patient to an appropriately qualified therapist.

5

SELF-HYPNOSIS

INTRODUCTION

The primary purpose of employing hypnosis in clinical practice is to facilitate or intensify a treatment process, whether in the form of control of physical states, in behaviour modification, or in analytic therapy. However, it is worth bearing in mind that the ability to enter trance is for most people in part an acquired skill that requires practice. For many patients, especially those in whose condition there is a major degree of anxiety and those who have substantial obsessional defences, entering hypnosis can be in itself a somewhat alarming experience and this alarm needs to be allayed, again through practice, especially practice alone, where no threat, such as from anticipated treatment strategies, is imminent.

Where chronic anxiety or repeated anxiety attacks are present, or where physical symptoms or pain are the target of treatment, the patient's ability to enter the hypnotic state while alone is a vital strategy in itself. Once well-trained in self-hypnosis the patient will be able to reduce anxiety, pain, etc. whenever he needs to do so. In virtually every case where hypnosis is to be used, it is helpful to include training in self-hypnosis at the beginning of treatment and encourage the patient to practise, thus making the purpose of such practice explicit.

Once again, it must be emphasized that hypnosis or experiencing the hypnotic state is not a treatment in itself, but that spending time in trance is often comforting and generally helpful. A patient who spends most or all of his waking hours (and many while asleep as well) in a state of heightened arousal will benefit significantly from spending one or two periods each day in a state of deep relaxation and detachment. Patients who have had no more than a trial induction, with deepening and some comforting and pleasant imagery, often leave the consulting room in a state of relaxation and even sometimes euphoria, and with confidence and hope that were notably lacking earlier in the session. Most patients will find, once they master the knack of entering the trance, that they are able to re-capture those good feelings at home and to use the trance to gain respite from anxiety, depression, pain and so on.

Since one of the principal ways of using hypnotherapy is to assist the patient to gain mastery of his own behaviour, reactions and experiences, it follows that the patient needs to learn the art of entering the trance and of employing it to achieve the desired mastery.

Finally, when treating physical problems such as pain, eczema, migraine, etc., or when treating addictions or compulsive behaviour, the patient needs a tool to reduce the pain, itching, feelings of compulsion and so on, and here self-hypnosis may provide him with what he needs.

To repeat: it is good practice to include some training in self-hypnosis in the first hypnotherapy session with any patient and to advise or even strongly suggest that he should spend time in a self-induced trance daily. If it is intended to use hypnosis in further sessions in, for example, uncovering and exploring traumata, the patient will become more confident as well as more adept in using the trance in therapy through regular practice. He will lose any remaining fear of the state and learn, at both conscious and unconscious levels, that the process is under his own control and that he can escape if need be to the safety of his 'private place'. In some cases, the development of self-hypnotic skills is central to the patient's needs. For example, if the therapy is aimed at mastering chronic pain, then clearly one would need to emphasize right from the start a thorough establishment of self-hypnotic skills.

Just as in hetero-hypnosis, many patients do not require any elaborate ritual for self-hypnosis, but usually some attention-fixing routine makes the whole thing much easier. Once the patient has become really adept and comfortable with the process, the induction can be abbreviated to as little as a single key word. For example, a patient subject to anxiety attacks may learn to enter a shallow trance almost instantaneously by saying to himself a single word such as 'Calm' or 'Peace' and so abort an incipient panic. However, one would normally begin by teaching self-hypnosis through the use of an induction that has both attention-gaining and attention-holding characteristics, perhaps employing relaxation and breathing patterns to enhance detachment and dissociation, with such suggestive power as to lead the patient into trance even when preoccupied or anxious.

Patients who find self-hypnosis difficult, perhaps because of continuous anxiety, preoccupying or compulsive thoughts and the like, may need the assistance of a self-hypnosis routine as specific as that employed in the hetero-hypnotic induction used by the therapist. Thus one may suggest fixating a spot on the ceiling, or indeed any of the techniques described in chapter 3 that can be adapted to use alone. Alternatively, a tape-recording made by the therapist of an induction (usually best made with the patient present) may have to be provided. This is discussed in detail later in this chapter.

In general, it is helpful to conduct the instruction in self-hypnosis while the patient is in trance. The training can be done while he is in his normal waking state, but tends to be more effective and readily absorbed if he is actually in the trance state at the time. If the self-induction routine is presented while the patient is in a light trance, he will tend to sink into deeper trance through his attention to the presentation of the self-hypnotic induction. The experience of so sinking deeper and deeper conveys an implicit suggestion of the effectiveness of the self-hypnosis routine, and so enhances the effect of the routine being taught. Once the self-induction has been presented, it is useful to suggest that the patient should now return to the waking state and carry out the self-induction immediately himself while the therapist sits silently by, to ensure that the procedure is right for him, that he remembers it, and that he experiences its effectiveness. A typical training would be on the following lines.

████████████ Script 5.1

I am now going to tell you how to take yourself into this comfortable trance state. You will find it helpful to use this exercise once or twice a day and then, when you have

mastered it, you can use it any time you need to ... [reduce
pain, extinguish anxiety, control rage, etc.]. Just go
somewhere where you will be undisturbed for a little while; sit
or lie down and make yourself comfortable. Then, when you
are ready, close your eyes and relax. Draw a deep breath; hold
it for a moment, and then let it out slowly, counting as you do
so: One ... two ... three. You will feel yourself relaxing more
and more as you do this. Then draw another deep breath;
hold it for a moment and then let it out slowly, counting as
you do so: Four ... five ... six. As you are doing this, you will
feel yourself beginning to sink down into the same comfortable
state you are experiencing at this moment. Then take another
deep breath; hold it for a moment and then let it out again,
slowly, counting as you do so: Seven ... eight ... nine. You will
feel yourself sinking deeper and deeper. Then forget about
your breathing, let it go back to its natural rhythm, and
concentrate all your attention on the number ten. As you do
so, you will be able to sink into as deep a trance as you need
and want at that time. Then, if you wish, you can either let
yourself go back to that happy time and place you experienced
earlier in this session, or let any image you wish form in your
mind's eye, and enjoy it. Alternatively you can just let yourself
enjoy the peace and tranquillity of being so relaxed and
detached. After a few minutes[34] you will return to the normal
waking state, but bring with you all the calm and peaceful
feeling of the trance. Your eyes will open and you will become
fully alert. If, while you are in the trance, something should
crop up that requires your attention, or if some emergency
should occur, you will immediately leave the trance and
become fully alert so that you can deal with the problem.
When you wish to leave the trance you can just count
backwards from five to one in your head, and as you do so,
you will gradually waken and become fully alert by the count
of One.

The latter part of this script includes precautions that should be
added to every self-hypnosis routine: arousal in case of emergency and a procedure for self-arousal at will.

At the point reached in the above script, one would leave

the patient to enjoy his state for a few moments (having first told him that you will keep silence for a short while), and then resume as follows:

Each time you practise this exercise you will find it easier to do and you will be able to go a little deeper until you find yourself able quickly and easily to reach as deep a trance as you need. So, as you go on practising and become more familiar with the trance state, you will find it easier to go as deep as you need when you are with me. You will also find that, as you spend time in the trance each day, the effects of spending time in trance will become stronger and stronger and will last longer and longer. You will be able to remain calm and confident [or: free from pain, etc.] for more and more of each day.

In a few moments, I am going to ask you to come out of the trance and then to use this exercise immediately to go back into trance so that we are sure we have got it right.

The patient is then roused, the routine discussed and amended if necessary, and he is then asked to go into trance on his own.

Two further self-induction scripts may be found useful, the last with quite specific value in anxiety attacks, phobic reactions and similar situations. It is a particularly apt method for coping with 'exam nerves' or 'stage fright'.

Script 5.2

When it is time for you to go and do your self-hypnosis exercise, go somewhere where you will be undisturbed for a short while. Sit or lie down and make yourself comfortable. Then close your eyes and relax. When you are ready, roll your eyes upwards in your head as far as you can and at the same time draw a deep breath and hold it. Then let your breath out slowly and let your eyes return, still closed, to their normal position. As you breathe out and relax your eyes, you will be able to feel yourself beginning to sink down into the trance, just letting go as you release your breath and your eye muscles, letting go and sinking down, deeper and deeper.

If the patient found it difficult initially to enter trance, suggest that this routine should be performed three times, with increasing depth of trance at each repetition.

The same precautionary suggestions about arousal, length of trance, etc., are then added, as are suggestions of increasing ease in entering the trance and the effectiveness of spending time in this way in terms of general ease and comfort, as well as improvement in whatever may be the specific problem being tackled.

Script 5.3

When you need to go into trance very quickly and briefly, as for example when you find yourself becoming very anxious, just hold your left hand over your eyes for a moment as though shading them, close your eyes and think of the word 'PEACE'. Perhaps you would like to see it written or painted, or to think of hearing the word spoken. PEACE ... PEACE. ... As you think of that word, you will instantly go into trance for just a moment, just long enough for the anxiety to fade right away. And then you will open your eyes, take your hand away and you will be in control again, with the anxiety gone.

Some care has to be taken in choosing the stimulus word for 'instant trance'. A woman colleague with a particularly rich and warm voice reported using this technique when treating a young man for premature ejaculation. She used an approach much like that of Script 5.3, employing the word 'Calm', until the young man suddenly burst out with: 'If you go on saying that, I *shall* come!' The word 'Peace' can also cause difficulties if not pronounced with care.

Alternatively, one may simply use the same approach as in hetero-hypnotic induction, that is, to suggest to the patient that he go through the same induction that he has just followed with the therapist when he is on his own: staring at a spot on the ceiling until his eyes tire and close spontaneously, then visualizing the same scene, be it stairs, escalator or whatever has been used, counting himself down, and so on.

Some patients find the simpler approaches to self-hypnosis unsuccessful and need more elaborate self-inductions, including imagery. Even with detailed and lengthy self-inductions, some patients find that their ability to enter trance while alone wanes quite rapidly and, even if 'topped up' at weekly or fortnightly sessions, cannot use self-hypnosis successfully. Commonly, such patients give up the attempt after a few days. They can often be successful in reaching trance on their own with the assistance, as suggested earlier, of a tape-recording of the therapist carrying out an induction with them, plus imagery, ego-strengthening and so on.

Hypnotic inductions on tape can be purchased on the open market and some patients have used such tapes before seeking therapy. If a patient has found such a tape helpful it would be inappropriate to discourage him from using it, but we prefer to provide an individually designed recording for each person which employs that patient's name and which has specific suggestions for that patient. We generally find it more satisfactory to make such a recording with the patient present. It cannot be guaranteed, of course, that when the patient is alone he will react at the same pace as when the induction is carried out in person, but it is more satisfactory to pace one's delivery and the flow of suggestions, imagery and so on to the reactions of the patient rather than by one's judgement in his absence.

It is important to make a suggestion about instantaneous self-arousal in the event of some emergency occurring in the course of the taped induction, at an early point in the tape. When the induction is complete, the recording continues on lines such as the following:

For a few minutes now, you will not hear my voice, but in the silence, you can go on enjoying [*whatever the specific image or 'private place' may be*]. **When you hear my voice again, you will be ready to return to the waking state, bringing with**

you all the relaxation, well-being and ease of mind and body
that you have recaptured during your time in the trance.
Remember that if at any time something should occur that
requires your attention, you can quickly rouse yourself and
become fully alert by counting backwards in your head from
five to one, and by the count of One become fully alert. Now
just enjoy [the 'private place']. [Pause for whatever time has
been agreed, then resume:] Good. In a few moments, it will be
time for you to return to the normal waking state. I will count
backwards from five to one, and as I do so, let yourself
gradually waken, so that by the count of One your eyes will
open and you will be wide awake and fully alert. Bring with
you all the good feelings you have been experiencing during
your time in your private place, so that you go on feeling
relaxed and at ease in body and in mind. Five ... four ...
beginning to waken, ... three, ... two, nearly there. ... One,
wide awake.

Difficulties in falling asleep or returning to sleep after waking
during the night are commonly associated with a wide variety of
problems, both psychological and physical. For such patients,
one can make a dual tape with considerable benefit: one side
bears an induction followed by whatever therapeutic programme
is being used; the other contains a similar induction followed by
suggestions of progressive loosening of attention, the approach of
sleep, and finally a descent into sleep. One may add suitable
imagery for fostering sleep (see chapter 7 on disorders of sleep).

In the self-hypnosis tape, one will generally begin with an
induction that has been carried out 'live' with the patient. As
mentioned before, it is generally wise to include instructions
about self-arousal in case of emergency at an early point and
then repeat this towards the end of the routine. In the case of
a mother of young children it is also a good idea to give
reassurance concerning instantaneous arousal if anything
should happen with a small child that demands instant attention,
although obviously one would suggest that such a patient should
carry out her sessions of self-hypnosis during periods when any
small child in her care is asleep.

Imagery that has been used successfully with the patient

is followed by a period of silence in which he is to carry out pre-determined tasks such as anxiety dispersal, or simply focus on and enjoy the peace and comfort he is experiencing. One may repeat at this point the earlier suggestions concerning self-arousal if it should be necessary. Before leaving a silence, remember the need to warn the patient of this. At the end of the silent period comes a closing passage consisting of ego-strengthening, suggestions of improving skill and ease in entering hypnosis and its increasing benefits and, finally, arousal. The last can be in a dual form, leaving the choice to the patient. Thus:

In a few moments, I am going to count backwards from Five to One. As I do so, you will find yourself gradually returning to the ordinary waking state, unless you decide to stay in the trance a little longer. If you are ready to rouse, then, as I count, you will feel yourself gradually coming out of the trance so that by the count of One you are fully alert with your eyes open, alert and feeling very very good. If you decide to spend a little longer in trance, then, when you are ready to return to the ordinary waking world, just count backwards in your head from Five to One, and let yourself waken as you do so, so that by the count of One, your eyes are open and you are fully alert and orientated, feeling really good. Five ... four. ... [etc.].

Many patients appreciate being given a choice in this way. On the one hand, the suggestion of arousal following the therapist counting backwards is reassuring; on the other, the suggestion is being made of the patient's ability to determine the length of time he remains in trance and the manner of terminating it.

For those patients who experience difficulty in falling or remaining asleep, the other side of the cassette, which bears a similar induction, is followed by suggestions of progressively loosening attention not only to the current imagery but even to the therapist's voice, increasing diffuseness of awareness and a gradual drift into natural sleep. Suggestions are added concerning the restful and uninterrupted sleep to be expected, with normal and refreshed waking in the morning.

On such a tape, one needs to make allowances for the mechanics of the machine to be used by the patient. If it is of such a kind that it will not switch off automatically on reaching the end of the tape, one may suggest that when the patient hears the therapist say: 'Goodnight. Sleep well', he should reach out and switch the machine off without being in the least interrupted in his progression to sleep. Alternatively, one may suggest that either the patient will fall asleep immediately and not hear or be woken by any 'click' the machine may make on reaching the end of the tape, or that when he hears that 'click' he will fall into a deep, sound sleep.

It is by no means always necessary to check the appropriateness of a newly taped induction, but if the patient appears unconfident he can be asked to listen to the tape, let himself go into trance and then arouse himself as soon as the period of silence (if used) is reached.

Some patients never succeed in achieving much in the way of trance on their own, and many fail to practise regularly. It is obviously necessary to explore the difficulties in motivation this may disclose, but even when no trance seems to be achieved, the sheer relaxation and attention to one's own needs that the exercise involves is usually helpful to most people. Very occasionally patients report experiencing headache after self-hypnosis, and this needs to be explored. Similar experiences occur in the use of related techniques such as transcendental meditation.

The key feature of the use of self-hypnosis is the fact that it puts into the patient's hands the power and the responsibility for helping himself, and the awareness of this. This aspect of the process should be clearly understood by the patient, and if necessary repeated in the self-hypnosis routine and its embedded suggestions.

6

THE FIRST INTERVIEW

INTRODUCTION

Once it is known that a practitioner uses hypnosis he is likely to
receive referrals specifying hypnotherapy as the treatment of
choice. When this is the case it is nevertheless necessary to
prepare the patient as previously outlined, since relatively few
people have a realistic understanding of the nature of this
technique or of the experience which results from its use.
Naturally, when hypnosis has not been mentioned by the
referring agent or by the patient himself, the therapist will
introduce the topic if there is any likelihood of hypnosis being a
useful vehicle for treatment. It is generally wise to mention the
possibility of this early on: at the first or second interview. First, it
establishes more positive expectations in the patient if one
mentions it at the outset rather than if the topic is introduced at a
later stage, when the patient may well interpret the suggestion as
indicating that the therapist is losing hope of successful treatment.
In many instances hypnotherapy is suggested only when all other
forms of treatment have failed.

Secondly, it enables the therapist to assess whether this
approach is practicable with the patient before committing
himself to using this treatment mode, by carrying out a trial
induction. If the patient shows a good aptitude for hypnosis and
there is a high probability of using it, one may take the
opportunity of training the patient to respond to a brief or nearly
instantaneous induction for use on further occasions (see the end
of this chapter and also the section in chapter 3 on brief
inductions).

Thirdly, if some level of trance is achieved at a trial
induction, the patient will experience a degree of relief from

anxiety, depression, or other negative affect and therefore leave the interview in a more hopeful and positive frame of mind than may in all probability have been the case otherwise. Finally, in cases of clear-cut symptoms (especially if these are somatic), some symptom relief is likely to result in highly beneficial effects on the patient's attitude to the treatment planned and on his expectations.

Very commonly patients become quite alarmed at the mention of hypnosis. For example, a young man who had asked specifically for psychotherapy for a psychosexual disorder found the initial assessment interview interesting and congenial until he was asked how he felt about using hypnosis to facilitate the planned therapy. He lost his equanimity immediately, expressing considerable fear and, interestingly, betrayed then a very considerable anticipatory resistance to self-disclosure which had been heavily concealed up to that point. His marked ambivalence about either exposing himself or making any change in his behaviour, attitudes and lifestyle was now clearly visible and in this sense his response to the suggestion of hypnosis was of considerable clinical value. More commonly, in the absence of severe ambivalence about therapy itself, the patient will discuss the suggestion more or less comfortably and, if he has confidence in the therapist, will agree to a trial induction.

Our own practice is to conduct a fairly standard assessment interview with every patient, whether or not hypnosis was mentioned in the referral. Initially we seek to satisfy ourselves that the problem with which the patient presents is within our professional competence as psychologists and psychotherapists to treat. That is to say, we look for indications of physical conditions which might underlie an ostensibly psychological problem, the presence of major psychiatric illness, and so on. At the same time, in cases that present as or are described as 'depression', we seek to differentiate between appropriate depression of mood (such as grief at loss, reaction to major life changes such as job redundancy and so on), neurotic or reactive depression, and endogenous affective disorders.

Once we have concluded that some form of psychotherapy is appropriate, the next point is to clarify what manner or type is indicated by the nature and origin of the disorder, the personality of the patient, his personal resources, emotional strength and resilience, and his personal and social framework. For example, almost any form of personal therapy in the case of a married person will affect the marriage in some way, and such effects must be discussed with the patient before he can reasonably commit himself to treatment. It is often wise to interview the spouse, or perhaps the patient and spouse together, and in addition the spouse may be brought into the treatment contract in some way.

In addition, the question of who is asking for treatment also needs to be answered. This is especially the case with children and young people under some degree of parental control, where it may well be the parent who desires treatment or change rather than the patient himself. Indeed, on occasion a child is referred as a means of bringing therapist and parent together, either at the instigation of a referring agent who does not feel able to mention the need for help on the part of a parent directly, or by the parent him- or herself. This question is sometimes posed as: 'This is the client: who is the customer?' The customer (that is, the person requesting that change be obtained) is not necessarily the same as the client (the person in whom change is required), and it is important to identify both.

At a fairly late stage in the assessment process, the question of using hypnosis may be raised. If there is any likelihood of benefit, either through speeding up treatment or in enabling the patient to manage his life more successfully during the period of treatment (for instance by improving sleep, or reducing handicapping symptoms) or if hypnosis is considered by the therapist to be the most appropriate mode of treatment, the topic will be raised. This is of course much simpler if the patient is expecting and has asked specifically for hypnotherapy. Even in such cases, however, the initial assessment is mandatory.

Quite commonly patients are referred for hypnotherapy for apparently simple and limited problems such as tinnitus, back pain or smoking, when one nevertheless finds very quickly that this is only the tip of an iceberg and that help is really being sought for quite other and usually much more complex and distressing problems. It is not unknown for patients to be referred for 'relaxation under hypnosis' because of some minor stress reaction in whom even a fairly cursory examination discloses that they are actually depressed or otherwise more seriously disturbed.

At some point in the assessment interview, then, we will ask the patient how he feels about the use of hypnosis in the course of the anticipated treatment. As with everything else in therapy, the ease, comfort, and confidence of the therapist are crucial. If one suggests the use of hypnosis while feeling (and therefore conveying) that the idea is likely to alarm or disturb the patient or to make the therapist appear a crank or a quack, the patient will quite rightly refuse. Once you have indicated clearly that you will accept the patient for treatment, and he has accepted both his need for treatment and the offer of therapy whilst also believing that the latter can help him, you may continue on something like the following lines.

▇▇▇▇▇▇   **Script 6.1**

I find very commonly that it can be very useful, with this sort of difficulty, to use hypnosis. I do not know at this stage whether that will be the most appropriate form of treatment for you, but many people find it helpful. I wonder what the word 'hypnosis' means to you?

Each therapist will, of course, find his own way of introducing the topic to a patient who is not expecting it, but even when a patient is waiting for this to be discussed, the same question has to be asked: what are his preconceptions?

The next step is to clear away misconceptions, introduce a more accurate and realistic understanding and generally discuss the matter on the lines indicated in chapter 3 dealing with preparation of the patient. At this point the patient will be asked to identify a time and place earlier in his life at which he had felt completely well, relaxed, happy and confident.

Some patients, especially those who are more or less depressed, will have difficulty in identifying such an experience and may even claim that they have never felt good. Most such patients will be delighted when they discover, through the use of 'age regression' (see chapters 16 and 17), that there *were* such good moments in their lives, but even then a few will be quite unable, even with the use of regression techniques, to locate a good moment in their past life. In such cases the therapist may construct such an experience from elements and hints provided by the patient, or create one for him *de novo*. Quite obviously, an actual experience from the patient's life is likely to be more effectual than any invented by the therapist. On occasion, having used a fantasy built up by the therapist himself, the patient will remember a good experience of his own, to his surprise.

At this point one may move on to a trial induction. Some therapists like to use one or other of the various scales by which one may assess hypnotic talent, but we find it simpler and more direct to proceed straight into the patient's first experience of hetero-hypnosis. This serves several purposes, the first of which is to assess the patient's potential for using hypnosis. The formal scales of assessment of hypnotic talent or susceptibility (Barber,[15] Stanford,[16] Harvard[17]) indicate in a quantifiable way how well an individual responds to suggestion, imagery and so on, which is of value in any research on hypnosis; but the most reliable way of assessing a patient's response in clinical applications is by experiment. Secondly, since this is highly likely to be any patient's first experience of formal hetero-hypnosis, it gives him an opportunity of losing any remaining apprehension and anxiety and of finding it congenial and helpful in itself.

The first induction may not be a wholly reliable indication of how the patient will respond in the future, but it will give some idea of his acceptance of the procedure itself, an opportunity to assess the kind of induction, deepening, and imagery that should be used in future sessions, and some guidance as to the patient's willingness and capacity to use the technique. In addition, even if only a very shallow trance is produced, the patient will leave the session in a noticeably, and sometimes dramatically, improved frame of mind: more peaceful and more hopeful than he would otherwise have been.

The majority of patients will show some degree of hypnotic response. Writers differ considerably in their estimates of the proportions of the clinical population that show different degrees of hypnotic susceptibility or talent: some describe their 'success rate' as high as 95 per cent (Edelstien, 1981), while Kroger (1977) says: 'Failure to reach some degree of hypnosis is rare.' Our experience, and that of other practitioners in Britain with whom we have discussed this, suggests that there may be cultural differences involved, since it seems that in Britain a lower proportion of patients show a useful response to hypnosis than in the USA. We find that perhaps one out of three patients will respond satisfactorily to a first induction and score satisfactorily on assessment scales at this point. Rather more will show signs of (beneficial) relaxation, but no real response to suggestion or evidence of anything more than feeling rested.

When the trial induction has been carried out and the programme outlined below completed, the therapist must decide whether the hypnotic talent demonstrated by the patient in this trial induction is sufficient to facilitate the treatment programme being considered; if it is not adequate, whether it is likely to be developed through practice; if it would be helpful to the patient to use self-hypnosis for anxiety management and stress reduction even though his capacity for using hypnosis is not sufficient for the therapeutic procedures planned.

Having agreed with the patient to try out hypnosis, the therapist must select an induction to suit his personality. Some factors in this choice have already been discussed in chapter 3. For example, the more 'controlling' and perhaps obsessional the patient is, the more desirable it is to avoid inductions that employ limitations of his self-determination, that is using phenomena such as catalepsy or paralysis (the inability to carry out some normal action). The more anxious and apprehensive the patient is about hypnosis, the more one would choose an induction that is very permissive and gentle. In the initial stages it is probably wisest to use whatever induction can be delivered most confidently and smoothly. With experience, the therapist will be able to judge more readily what is likely to suit a specific patient, using intuitive processes as much as more formal cognitive decisions.

Occasionally the first choice proves uncongenial to the patient. Much more commonly, conscious or unconscious resistance persistently appears, manifested perhaps by giggles, open laughter or by the patient interrupting. Alternative inductions can then be introduced to allow for any specific difficulties the patient encounters, until either some degree of trance is achieved or agreement is reached to end the experiment. While avoiding becoming too persistent (and thereby perhaps exposing the therapist's anxiety to the patient), the therapist should not drop the whole idea if the first induction fails. Many patients seem to need a second try and do then achieve usable effects, the repetition allowing their resistances to weaken and often dissolve, presumably through the reassurance the patient receives in the demonstration of his ability to resist an induction successfully.

With most patients, a minimal level of trance will be reached. This can then be used in several ways. First, the opportunity should be taken to make suggestions of an easier and deeper response to induction on future occasions. Secondly, suggestions should be included of the value of practising regularly, both to increase the patient's skill in using hypnosis and to gain relief from tension, anxiety and other distress. In the case of physical symptoms and pain, the suggestions should be directed towards using self-hypnosis to gain control of the symptoms. Having carried out an induction followed by deepening where the patient appears to have achieved a useful level of trance (perhaps indicated by the production of one or two phenomena taken from one or other of the scales previously mentioned), continue as follows.

██████████   Script 6.2

Good. You are now very comfortable, relaxed, at ease and at peace. From now on, you will find it easier and easier to enter this deeply relaxed state and each time you listen to me in the way you have been doing, you will find yourself going into as deep a trance as you need more and more easily and quickly.[38] You will find that, as you practise going into trance on your own, it will become easier to do so and you will get more and more benefit from using self-hypnosis regularly.

The next step is to provide the patient with a routine for self-hypnosis. The self-induction can follow the lines of the induction that has already been used in the session. For a rapid induction it may be necessary to choose a form the patient can use whether at home or outside.

For example, if the problem for which the patient was referred is panic attacks when away from home, a dual approach might be employed. First, the patient may be asked to use daily or twice-daily sessions of self-hypnosis to work systematically on extinguishing panic responses to various more or less specific triggers. Secondly, it can be very helpful to the patient to have a technique for inhibiting the development of such attacks whenever one is imminent, wherever he might be at the time and without even having to close his eyes. Various self-inductions, covering both the more gradual approaches to be used for regular self-treatment and 'instant' techniques, have been covered in chapter 5.

One will then go on to 'ego-strengthening'. Reading scripts for this such as those by Hartland (1971) reminds one of the Abbé Coué. Self-suggestion of improvement in peace of mind or symptomatology will appear more than a little fatuous in the cold light of print, yet in the setting of trance can sometimes prove astonishingly helpful and effective. For example:

Script 6.3

As you practise self-hypnosis each day, you will find yourself experiencing more and more a sense of peacefulness and ease while you are in the trance, and you will find that, when you open your eyes and come back to the ordinary waking state, that sense of peace, well-being and ease will last longer and longer. You will find with regular practice that you will gain more and more benefit from your periods of self-hypnosis, and bit by bit find yourself able to master the problems that have been interfering with your life. You will become more and more able to disperse and get rid of anxiety and tension and to lift your mood. To help you do this, we will now carry out a little experiment.

At this point, the 'private place' will be introduced. The principle underlying this exercise is that in recalling a good time when the patient felt happy, strong and hopeful, or experienced a sense of mastery, he will also recall (or rather *recapture*) those feelings and in re-experiencing them will be able to counter current feelings of anxiety, depression, despair and so on. These three approaches are illustrated in the scripts that follow.

Script 6.4

I would like you now to let yourself go back in time, back through your life to that time and place we talked about earlier, that time and place when you felt completely happy and relaxed, when everything was fine. You are going back to [*when you first rode a horse/were lying on the beach in Crete/stood on the top of Snowdon/played the MOONLIGHT SONATA to your sweetheart/built a sandcastle with your father*]. Let yourself go back to that time, back to that [*horse/beach/mountain*], feeling the [*movement of the horse under you/the sun on your body/wind playing over you*] listening to the [*sound of its hooves/the splash of the waves on the shore/the silence of the mountains*]. For a little while, just enjoy being back there, back [*on the horse/on the beach/on Snowdon/at the piano/five years old*] feeling completely at peace, happy and content, feeling that all is good. Let yourself soak up all the good feelings of that time, so that when you come back to the ordinary world in a while, you will go on feeling just as good, relaxed and happy as you do now, completely at ease, relaxed and good.[39]

Script 6.5

Let yourself go back in time. Let yourself feel that you are going back through your life, just going back, getting younger and younger, so that you find yourself experiencing some of the good things which happened in the past. Let yourself go backwards through time until you come to a moment that was especially good. A time and place when you felt really good, happy and at ease. You need not tell me about it if you do not wish to. Go back until you find yourself at such a moment and then stop there; let me know when you get there, and then let yourself enjoy whatever good feelings you are experiencing so that, when you come back to the present day again, you will go on feeling all the good feelings of that time and place.[40]

Script 6.6   The photograph album[41]

What I would like you to do now is to imagine that you have
a photograph album in front of you. This photograph album is
a collection of all the good times in your life, of all the times
you have been happy, enjoyed yourself, and felt confident. It is
a photograph album <u>only</u> of the good times, and will include
all the good things that have happened to you from when you
were very small right up to the present time. What I'd like
you to do is to begin to turn over the pages of the album until
you come to one of those times, one which you would like to
focus on today. Just take your time leafing through the album
until you come to a particularly good time and let me know
when you have found the one you want to think about
today.[42]

It might be a time from long, long ago ... or a time from more
recently. It might be a time when you were on your own ... or
with other people. It might have been a special occasion ... or
something that happened regularly ... or over a period of time
in your life. It might be indoors ... or out in the countryside.
Just take your time until the right one seems to turn up, and
then let me know.[43]

[When the patient signals, go on with the next stage.] Good.
Now I would like you to re-create that event and that time in
your life as if it is happening right now. Let yourself become
completely absorbed in the picture and take careful note of all
the colours and shapes around you, ... the sounds you can
hear that are associated with this place. ... Now, you might
like to tell me about this time in your life ... or you might like
to keep it to yourself. Would you like to tell me about it?[44]

Now that you can fully experience that *[lakeside picnic/
summer holiday/birthday/time in your life],* just take a few
moments to notice the feelings connected with this place.[45]

As these feelings get stronger and stronger, just allow yourself
to enjoy them, ... to enjoy the sensations of strength,
confidence, and being at one with the world. ... It is as if until

now you have been sitting on a powerhouse but had lost the key. Now you have found the key, and can use these internal sources of strength and understanding. ... You can feel increasingly, too, the feeling of being able to take control of your life, ... the ability to take actions and make decisions that will bring you satisfaction and a sense of achievement. ... You can enjoy the sensation of mastery ... and at the same time a feeling of growing freedom. ... Notice how good this feels. In future, the more frequently and regularly you come to this place, the more quickly and strongly you will be able to get in touch with these feelings, and the more they will begin to spread out into your everyday life in ways that will bring you enjoyment and satisfaction.

Script 6.7

You remember you told me that you get feelings of peace and calm when you are in a wood. I would like you to let a picture form in your mind as I describe it. Imagine that you are walking through a field towards a wood. You are walking through the grass ... feeling the sun on your back ... really warm and comfortable ... and feeling a warm soft breeze playing round you. ... Perhaps you will be able to smell the grass drying in the sun. ... You are coming closer to the wood now ... you can see how it is much darker inside the wood ... with patches of sunlight dappling the ground here and there. ... Walk right into the wood now ... notice that it is cooler there ... how quiet it is. ... Notice the wild flowers here and there ... perhaps you can identify some of them ... and maybe bracken and undergrowth ... bramble bushes ... or just a level carpet of leaves or needles and twigs. ... There may be moss growing on the trunks of trees ... and some old tree stumps ... ivy climbing here and there. ... Notice the young saplings shooting up between the larger trees ... the soft green of the leaves with flickers of sunlight catching them here and there ... the scent of the trees ... the earthy scent of leaf mould. ... Just ahead of you, I would like you to see a large old beech tree, reaching up high above you. Lean against the trunk or sit by it for a moment, ... perhaps in a pool of sunlight, ... and rest against it. Listen to the silence, broken only by a gentle rustling of the leaves and an occasional creaking sound where one branch rubs on another. Let yourself soak up the peace, quiet, calm, warm peace of that place. ... Let yourself become one with the trees and the peace, so that all the tensions and unhappiness you feel begin to drain away from you. Let all those bad feelings drain away, fade away, so that in a little while, when you come back to the ordinary world, you will still feel something of the good feelings of that place. You will be able to recapture those good feelings every time you go into trance and find yourself in this wood again.

It can be helpful also to include imagery to assist in the diminution of negative affect. The affect may be symbolized by any weight or burden which the patient loses or rids himself of. For example, depression can be symbolized by a dark, heavy, oily fluid filling the body, making it feel heavy and sluggish; this fluid is then visualized as draining out of the body, perhaps through the fingers and toes, and as it drains away, so the body begins to feel lighter and more free. Or the patient's worries and fears can be visualized as written on many small pieces of paper which are then thrown one by one into the stream or river beside which the patient is sitting.

Even with such apparently innocuous images, one can run into trouble. One of the authors used this image with a young man whose favourite pastime and happiest memory were fly-fishing in a stream in Northern Scotland. The suggestion of throwing his troubles into the water in the form of scraps of paper stored in his pocket appeared to be well accepted, but after the session was over the patient explained he had begun to do so and then realized with horror that the bits of paper were polluting his beloved river, and so had stopped throwing them in. This, although overtly reasonable, disclosed some important aspects of his reluctance to lose his problems and the ambivalence he was experiencing concerning therapy. It also illustrates that the image used must be chosen with some care if it is not to result in increasing stress and distraction rather than reducing stress. One cannot rely on patients (especially those with significant ambivalence concerning change) remembering and employing the injunction given earlier in their treatment to change any image or suggestion they find uncongenial.

Another image, of a largely somatosensory nature, that we use commonly is that of a warm glow at the centre of the body, rather like the feeling of holding a hot-water bottle to the abdomen and allowing the feeling of warmth to spread outwards through the whole body, inducing peaceful calm feelings and soothing away all tension and distress of any kind. Repeat suggestions of increasing well-being following each session of self-hypnosis, remembering that such suggestions will be more deeply accepted while the patient is actually experiencing what you suggest than at other times.

Finally, it is as well to include suggestions about the future use of hypnosis in treatment. The detailed content of such suggestions will naturally depend upon the treatment plan. If it is intended that treatment will be largely through hypnosis, the suggestions should be direct and to the point.

Script 6.8

You will find that when we begin to use hypnosis in the way that we agreed, to deal with your difficulties, you will find it easy to go into just as deep a trance as you need, and when you return to the ordinary everyday world you will feel relaxed and confident, at ease in mind and body, having mastered your difficulties a little more each time, until you have achieved what you want, and are able to do whatever you need in order to feel good.

If, on the other hand, the trial induction was carried out only as a preparation for later use of hypnosis, one would proceed more on the following lines:

■■■■■   **Script 6.9**

**You will find that using your self-hypnosis routine every day,
or whenever you need, you will be able to calm your mind
and step aside from your problems for a little while. Then, at
any time that you and I agree to use hypnosis to help in
solving your problems, you will be able to go into the trance
state easily and comfortably and to go just as deep as you
need at that time. Any time we use hypnosis in our sessions,
you will find the experience helpful and pleasant, and feel
really relaxed, comfortable and confident.**

This is usually sufficient for the initial hypnotic session, except for
any specific suggestions that may have been agreed at the outset.
With further suggestions of well-being, confidence and comfort,
the patient can then be returned from the trance. Anyone who has
been in even a fairly shallow trance needs some time to collect
himself on returning to normal alertness. Every patient should
therefore be allowed a little time after opening his eyes before the
session continues. One of the aspects of using hypnosis that is
especially rewarding to the therapist is the deep sigh of peace and
calm, usually accompanied by a broad smile, that most patients
produce as they emerge from the trance.

If it is felt that any self-induction routine taught in the
course of the period in trance needs to be practised, or an
abbreviated hetero-induction tried out, this is then done. Following this, the whole experience needs to be discussed in some detail.
The concluding discussion is important since the patient may
need an opportunity to talk about what, quite frequently, will
have been a quite moving and unexpected experience for him.
Furthermore, discussion often discloses that it is necessary to
amend the procedure in one or more aspects to make the
technique more acceptable, congenial or effective for the patient.

As discussed in chapter 3, it can also be useful to devise and
practise an abbreviated induction for use in future sessions.
Generally this is practicable at this stage only with patients who
respond easily and well to induction: that is, who go easily into a
substantially deep trance. Less apt subjects will need repeated full
inductions before becoming able to respond satisfactorily to

abbreviated or 'instant' inductions. If then it appears that a given patient would respond well to such inductions in the future, the abbreviated form is presented with appropriate suggestions while the patient is in trance, and after arousal taken back into the trance with the abbreviated form there and then, before the final de-briefing.

PART II

TREATMENT STRATEGIES WITH ADULTS

7

HABIT DISORDERS

In any therapeutic practice, referrals for habit disorders are common. The request may be for the extinction of patterns of behaviour that have become habitual to the point of compulsion such as smoking, hair-pulling, nail-biting and so on, or for the re-establishment of lost habitual behaviours such as sleeping, sphincter control, etc. In this chapter a number of such conditions will be considered and treatment strategies outlined, but it is important before embarking on such or any treatment to distinguish between habitual behaviours, obsessive-compulsive rituals and other psychoneurotic disorders and inability to perform natural functions. As always, a careful diagnostic assessment must be performed before deciding upon treatment.

The borderlines between such categories can be vague and difficult to clarify. Smoking, for example, commonly straddles such a boundary in that some smokers who have been advised to stop or wish to do so for other reasons continue to smoke because of the habitual nature of the behaviour, while others do so as a part of an 'over-determined' process, that is, smoking fulfils for them a number of neurotic needs or relieves neurotic pressures. For this latter group, which seems to be the majority, extinction of the habit by means that do not simultaneously deal with the underlying neurotic processes and relieve or discharge the anxiety that fuels the habit is unlikely to be successful, or if successful may be so only for a short period and is likely to result in the emergence of other symptoms. These, whilst perhaps not as unhealthy as smoking, may be equally undesirable or deleterious to the life of the patient.

A useful phrase employed by some authors (for example Crasilneck and Hall, 1985) is 'empty habits'. Many habitual and near-compulsive behaviour patterns originated as neurotically determined actions: 'symptoms' which once had significance and function in the life of the patient but which have now outlived the processes, conflicts, anxieties and so on that created them and gave them that significance. For instance, many young people begin to smoke as a means of asserting themselves and signalling, as much to themselves as to the outside world, that they are adult, independent, 'one of the lads' and so on. The habit, however, persists long after the need for such assertion has been outgrown and has in this sense become empty. For some smokers, however, the habit is not 'empty' in that they continue to have underlying and probably wholly unconscious unease and insecurity about their adult status, independence and self-determination.

In the former case, the patient will need very little help with giving up the habit once he has decided to do so, while in the latter group patients will continue the habit even with strenuous exertions and elaborate treatment, or resume it after a very short interval, as long as the underlying determinants remain untouched. Indeed, in such cases treatment is perceived by them at deeper levels as an assault on this rather fragile independence, and resistance will manifest itself quickly and strongly. In the assessment of the patient requesting help with such problems, one of the primary objectives is to assess the degree to which the target behaviour is in fact such an 'empty habit' or what unresolved anxieties and conflicts may underlie it and continue to require expression and relief through performance of the actions concerned.

'It may be a bad habit but it is *my* habit' is sometimes an unspoken message in what the patient presents. Habitual actions and often the accoutrements of the habit (the lighter, the pipe, etc.) become an integral part of one's self-image as well as of one's public image, and giving up a habit will involve some change in the way an individual perceives himself and also in the way he believes and expects others to perceive him. Such a change can be difficult to achieve and can arouse considerable and essentially involuntary resistance, even when the change is strongly desired at a conscious level. What is desired is *some* of the consequences of change, but not the totality. Thus some people presenting with a desire to stop smoking wish to free themselves of the health hazards involved, or of the symptoms of damage that they are already experiencing, or the financial drain on their resources, but they do not wish to become *non-smokers*, or have not grasped that this is a necessary corollary of the change they are seeking. Were it not for just such underlying sources of resistance, smokers, nail-biters and others would be able to decide to stop smoking, nailbiting or whatever without further ado. Helping strategies must, if they are to be successful and maintain success, be directed as much at the underlying processes and forces as at the manifest behaviour.

This chapter will deal first with the extinction of habitual behaviours, while the treatment of disordered or lost adaptive patterns (as in, for example, enuresis and loss of bowel control, sleep disturbance and so on) will come later.

Many treatment plans for smoking and similar behaviours address themselves to ego-strengthening suggestions associated with extinction of the target behaviour: 'You will feel proud and satisfied that you have broken the old habit', or: 'You will feel relaxed and comfortable at the thought of being a nonsmoker.' Emphasis in such approaches is put on the anticipated good consequences of no longer smoking, such as improved health, increased pleasure in food and its taste, absence of stale smoke and smell around the person, financial benefits and so on. While such suggestions are a useful component in any programme and should be included, our experience is that a more powerful approach is one that explicitly tackles the behaviour itself and at the same time provides some relief and compensation for the sense of deprivation involved in 'giving up' and for any underlying anxieties (and other unconscious processes involved). This is essential if the treatment is to prove successful and the change to be maintained.

Other approaches advocated in the literature (e.g. Kroger, 1977) are on the lines of aversive conditioning, emphasizing the unpleasant aspects of the behaviour and its unwanted consequences, often attempting to establish additional unpleasant experiences rather on the lines of the use of Antabuse in alcohol dependency: 'Every time you light a cigarette, you will feel nauseated just as you do when you smell ... [whatever the patient has identified as his most disliked odour].' 'You will notice how the smoke feels revolting in your mouth and nose, how it stings and tastes foul.' When such an approach is used *in vivo*, such as in the traditional treatment of nail-biting by coating the nails in some foul-tasting substance, the success rate, although perceptible, is low. The same is true of *in vitro* or imaginal treatments of this kind: they work sometimes. In both cases, the patient feels (rightly) that he is not in control but is being managed or manipulated. This reaction is distinctly counter-productive if the behaviour concerned embodies some thread of self-assertion, anxiety about independence, and so on.

In fact, many people asking for help with habit extinction have actually decided that they are going to give up the habit and are really asking for some sort of face-saving ritual and something to mark the transition from habitual performance to non-performance. Such people will respond well to any form of treatment, because any ritual will perform the functions they seek.

The identification of the target behaviour and the delineation of the part it plays in the life of the patient are obviously the first steps in assessment for treatment. The next is to identify the situations in which the behaviour occurs, the stimuli that trigger off its performance, the associated and subsequent experiences and the consequences anticipated, often at the boundary of consciousness, at cessation or non-performance of the behaviour. The strategies and imagery to be employed in treatment will, of course, be drawn from this information. For example, smokers commonly report that they feel the urge to smoke immediately they take a break from work and have a cup of coffee, or after a meal, and that smoking is an integral part of this relaxing and refreshing experience. Others may report that they smoke more when they are taking a drink with friends at a party or in the pub, again in the context of relaxation and pleasure.

In this latter situation one commonly sees a paradoxical thread of anxiety and tension through the self-consciousness and unease inherent in such accounts. In smoking, nail-biting, hair-pulling and so on, it is frequently the case that both relaxation and tension precipitate the behaviour. It is performed when the patient is relaxing and feels at ease (while reading for pleasure, watching television and so on) and equally when rendered self-conscious and tense by, for example, a social situation. The treatment plan should encompass both these aspects and all typical precipitating situations and use as many as can be reasonably managed in the course of the imaginative exercises employed. In each situation employed, the focus is on extinguishing the link between the target behaviour and tension reduction and substituting a link between *non-performance* of the target behaviour and tension reduction.

An integral component of most treatment plans for such behaviour, whether or not these are mediated by hypnosis, focuses on bringing the normally automatic and barely conscious behaviour vividly into consciousness to make it accessible to conscious decision-making and control. The technique of 'paradoxical intention' and related approaches work in part on these lines: the patient is constrained to perform the target behaviour to order, repeatedly and frequently in the treatment sessions, so that he becomes more and more vividly aware of the action and its associated sensations. In so doing he becomes 'sensitized' and aware of the sensory components of the behaviour which, when it is performed automatically, are out of awareness.

For example, the patient may be instructed to bite his nails for a set period every time the therapist gives a signal in the course of the session and, as he does so, to focus his attention on the sensations he receives from his lips, teeth, jaws and finger. This may be re-inforced by practising nail-biting in front of a mirror at home between sessions, with instructions to watch himself carefully while so doing. Such heightening of awareness of the actions involved in performing the habitual behaviour is a necessary ingredient in the treatment of habits and should be included, even though on its own it has a relatively low success rate.

Our favourite model of treatment embodies all these aspects but emphasizes two in particular: on the one hand, it is designed to create a feeling of mastery and satisfaction, while on the other, it provides a counter to any underlying neurotic need symbolically fulfilled by the habit. At the same time it is designed to evoke relaxation, ease, comfort and pleasurable feelings at non-performance of the behaviour. The following script can be applied, *mutatis mutandis*, to a wide range of habitual behaviours. It can be used more or less as it stands, or taken as an outline model.

Before embarking on induction, the treatment plan is discussed and agreed with the patient. Emphasis is put on the fact that he has decided that at an as yet unspecified date in the future he will become a non-smoker and that in the meantime he will practise regularly the exercise that is about to be taught. He is to make no effort to stop or reduce his smoking since the treatment will ensure that smoking reduces and stops without effort or struggle, as though automatically. A 'private place' is identified and the situations in which the patient smokes are noted, as are any trigger events and stimuli.

The patient is assured again that he should make no direct effort to avoid smoking if and when he feels the urge to do so, especially since any such effort will turn the process into a battle and thereby arouse internal resistances. However, each time he feels the impulse to smoke he is to rehearse the exercise first *in vivo*, that is, without hypnosis but with the actual cigarette, and then, if he still wishes to smoke, he may do so, knowing that this urge will diminish progressively. He is told that he will find, more by hindsight than at the time, that his smoking diminishes, that he will feel no 'withdrawal symptoms' and that he will not miss smoking, as long as he practises the prescribed exercise regularly and frequently. He is to do this in imagination while in a self-induced hypnotic state at least twice a day, at agreed times, and again without hypnosis each time he feels the urge to smoke. He will then find, after some time, that he has naturally and easily become a non-smoker.

Induction is then carried out, with deepening and the usual ego-strengthening, including the anticipated pleasures and rewards of change. The patient is then taken to his 'private place'. Ideally this should be a scene in the open air, a beach, mountain or something of that kind where emphasis can be put on the clarity, purity and freshness of the air being breathed or on the pleasant scents of flowers. These anticipated pleasures are stressed and associated explicitly with the future time when the patient has become a non-smoker. The scene is then changed to one or other of the situations in which the patient most frequently smokes.

Script 7.1

You are sitting at home. It is evening, and you are watching television. You have a drink on the table beside you. You are feeling quite relaxed and at ease and now you are beginning to feel you would like a cigarette. The urge to smoke is getting

stronger, so you pick up your packet of cigarettes. Notice how
the packet feels in your hand. You open the packet and take
out a cigarette and put the packet down again. Notice the feel
of the cigarette between your fingers; roll it between your
fingers and notice also the difference in texture between the
paper and the filter. *[Pause]* Bring the cigarette slowly up
towards your mouth until you can just smell the tobacco.
[Pause] You put the cigarette between your lips. Notice the
smell of the tobacco in your mouth and nose, stronger now,
and notice the feel of the cigarette between your lips. *[Pause]*
Stop there for a moment and concentrate on the sensations of
touch, smell and taste. *[Pause]* Now take the cigarette out of
your mouth again and slowly lower your hand, holding the
cigarette. Notice as you do so how you feel yourself relaxing,
relaxing more and more. The further down your hand goes
with the cigarette in it, the more relaxed and comfortable you
feel. You put the cigarette back in the packet, and close it.
Notice how good you are feeling, relaxed and comfortable. You
push the cigarette packet away from you a little and again
you feel even more relaxed. Notice a sense of well-being and
ease growing inside you as you push the packet away. Good.

Now, pick the packet up again. As you do so, notice how it
feels in your hand, and notice too a feeling of uneasiness,
perhaps in the pit of your stomach.[46] Take a cigarette out, and
feel it between your fingers, and notice the uneasiness and
tension growing in your stomach. Raise the cigarette towards
your mouth until you can smell the tobacco, feeling more and
more uneasy and tense, becoming increasingly uncomfortable,
uneasy and tense. Put the cigarette between your lips, noticing
the smell and taste of the tobacco more strongly, and as you
do so, you can feel yourself really very uncomfortable now,
very uneasy and tense. Take the cigarette out of your mouth
again and hold it for a moment, and notice that the tension
and uneasiness immediately diminish a little. Lower your hand
holding the cigarette and feel the tension and unease ebbing a
little more. As you move the cigarette away from your mouth
you feel a little more comfortable, as the uneasiness and
tension get less and less. Put the cigarette back in the packet
now and close it and as you do so, feel the relaxation and ease

welling up inside you, the tension and uneasiness fading away. Push the cigarette packet away and notice the feeling of well-being and comfort welling up inside you and spreading through you, so that you feel more and more comfortable, relaxed and at ease, feeling really good.

This process is repeated with increasing emphasis on these sensory and affective components. The patient is again instructed (whilst in hypnosis) to practise this exercise while in a self-hypnotic state, twice daily or more. He is then instructed to go through this exercise without hypnosis every time he feels the impulse to smoke. That is to say, when he feels that impulse he is to take a cigarette out, hold it in his fingers and carefully note the sensations he receives, bring it up to his mouth, and so on right through to the point where he pushes the packet away from himself while focusing on the pleasant affect he experiences as he progressively distances the cigarette. He may then, if he wishes, smoke, but next time he feels the urge to smoke he must repeat the exercise first. Naturally, strong suggestions are made that at the end of the *in vivo* exercise the urge to smoke may well have evaporated, in which case he will no longer need to smoke on that occasion.

Finally, the patient is asked to project himself into the future and picture himself some days or weeks ahead in one or a series of situations in which he has commonly smoked in the past and to note his feelings of confidence and self-assuredness in his new identity and character as a non-smoker. He is then returned to his 'private place' to enjoy the affect associated with it for a while, again emphasizing the clean and fresh smells, which he will enjoy the more as a non-smoker.

Additional suggestions can be made relating to the benefits he can expect to result from the change to non-smoking in terms of freshness, cleanliness, improvement in health and so on, but maximal emphasis is laid on the sense of mastery, self-control and confidence.

– Note that the phrases: 'stop smoking', 'give up smoking' and the like are not used at any time. The sense of loss or deprivation that most people have experienced or expect to experience in previous, unsuccessful attempts to stop smoking are enough in themselves without being reinforced by the therapist! If one refers to the target in such terms it obviously leads the patient to expect that he will feel deprivation, whereas the treatment strategy we advocate embodies an implicit suggestion that no sense of deprivation is to be anticipated.

This strategy may be modified according to whether the patient has decided to stop smoking there and then or at a date in the near future. Some writers advocate setting a definite day: 'Q-Day' (Quitting-Day) on which the patient enters his new life as a non-smoker. Others suggest that the next session with the therapist should be the target. The suggestions to be made about becoming a non-smoker will be tailored to the decision made by the patient. Our experience with the approach outlined above is that the majority of patients who have decided to cease smoking of their own accord rather than under pressure from physicians or relatives stop either at the time of their first interview or within a few days, often without having set a date at all.

Giving up a pleasure-yielding habit of many years' standing involves not only major changes in self-image but also an appreciable and sometimes major degree of deprivation. For any treatment strategy to be successful, therefore, this experience of deprivation and self-denial must be more than balanced by concomitant gains or rewards. Many writers, Kroger, Crasilneck and Hall amongst them, advocate the application of the principles of aversive conditioning as the method of choice for smokers. This is against the mainstream of contemporary British behaviour modification practice and is additionally uncongenial in principle to most practitioners, who find its somewhat punitive style contrary both to taste and to effective practice.

It may well be that there are cultural differences involved in this. The more recent literature in behaviour modification gives one rather little confidence in using such an approach in the treatment of any condition, and our own experience is that such methods tend to be counter-productive, that any gains are ineffectual or very short-lived. Such an approach tends to emphasize the stresses of the change and predictably, therefore, often results in withdrawal symptoms or substitute behaviours, in themselves as unhealthy as the original behaviour. The follow-up studies reported by advocates of the aversion approach (for example Kroger, 1977) suggest that their long-term success rates are rather less than those to be obtained by the more positive and rewarding technique described here. Furthermore, this approach does not appear to generate withdrawal symptoms (even in the heaviest smokers), suggesting that smoking is frequently not an addiction but a habit. Substitute activities are also rare. Occasionally a period of sucking sweets may follow Q-Day, although this is usually short-lived.

The principles involved in this method are no doubt clear, but may be worth spelling out. The first stage of the exercise (the 'private place') sets the affective scene, with quite indirect suggestions, not linked at this stage at all with the target or task in hand, concerning the freshness of the air, flower scents, and so on. This prepares the way for more explicit suggestions at a later stage, referring directly to some of the benefits to be obtained from becoming a non-smoker. By leaving the link unstated we allow the image and its related affect to be established quite uncontaminated by any hesitation, ambivalence or reluctance on the part of the patient. When this image is firmly established, it can then be called on in its entirety at the appropriate moment.

The first repetition of the next phase of the exercise (going through the opening phases of the smoking process, in imagination) contains no suggestions of discomfort, stress or other negative affect, and relies simply on suggestions of increasing comfort and ease as the cigarette is removed from the mouth, onwards to its total rejection. It appears to be helpful to keep the association between the affective experience and the associated events unstated: that is to say, the two are associated by temporal contiguity but the functional connection is not stated.

The intention in structuring the process in this way is to establish a stimulus-response pattern on the lines of classical conditioning, and at the same time to avoid any possible interference with the establishment of the conditioned response being sought by both conscious and unconscious thoughts and feelings. The second and subsequent repetitions of the exercise introduce and gradually expand both the suggestions of negative affect associated with increasing proximity of the cigarette and the suggestions of increasing comfort with separation from and refusal of the cigarette. These suggestions, both of discomfort and of comfort, are not linked explicitly in any way to the refusal to smoke: the patient is asked to notice almost incidentally that he becomes increasingly tense and uncomfortable as (rather than because) he raises the cigarette to his lips, and similarly to notice that he experiences increasing relaxation and ease as he distances himself from the cigarette again, culminating in feelings of well-being and mastery as he removes the cigarette packet completely.

This approach is in sharp contradistinction to the aversion method in several ways: first, the association of affect is made at a peri-liminal level, which is generally more effective than suggested associations made explicitly and at a fully conscious level. Secondly, the distastefulness of the nausea, approaching vomiting and so on characteristic of the aversion method makes it less likely that the patient will accept and practise the treatment strategy himself. Thirdly, if the patient does indeed feel nauseated at the smell of tobacco or of smoke, that is, if the treatment is effective, he has no opportunity of feeling that *he* has mastered the habit and has taken control, but rather that control has been taken away from him. Indeed, if such a treatment were entirely successful, the patient would be incapacitated from working, travelling or living anywhere except in a wholly smoke-free environment.

Putting the emphasis firmly and unequivocally on the positive aspects and gains of feeling relaxed, at ease and comfortable provides an automatic compensation for the deprivation of giving up smoking. This is then enhanced or re-inforced in hypnosis by re-entry into the 'private place' and accompanied by more direct suggestions of cleanliness, freshness and the pleasant smell of the air, now more explicitly linked to the concept of being a non-smoker.

The language used in this process is important. To re-iterate: at no time is the phrase 'giving up smoking' used because of its suggestion of loss and deprivation. In our experience patients who become non-smokers through this method simply do not experience feelings of loss, deprivation or withdrawal, even if, as in some cases, they have been smoking as many as eighty cigarettes a day for many years. Whether the hypnotic practice dissipates or disguises any withdrawal feelings, or whether despite popular belief tobacco does not contain addictive compounds, is not clear. It does seem that the appearance of withdrawal symptoms depends upon the affective tone of the experience of giving up. If this is felt to be one of loss, deprivation and submission, such symptoms appear, whereas if the tone is one of relaxation, ease, mastery and satisfaction they do not. It could be argued that feelings of ease and mastery are experientially incompatible with feelings of dependency and neediness, and that if strong enough, the former extinguish the latter.

The same approach can be adapted to other habits or compulsive actions, especially those that are related to tension reduction or self-comfort. For example, nail-biting and hair-pulling often appear to be related to both these: that is, they tend to be performed when the patient experiences either anxiety or lowering of mood. In addition, the self-stimulating aspects of the behaviour (including, of course, smoking) may fill a further need. If in a particular case this later emerges as a prominent feature, the programme can be adapted so that self-arousal, or the fulfilment of a need for stimulation, is obtained in a more acceptable and satisfying way through the use of imagery and hypnotically-aroused sensation.

In some cases of habitual behaviour we have found it useful to add a suggestion of momentary catalepsy or paralysis of the limb engaged in the target behaviour at the moment before the relevant action actually occurs. In hair-pulling, for example, we go in some detail through the movements leading to pulling out a hair. We suggest that the hand normally used to pull out a hair approaches the head, then finger and thumb select one or a few hairs (this is the common practice, although sometimes a small bunch of hair is wound round a finger instead). The fingers are about to pull. At that moment suggestions of instant catalepsy are made, so that the hand feels immovable for a short while. It remains thus in position for a few moments, locked rigidly in place, and then the fingers loosen their grasp on the hair and the arm relaxes again and sinks down, with (of course) associated feelings of tension reduction, ease and so on. This procedure is carried out very slowly; imagery of performing the action as though on a slow-motion film makes every step in the process more vividly conscious.

With appropriate modifications, such a programme can be applied to virtually any habitual or compulsive behaviour, bearing in mind, as noted at the beginning of this chapter, that only 'empty habits' can be treated successfully in this way. Habitual or compulsive behaviours that still express or otherwise stem from unresolved and unconscious conflicts, anxieties and so on require exposure and resolution of the underlying determinants before they can be successfully eliminated.

Disturbance of normal and habitual behaviour or loss of normal habits, for example, loss of bladder and bowel control, are approached rather differently. Such conditions are relatively rarely found in adults without organic or major psychiatric pathology, except perhaps in old age. In children nocturnal enuresis, both primary and secondary, is common. Diurnal enuresis, although much less common, also occurs quite frequently. Treatment of childhood incontinence is dealt with in chapter 12. In adults, a combination of training to increase alertness to sphincter, bladder and rectal sensations and ego-strengthening and anxiety reduction can be effective.

The primary ingredients in programmes to re-establish disturbed or lost habits are, just as in the extinction of undesired acquired habits, on the one hand, feelings of ease and mastery at achieving the desired result and on the other, heightened awareness of and therefore choice in the performance of the target behaviour.

Some patients suffering from urinary incontinence have blocked or reduced the sensations that normally signal a need to void and can therefore neither strengthen sphincter control nor take appropriate action. Others, however, experience incontinence and both urgency and frequency of micturition, normally associated with a high level of anxiety over access at all times to a lavatory. This latter group, whose incontinence is usually secondary to these other symptoms, will as a rule be found to suffer from hidden neurotic processes, that is to say, the urinary problem is a displaced symptom and enquiry will fairly readily disclose a more complex neurotic process than the presenting complaint would suggest. This group requires treatment of the underlying condition rather than a symptomatic approach.

The first step in treatment of those patients where a symptomatic approach appears to be appropriate is to ensure that the patient has a working knowledge of the relevant anatomy and physical mechanisms, especially of the sensory and motor nerves involved. This does not need to be of the standard required by an examination in neuroanatomy. Hans Eysenck (in an untraceable paper in the 1960s) reported his treatment of diurnal enuresis in a dancer. He arranged that she should be fitted with an indwelling catheter connected to a manometer which she then monitored regularly while otherwise engaged in her usual activities. This procedure was carried out so that she should develop awareness of the sensory stimuli relating to different levels of hydrostatic pressure in her bladder, an awareness which she had in effect lost. Such sensory training can be enhanced by getting the patient to postpone micturition (or defecation in the case of bowel control difficulties) for longer and longer periods to heighten bladder or bowel sensation and simultaneously to practise voluntary control of the sphincters.

It appears that increased concentration, one of the characteristics of the hypnotic state, amplifies the effect of such exercises quite considerably. Since normally autonomous neural processes can be brought into awareness and so under control in hypnosis, any training programmes of this kind can be more effectively carried out in hypnosis than without it. The following treatment strategy can be employed, making whatever changes may be appropriate to the patient and his condition.

The patient is asked to picture a diagram representing his bladder and the nerve endings in it which mediate sensation. He is to imagine that as the bladder distends, the nerve endings will be stimulated and send messages along their fibres through the spinal cord to the brain, perhaps in the form of little blobs of light moving along the fibre. When these signals reach the brain, the result can be imagined rather like the explosions that form an integral part of 'Space Invader' games. This response in turn triggers off further similarly represented messages which spread through the brain, representing a growing awareness of these sensations and triggering off signals along the efferent nerves which control the sphincters. As these messages reach their targets in the sphincter muscles, they result in further little explosions of light as the sphincter muscles receive the signals and respond by increased tension. As the bladder continues to distend, the signals become more frequent and in consequence the sphincter muscles contract progressively more strongly.

An alternative strategy, or one that can be added, would be to suggest the presence of switches in the spinal cord which can interrupt the movement of the impulses in those efferent fibres, mediating opening of the sphincter through muscle relaxation. In this way the action of voiding is blocked until the patient *chooses* to do so by 'switching' those fibres back on. At the same time, the efferent impulses involved in sphincter contraction remain active in proportion to the signals of fullness.

Having used such an approach in the hypnotic sessions and having instructed the patient to rehearse such exercises in his self-hypnosis sessions, he is then asked to practise *in vivo* both by postponing micturition and by interrupting micturition, in both cases to enhance the feelings (and actuality) of voluntary control and of sensation.

Such imagery may sound somewhat over-simplified or even far-fetched, but it tends to give patients a sense of relief in gaining a conceptual 'handle' on what is happening: a way of thinking about their problem which is value-free and can be mechanically applied.

Sleep difficulties may occur either on their own or as a by-product of other difficulties. In this context, the similarity between hypnosis and the relaxation and detachment that immediately precede normal sleep is useful. The first point to tackle, however, is the patient's feelings about his problem. It is generally believed that without adequate sleep one will collapse or disintegrate, probably mentally as well as physically. The anxiety experienced by the typical insomniac revolves around this: a desperate longing for sleep and terror of it not coming. In fact, of course, almost everyone can survive happily on very little sleep, and most people have had the experience of doing so: for instance at parties which have left them feeling good even though tired. The fear and disturbances of thought and feeling that follow sleeplessness are generally related to usually unconscious feelings of resentment, anger, anxiety and so on towards the cause of sleeplessness, and not to the lack of sleep itself. Obviously this does not apply entirely as it stands to severe and prolonged sleep-deprivation, such as when one has a small child who is ill and demands continuing attention throughout more than a small number of successive nights.[47]

In insomnia, however, the fear of not sleeping is one of the principal factors maintaining the insomnia itself. Reassurance on this point is therefore given, preferably after obtaining from the patient some reminiscence of all-night jamborees or other happy occasions when he did without sleep and yet was happy and subsequently functioned well. The patient will almost certainly recognize the fact that he adds to his wakefulness by anxiety at not sleeping.

Sleeplessness often represents fears on the part of the patient concerning death and dying, and the presence of such fears and associated neurotic fantasies needs to be explored before proceeding.

███████   Script 7.2

[Induction and deepening have been carried out. The patient is then taken to his 'private place' and whatever tension-reduction images have been agreed are then employed.]

In a little while, you are going to have a short sleep. I would like you first to picture that a slight mist is drifting into *[the private place]*, so that bit by bit it is all shrouded in mist. The mist is getting thicker, but it is still very warm and pleasant. The mist is getting thicker and thicker until you cannot see anything except a soft warm mist. You will also notice that the various thoughts, memories and feelings that drift in and out of your attention while you go on listening to my voice become less and less clear. They are all becoming misty and vague. You may find all sorts of things appearing in your mind, but they simply float in and out of your attention. Notice that as time goes on they seem more and more misty, diffuse and vague. Let your attention gradually become more and more diffuse. Perhaps it will seem to you as though my voice is becoming more and more distant and you seem to hear what I say less and less clearly. In a short while you will find yourself drifting off into a natural comfortable sleep, and as you drift away, my voice and what I say as well as the other things that may enter your mind from time to time will seem to be vague, misty, unclear and far away. You are slowly and comfortably drifting into a sound, natural sleep. You will sleep for a short while, and then, after a short while, even though you are deeply asleep, you will hear my voice saying your name. When you hear me say your name, you will come out of your sleep and return into the trance state for a short while. You are drifting off to sleep, off to sleep. Just let everything become diffuse, vague and distant as you drift off to sleep. Drifting off to sleep ... sleep ... sleep.

[Judge the moment at which to lower your voice by the change in the patient's respiration to a sleep pattern, and then leave two or three minutes' silence. Then say the patient's name clearly and slightly more loudly than you were speaking towards the end of the last passage.]

Good. From now on you will be able to drift off to sleep any time that you wish. You will go into the hypnotic state when you are ready to sleep, and then go into your private place. Let yourself become free of all tension, anxiety and worry, and when you feel completely at peace and at ease, let your private place gradually fill with mist and fade away, so that you can then drift off easily and naturally into sleep. You will be able to sleep for as long as you need, and if at any time you are woken during the night, you will be able to return into natural sleep by repeating this exercise.

It is often possible to get the patient to drift into normal sleep in the course of a session by this process. Once this has been done, suggestions of sleep following self-hypnosis and some sort of imagery that represents a loosening and gradual loss of attention can be given either as described in the script above or in any other way appropriate to the patient concerned. A tape-recording of the therapist reciting an induction which ends with suggestions of sleep is often successful. It is wise to include on the tape suggestions that provide for the operating characteristics of the machine the patient will use. If this is of the type that switches itself off at the end of the tape, the noise made by the machine can either be ignored in sleep or used as the signal for the onset of sleep. If the machine must be switched off by hand, then this action is incorporated into the suggestions again as the immediate prelude to sleep, representing perhaps that the patient, in switching the machine off, also switches off his day-time self.

Disorders of eating are sometimes treated as though they fell within the category of habit disorders. Both anorexia nervosa and its variants and bulimia involve a strong habitual element, but they are invariably symptoms of complex over-determined neurotic processes and must be treated as such. Behaviour modification programmes are reported as moderately successful in anorexia nervosa, but the relapse rate is high and patients suffering from this condition are notoriously unco-operative. Even when overtly well-motivated for treatment and personal change, the patient will find ways of undermining the treatment programme. Much the same is true of bulimia patients. With such fragile and incomplete co-operation, hypnotic techniques are of little use. In combination with pharmacological treatment and rigid behaviour methods, hypnosis can offer some help, largely in enabling the patient to manage distress and tension. When dynamic therapies are employed for such conditions, hypnosis can be very helpful in uncovering repressed material, but the techniques designed for habit control are of little, if any value.

8

PHYSICAL AND PSYCHOSOMATIC DISORDERS

INTRODUCTION

It is fully recognized nowadays that psychological factors are doubly involved in all physical illnesses and disorders. Emotional and behavioural effects both stem from the presence of physical illness or trauma and also in turn contribute to the progress of the condition. The converse, of course, is equally true: all psychological disorders and problems have physical manifestations and involvements. It is virtually impossible, therefore, to establish clearly and positively whether psychological features are among the effects of physical illnesses or traumata, or whether physical conditions either have their origin in psychological stresses or the latter play a significant and readily discernible part in the aetiology and progress of physically manifested disorders. The term 'psychosomatic' must necessarily apply to all conditions to some degree, whether the symptoms are physical, emotional, behavioural or a combination of any of these, in that mind and body are inextricable parts of a single organic whole or organism.

Some current trends in medicine, usually termed 'holistic', emphasize this integrated approach, and it is increasingly accepted that physical treatments alone are not sufficient in the treatment of physically manifested disorders. In other words, if involvement of other aspects of the patient as a whole being is neglected, the effects of psychological processes can reduce or negate the effectiveness of the physical treatments applied, or otherwise prolong the illness and its aftermath. Similarly in psychotherapeutic practice, the effectiveness of psychological methods of treatment can be undermined and the disorder prolonged or fail to respond to treatment at all if the physical condition of the patient and the physical circumstances of his life remain such as to maintain either a level of general stress that is pathogenic to that individual, or if specific stresses remain unchanged. The influence of the social environment must also be included.

Hypnotic techniques may play a part in the management and treatment of disorders at any point in the physical–psychological continuum. In this chapter, conditions of primarily physical origin and nature will be considered first, followed by discussion and description of the role of hypnotic techniques in the treatment of accidental injuries. Conditions in which psychological and psychosocial factors appear to be primarily causal will be considered later. In addition, the use of hypnotic techniques in reducing pain, discomfort and distress occasioned by medical and surgical procedures will be described. Detailed description of the use of hypnosis in the management of pain is, however, to be found in chapter 10.

The reaction of an individual to the occurrence of trauma or disease which interferes with his enjoyment of life and the execution of his normal activities varies in response to his basic personality structure, social situation, support systems and so on. At one extreme is the individual who takes such an event 'in his stride', accepting what he may regard as a temporary inconvenience and discomfort but not reacting to the illness or accidental injury as reflecting on or affecting his role, status, function and value, especially self-value. Such a person will be whole-heartedly committed to recovery from the disability and so accept and utilize the treatments provided, co-operating with those treating him without sabotaging their work, and his single-minded determination to recover and to resume normal life will support their treatment. His determination to recover may indeed be regarded as more important in ensuring his recovery than all the medication.

An opposite reaction to this is exemplified by the patient whose response to illness or injury is resignation. He will accept the illness as in some way his due and consequently sabotage (often without conscious awareness of the nature of his actions) the treatments offered, either by failing to co-operate in quite overt ways, or more subtly by ensuring that his overt co-operation is matched by actions that will lead to lack of success. His despair will militate against recovery. Similarly, a patient who experiences disability through illness or accident as a major blow to his role and status, and whose self-esteem and self-value are thus reduced or destroyed, will react in such ways as to prolong his illness, usually again by more or less subtle sabotage of the treatments applied, while at the same time exhibiting cognitive, affective and behavioural regression.

A variant of this picture is the patient whose pride or insecurity will not allow him to recognize the fact that he is ill, requires treatment and needs, for the sake of his full recovery and continued health, to retire for the moment from normal life and devote himself to treatment and rest.

The reactions of many adolescents to serious illness or injury may appear to fall within the second type described above, and many of the overt features may seem closely similar. In adolescence, however, disturbance of or interference with bodily integrity is generally a more severe blow to the individual's security of identity. Regression and passive resignation occur commonly, sometimes as a transitory stage, sometimes more severely, yet with a rather better prognosis than if such a reaction occurs in an adult. Nonetheless, this regressive and maladaptive reaction needs sympathetic and constructive management if the patient's potential for recovery and re-adaptation is to be mobilized effectively. This involves positive and insightful handling of the usually well-hidden and often totally unconscious interpretation by the patient of the personal significance of the illness or trauma and the treatments and procedures applied. The regressed ego state of an adolescent in this situation can be very effectively comforted and reassured with hypnotherapy, especially by the use of metaphors and age progression.

The adolescent patient, having been taken into trance, can be asked to visualize a scene from a period earlier in his life in which he had been frightened, ill, injured or distressed and then received comfort and reassurance followed by relief. The link with the present-day situation is left unstated. Alternatively, the distressing feelings can be projected on to an imaginary and younger child whom the patient will then comfort and reassure, again without any explicit reference to him and his current situation.

It is arguable that psychological adjuncts to treatment, including the use of hypnosis, should be considered even for the patient whose unambiguous commitment to recovery seems to make such interventions redundant. At the most superficial level, hypnotic techniques would enable him (if he is adequately responsive to hypnosis) to reduce discomfort and pain resulting from his condition and involved in the procedures that have to be undergone. Increased comfort will in turn improve his response to treatment, as well as making a substantial and worthwhile contribution to his well-being. At a more profound level, reinforcement or support of the 'will to health', in addition to his conscious determination to get well, is likely to contribute effectively to mobilization of the natural resources of his body and thus the efficacy of the treatments. For instance, control over the autonomic nervous system may be enlisted: for example, increasing the blood flow to a broken limb or reducing oedema in spinal injuries by suitable strategies in hypnosis.

Regression (reversion to earlier forms of intrapsychic organization in cognitive, affective and behavioural terms) is a common, even normal, reaction to the onset of disease or to accidental injury. The more severe the condition, the more helpless the patient becomes in fact as well as in his own perceptions, and therefore the more dependent he feels upon those responsible for his treatment. This regression predisposes most patients to accept hypnotic suggestions. One might, perhaps, expect that a patient who has been severely injured and is experiencing both intense pain and fear will be unwilling or unable (or both) to attend to an hypnotic induction. In fact, at such a moment, patients will respond more rather than less readily to a confident, reassuring and positive (even authoritative) induction, and display more 'hypnotic talent' than they would in a less disrupted state. This can be of value in Accident and Emergency Units as well as less formally at the site of an accident.

It is, however, in cases where spontaneous reaction to illness is counter-therapeutic that hypnotherapy may be applied with the greatest benefit. In the first instance, efforts may be directed towards modifying the patient's pathological and pathogenic attitudes through, for example, ego-strengthening. This may then be extended in a more generally psychotherapeutic direction, essentially independent of the illness, to disclose and resolve the patient's self-punitive, despairing and entropic or 'Thanatos-directed' drives. Therapy would be focused on uncovering the unconscious significance of the illness and the part it is playing in the patient's fantasies, as well as the use the patient may be making of his illness in his transactions with his life-situation and his significant relationships. This is especially so with adolescents, whose need for assistance in restoring and maintaining their sense of personal, especially bodily, integrity is particularly great, as is their need for reassurance and comfort of the regressed ego, however disguised that need may be.

MAJOR ILLNESS AND SURGERY

The management of the psychological aspects of major illness, and especially of major surgery, has been well documented. Caplan (1964) reports results of experiments examining the influence of giving patients a thorough cognitive preparation and systematic desensitization on their reactions to and recovery from surgery. He notes that the more a patient understood the nature of the intervention and was informed about the experiences that would follow, the less he showed resulting emotional disturbance, the more quickly did post-operative recovery occur and the less demand was expressed for reassurance, and especially for analgesic medication. The preparatory sessions held with patients in some of the researches involved the use of very vivid imagery, the patient being told in graphic detail not only what was to be done but how he would experience the sequelae of surgery. No overt hypnosis was employed and the word itself does not appear in the relevant literature, yet the techniques (except that no induction was carried out) parallel desensitization in hypnosis.

MANAGEMENT OF PAIN

Turning to the management of pain by hypnotic methods, the most important caveat in the generation of hypnotic anaesthesia or analgesia is that the symptom or pain that is the target of treatment should never be eliminated totally from awareness. First, it is important that the patient should be able to report any changes in his subjective experience of pain, since such changes may be the only indication of worsening of the condition requiring medical or surgical attention. Secondly, while total analgesia and anaesthesia can sometimes be obtained, failure to do so when this is the express objective or expectation of the patient will undermine his confidence in the procedure or in the therapist (or both) and thus deny him the relief he could otherwise gain.

Within the limits of safety and the abilities of the individual patient to utilize hypnosis, discomfort and pain may be reduced and distress, anxiety, apprehension and sometimes despair, together with regression and its manifestations in terms of demanding, crotchety and unco-operative behaviour, may be alleviated.

Techniques and strategies for reduction of pain are detailed in chapter 10. The management of the affective components of physical illness and post-operative states relies on three main aspects: reduction of anxiety, confusion and despair; 'age progression', that is, imaginative projection into the future in which the patient visualizes himself recovering progressively (within the realistic limitations of his condition) and resuming normal life; ego-strengthening to counter the regressive reactions he may be experiencing or demonstrating. The script which follows includes all these components.

██████████ Script 8.1

[Induction and deepening have been carried out. Obviously, the precise imagery used depends upon what has already been elicited from the patient; the following is suggested only as an example.]

Now I would like you to let a picture form in your mind of your special private place. Bit by bit, let that picture form in your mind until you find yourself sitting beside that stream, running through the woods you told me about, leaning against the trunk of a tree, feeling its bark rough against your back. There is a little birdsong from here and there in the wood. The sun shines down on the grass and wild flowers in the clearing in front of you, and glints here and there on the water. There is a soft scent of leaf mould and of fresh growth. You can hear the wind in the upper branches of the trees, and an occasional creak as one branch rubs on another as well as the rippling sound of the stream. Now and again you can hear the harsh shriek of a jay, and from time to time a cuckoo calls in the distance. It is very peaceful. Perhaps, as you remain still and quiet, you will see a squirrel or a rabbit on the other side of the stream, feeding there, or just playing. *[Pause]*

Feel the stillness. Let it soak into you, and as you absorb the stillness and beauty of this place, you can feel all the tension and anxiety, the fears and confusions and all the experiences of the last few days easing away, draining out of you as though it were all far away, far away. Feel yourself easing and relaxing as all the bad feelings fade away and you feel more and more at one with the wood, the stream, the sunshine and the peace of this place. Let all the stresses and strains you have accumulated drain out of you and evaporate. Feel yourself becoming more and more at peace and at ease in body and in mind as you absorb the good feelings of this place, bit by bit feeling more and more as you did in the days when you used to come and sit by your stream, totally at ease, at peace.

[Pause for a short while and then ask the patient if he has achieved such a degree of ease before continuing to the next phase.]

Now let that picture fade from your mind, but hold on to the peaceful and happy feelings. Go on feeling just as you always do by your stream: peaceful and at ease. *[Pause]* Imagine now that you are going forward into the future, going forward through time, and let yourself be four weeks ahead, four weeks ahead of now. You have been discharged from hospital, and you have been at home for several days now. You are sitting at home, perhaps in the garden or in your sitting-room. All the stress and discomfort is now behind you, and you can look back on it in memory if you wish. Notice how much better you are feeling now it is all over and you are recovering more and more. Notice how comfortable and relaxed you are now it is all over, how good it feels to be back at home and gradually beginning to take up the normal threads of your life.

You are looking forward to all the other things you are going to do again as you resume all your normal life. *[Then elaborate in line with the activities and situations that have been detailed in preliminary discussion with the patient.]*

Now let that picture fade from your mind again. Notice that you feel relaxed and at ease, looking forward to returning to your normal life, and feeling confident and comfortable. Let yourself feel still the ease and peace of your special private place. Each day that you go into self-hypnosis and spend time enjoying your private place, you will free yourself again of any stresses and tensions and feel relaxed and peaceful again, looking forward to recovering completely and to all that you will do, confident and relaxed, comfortable and at ease.

Further ego-strengthening can be added as appropriate to the particular patient, his experiences, condition, background, etc.
    Reactions to post-operative conditions, especially those involving mutilation (mastectomy, ileostomy, amputation of a limb, etc.) can be powerfully modified by hypnotic work. The effect of such mutilation on the self-esteem and perception of self-worth of the patient is likely to have profound consequences in his future life, general adaptation, and relationships. Discharge of grief, anger, resentment and regressed feelings can be readily mediated under hypnosis, the more so since display, or even admission, of such feelings may be in conflict with the patient's conscious determination to maintain a mature façade. It may also, of course, be felt at a deeper level that these feelings are too threatening to permit entry into consciousness. Under hypnosis, such defensive strategies can be by-passed, the patient's hidden reactions exposed and explored and, with or without imagery, finally discharged and left behind. Ego-strengthening will then assist in rebuilding self-esteem, confidence and positive attitudes towards the future.

ACCIDENTAL INJURIES

In all texts on the use of hypnosis in dentistry, it is well documented that simply being in trance, without any specific additional suggestions or techniques, appears to reduce bleeding after extractions. No successful explanation of this phenomenon has been offered. Nonetheless, this reaction to hypnotic induction can be exploited in any situation where control of bleeding is desirable. Naturally, in accidental injuries whether mechanical, chemical or through burning or scalding, diminution of pain is to be desired and can be readily achieved. Many studies suggest, usually implicitly, that the arousal following injury heightens susceptibility to induction, as well as the factor of regression that has already been discussed.

In the management of burns, most writers report substantial benefits in various aspects of the management of dressings and post-trauma lack of appetite gained through hypnosis. The use of suggestions of coolness in the affected area has been shown repeatedly to reduce the physical damage through heat and to promote healing. An unpublished paper by Dabney M. Ewin of the Medical School at Tulane University reported a case in which such suggestions were utilized in a case of severe burns to the hand, arm and shoulder. The therapist had been unaware of the injury to the shoulder and had limited his suggestions of coolness and comfort to the hand and arm. Although the shoulder had been less severely injured than the hand, the latter healed more quickly and successfully and did not require skin grafts while the former, for which no hypnotic suggestions had been made, required repeated grafts and remained much more badly scarred.

Many experimenters have demonstrated the appearance of blisters like those produced by heat injuries in uninjured subjects, in response to hypnotic suggestions of contact with a hot object. Claims have also been made of the suppression or diminution of blistering in response to experimentally applied heat (Chapman, Goodell and Wolff, 1959). Clinical application of hypnotic imagery for these purposes in the Accident and Emergency Unit does not appear to be widely practised as yet, but such reports as have been published suggest strongly that it would be of considerable value.

██████   PSYCHOSOMATIC CONDITIONS

1. Hypertension

The most obvious applications of hypnotic techniques is in the management of conditions known to have a major psychological determinant. For example, essential hypertension is well known to be substantially due to chronic heightened emotional arousal, usually involving suppressed and intense anger on the part of the patient (who may be less aware of the aura of rage around him than the people to whom he is close). Other common instances, again often more patent to the observer than to the patient himself, are asthma and disorders of the skin such as eczema and psoriasis. In all such conditions, relaxation and discharge of negative affect may show immediate and marked results. The effects of hypnotic intervention, especially if maintained and enhanced by well-motivated and systematic practice on the part of the patient, are often marked and can be dramatic.

For conditions in which emotional states and processes are powerful determinants in the onset and continuation or exacerbation of the symptoms, one may use imagery of the psychosomatic processes to modify the physical responses involved. For example, in hypertension it is possible to use visualization of the arteries, and the fact that their rigidity and constriction causes increased pressure in their contents. The arteries are then visualized as softening and becoming more elastic, thus allowing the pressure of the blood flowing through them to reduce. This imagery appears to establish some degree of direct personal control of arterial function.

██████   Script 8.2

[Induction, deepening and anxiety discharge have been carried out. The patient may be taken to his 'private place', or asked simply to turn his attention inwards to his body tissues.]

I would like you now to let yourself become vividly aware of the flow of blood through your body. It is pumped out of the heart and flows through the arteries, pushed along by your pulse, through to smaller and smaller vessels until it flows through the tiny capillaries in your body tissues. Then it reaches the smaller veins, and from them goes into larger vessels until it flows back towards the heart. Let yourself become very conscious of that flow of blood, pulsing through your body and its tissues. Concentrate especially on the arteries, and notice the way the arteries pulse, contracting and then widening, as the blood flows through. Picture the arteries like tubes, or hoses. Notice that the tubes constrict and then widen as the pulse beat moves along them. Notice that these tubes seem rather stiff, and that they contract and expand again rather stiffly, and that the blood seems to be forced through them as though reluctantly. Now imagine that the tubes are softening slightly, bit by bit, as you let yourself become more and more relaxed, softening and easing, so that the pulse beat moves along them more easily and smoothly, the walls of each tube becoming softer and more elastic as you relax, so that the blood is beginning to flow more easily and smoothly, more gently and more freely. Feel the easing of the arteries and the easing of the blood flow, becoming smoother and easier, smoother and easier, and so your heart can beat more gently and steadily, more smoothly, smoothly and easily.

Such imagery can be elaborated and expanded, or the flow of blood and action of the arterial walls likened to or represented by other images, not necessarily explicitly. For example, once the patient's attention is turned to an image of the arteries and their function, he may then be asked to picture a river in its early or upland stretches, rushing and tumbling and then, as it reaches the lower reaches slowing and easing, flowing more steadily and smoothly. This may be done as a metaphor, without making the application of the image explicit.

Ideally, the therapist would monitor the patient's blood pressure continuously through such a session in order to shape the imagery and the suggestions he makes to a continuous indication of effect. Current techniques for continuous monitoring are, however, either surgically invasive and impracticable or rely on periodic inflation of a cuff. This, although automatic and linked to periodic automated reading, tends to be somewhat disruptive to the patient's attention and to his ability to maintain relaxation. No literature appears to have been published as yet on the use of automatic monitoring of such treatment strategies, and research is highly desirable.

2. Skin disorders

Research on the treatment of eczema by hypnosis appears to be in its infancy. The literature so far contains only passing references to this application of hypnotic techniques although one clinical trial, of a sample of only seven subjects all but one of whom were small children, was reported by one of the authors (Karle, 1985). A further trial, of a larger number of children, is in process at the time of writing at the Hospital for Sick Children, Great Ormond Street, London. Jackson and Merrington (in Burrows and Dennerstein, 1980) suggest, as does Collison in the same work, without quoting any research findings, that uncovering techniques to reveal underlying psychological stresses and conflicts is desirable in all skin conditions.

While repressed or suppressed affect is improbable in eczema in neonates, it is highly probable that the distressing experiences inevitably associated with severe infantile eczema do indeed lay the foundations for stresses of this kind. That is to say, the condition of the skin, the sometimes extreme physical discomfort and distress resulting from this, the reactions of the significant adults in the child's life and the effects of all these on the child's self-image and relationships may all contribute to the establishment of an underlying reservoir of anger, frustration and distress which may be responsible for maintaining the eczema into later years. In the absence of such early stress, the condition might otherwise have improved with maturation. Where such stresses are present exposure and discharge of these accumulated and previously unacknowledged feelings are indeed likely to be beneficial.

A number of writers suggest that visualization of any experience which relieves itching, reduces the impulse to scratch and even improves the state of the skin itself can produce the same effect as the actual experience. For example, if immersion in cool water relieves irritation, picturing such immersion can reduce the actual irritation experienced.

One patient, a woman aged eighteen, found that sunbathing produced improvement in both the actual state of her skin and the itching that distressed her. She was asked to return in hypnosis to her favourite beach and there lie in the sun. As she complied, the skin of her face visibly changed, the angry redness diminishing. After the session was over, the patient reported that the itching she had been experiencing at the outset over her back and elsewhere had disappeared. The following week she reported that her skin had maintained its improvement and even improved further in both its physical state and reduced sensations of irritation. Longer-term follow-up followed the same pattern and, to her delight, this patient became able to tolerate showering and swimming without having to use emollients. She was, however, not only highly motivated, as most such patients are, but conscientious and systematic in her use of self-hypnosis.

Hypnotic treatment of eczema along these lines, using imagery as well as general relaxation and anxiety discharge, appears to be most effective with young children, but too little is known as yet of its application with adults to assess the value of such procedures beyond puberty. A number of individual case studies have been reported, and it is curious that conditions which are notoriously linked to emotional states, especially tension, do not appear to have attracted much attention from researchers in the field of hypnotherapy. Detailed treatment programmes for eczema in children are described in chapter 13.

Relief of itching and inhibition of scratching are always important in the management of skin conditions such as eczema and psoriasis, even if the physical state of the skin is not explicitly the focus of treatment. This is commonly achieved, often quite easily, either by training the patient to produce local anaesthesia or by using visualization of a relieving stimulus which is then associated with a touch of a hand. For instance, if the patient finds that application of cool water relieves the itching and the need to scratch, this is repeatedly visualized in hypnosis, and then the sensation of cool water associated with touch by one hand. Thus the patient first visualizes and then practises placing one hand over the itching body part and feeling the same soothing and relief as from cool water. He is then instructed that whenever in daily life he feels an itch developing, he is to close his eyes momentarily (obviously with suggestions that the latter is done only if appropriate and safe at the time) and place one hand over the affected area, when he will experience relief and comfort just as he has been doing in the course of the training.

3. Asthma

Many writers report that asthma is a highly appropriate condition for treatment by hypnotherapy. It is usually found that, however clear an allergenic factor may be, there is a significant psychological contribution to this condition. Asthma attacks in response to the proximity of an artificial flower of the kind the patient believes to be responsible for precipitating attacks may trigger off such an attack if he believes the flower to be real. Similarly, if one incautiously suggests in hypnosis that a patient who is allergic to grass pollens should wander through a summer meadow, hay fever or an asthma attack is likely to result immediately. It is commonplace for asthmatic episodes to be intimately related to life events and the emotional state of the patient at any particular time.

Some degree of caution has been advocated in the use of hypnosis in asthma in that while the patient is dyspnoeic and in a state of bronchial spasm, induced relaxation may endanger continued respiration.

General relaxation, discharge of tension and the exploration of underlying anxieties, frustration and anger can all be highly beneficial in reducing the incidence and severity of asthmatic episodes and of more or less chronic bronchospasm. In addition, the use of imagery directly relating to freeing the bronchi and the muscles of the chest can be helpful in giving the patient some degree of direct control over his own body, especially when he feels an attack beginning, when he can use such imagery prophylactically.

In virtually all conditions and experiences which involve pain, anxiety and tension, hypnosis is likely to be of benefit, if only through alleviating the patient's affective distress. In many instances anxiety or other negative affect is an added handicap to the improvement of the condition or response to treatment, and its reduction or removal will mediate quicker and more complete recovery. If indeed, as is suggested by some reports and experience, the attitudes, expectations, feelings and imagery of the patient can affect bodily functions directly, then substantially greater benefits can be expected. We take for granted that emotional states and cognitive processes affect bodily functions such as blood flow and its distribution, digestive functions, heart rate, blood pressure, etc. It follows that modification of cognitive and emotional processes can be used deliberately to influence such bodily processes to minimize damage from trauma or illness and to facilitate healing and recovery. Relaxation and tension discharge are the first recourse in such intervention, while more specific and direct or indirect suggestion, such as through metaphor, may well also serve to enhance normal healing and recovery.

9

ANXIETY

INTRODUCTION

This chapter presents treatment strategies for a range of conditions sharing as one of their principal features the common
thread of anxiety. The spectrum across which this ranges could be
described as beginning with mild and generalized ('free-floating')
anxiety, through anxiety attacks, to severe phobic reactions. The
various approaches described here can be applied to treat anxiety
as it occurs in other conditions, such as depression with anxiety,
but the main target of this chapter is anxiety reactions and states
as such.

Many conditions can be dealt with therapeutically quite
effectively at a symptomatic level and although this is often also
true of anxiety states, one more frequently finds that attempting to
disperse the anxiety alone, although helpful, is rarely adequate.
One commonly finds that whether this problem is generalized or
episodic anxiety on the one hand or phobic reactions to one or
more specific stimuli on the other, the anxiety is a manifestation of
an underlying disturbance. It will therefore diminish satisfactorily
only if the symptom-directed treatment is accompanied by some
degree of recovery and resolution of the underlying processes.
Most writers therefore advise that 'uncovering' techniques should
be employed in such conditions. The symptom of anxiety frequently has its roots in traumatic experiences, most often in
childhood, and the recovery into consciousness of a previously
repressed memory of such an event or, where the event itself was
normally accessible to consciousness but the affect repressed,
recovery of the affect may produce relief. More commonly,
however, recovery of repressed material relating to a trauma is not
enough, and dynamic or analytic 'working through' of the

recovered memory is necessary before the condition and symp-toms are resolved. These techniques belong in the field of dynamic or analytically orientated therapy and are dealt with in Part IV. They will therefore not be described in detail here, although examples will be quoted.

Wolpe (1958) is generally regarded as the father of the behavioural technique called 'reciprocal inhibition', the underly-ing principle of the treatment known as systematic desensitiz-ation. In brief this can best be described as based on the observed fact that anxiety and tension cannot co-exist with relaxation and peace of mind. Thus if an individual is either rendered anxious experimentally or becomes so spontaneously, and then relaxation is induced, the anxiety will diminish and even cease. If this cycle is repeated frequently enough, the anxiety produced in reaction to the original stimulus, even if biologically appropriate, will be extinguished.

This is of course diametrically opposite to the cycle experienced by, for example, phobic patients, who either force themselves to endure the situation and their own reaction (in the hope that repeated exposure will extinguish their response) and experience relief from anxiety only when they finally escape from the situation, or simply avoid the action or situation they fear. In practice, they find (as one would predict) that their condition is made no better by this practice and may even increase in severity. Similarly, those who retreat as soon as anxiety rises and thereby gain relief through avoidance perpetuate their condition, since the reduction of anxiety acts as a positive reinforcer to the act of avoidance. In consequence the phobic stimulus remains associ-ated with anxiety; therefore the conditioned response pattern remains unchanged. In neither pattern is relaxation or release from anxiety experienced at the very point of proximity to the phobic stimulus that aroused the conditioned response of anxiety.

Phobic patients actually perpetuate and even intensify their condition by the very efforts they make to conquer it, and often approach the concept of systematic desensitization, when it is offered in therapy, with considerable scepticism, since they fail to perceive the distinction between their own efforts to attain some sort of negative adaptation and the treatment programme offered.

The technique of Systematic Desensitization is closely similar to that used in Infantry Training where recruits are conditioned into the use of the bayonet. The reluctance of the average man to stick a large knife into the body of another person is strong, and in conventional Infantry Training this reluctance is overcome by creating a general arousal in the trainee and especially arousing fear and rage through the manner in which the training session is conducted in order to blot out the normal or natural hesitation. Military experience bears witness to the efficacy of this procedure in suppressing a deeply ingrained reaction. In parenthesis, one might note that the casualty rate in such training, in terms of emotional distress generated by the conflict which the trainee experiences, is substantial.

If a stimulus such as a word is made the conditioned stimulus[48] for arousal and attack, then no matter how pacific the soldier is by nature, he will be aroused to aggressive action. Similarly, if the conditioned stimulus is associated with relaxation, then it will trigger off that reaction no matter how tense the individual may be at that moment. If the reduction in anxiety and arousal is temporary, repetition of the conditioned stimulus or 'key word' at suitable intervals will suffice to keep the anxiety at a manageable level, and such repetitions will tend progressively to extinguish the anxiety. In systematic desensitization the cycle of anxiety arousal-> key word-> relaxation-> anxiety arousal, etc. is repeated at progressively closer proximity to or intensity of the anxiety stimulus, and ultimately the anxiety reaction is extinguished completely.

This process of reciprocal inhibition can be very effectively applied to general high arousal such as constant free-floating anxiety, as well as to attacks such as more or less abrupt arousal of intense anxiety and panic unrelated to any overt or observable cause or stimulus.

It is clearly important to discriminate between anxiety which occurs inappropriately (in the form of free-floating anxiety, phobic reactions or panic attacks unrelated to any identifiable stimulus) and anxiety engendered or triggered by situations in which anxiety is biologically or socially appropriate and where such reactions would be shown by most people. Examples of this latter category include the arousal experienced by almost everyone when appearing on stage or when placed in a situation of real danger. There is, however, a middle ground in the form of anxiety experienced in a particular situation or in the face of a specific stimulus that would create some degree of arousal in anyone, but where the degree or intensity of arousal is out of proportion to its object and significantly greater than would be experienced by most people.

To take this last group first: it is common in clinical practice for patients to complain of an uncomfortable or even disabling level of anxiety in situations or in response to stimuli that may arouse some degree of anxiety in anyone. The reaction is realistic in character but disproportionate in degree, and so becomes damaging or handicapping. This is in contradistinction to phobic reactions where the overt focus of the phobia does not necessarily have an intrinsic fear-stimulating character, may have been previously innocuous to the patient and does not necessarily represent a real danger.

For example, most people will feel a degree of anxiety (which for some is quite intense) when about to address a meeting or appear on a stage, but can nevertheless without concurrent or subsequent serious suffering or damage carry out the required task. Indeed, for most people a degree of such arousal ensures a better performance. Such feelings are generally felt to be reasonable and appropriate and it is only if that anxiety is exaggerated in intensity or duration, prevents execution of a required task or otherwise interferes with the sufferer's life to a significant degree that one begins to regard the reaction as pathological.

In contrast, most people do not react with panic if the door to the room they are occupying is closed or if they go out of doors or into a shop and so on. If an individual does suffer severe anxiety in these situations, to the extent of interfering with the way he functions in his everyday life, that reaction would be considered pathological.

Another category of pathological anxiety reactions are those attacks of panic held by some authorities to be relics of atavistic responses from the early days of man's evolution. Amongst these one would include phobic reactions to spiders, mice, rats and other small scuttling creatures such as snakes and lizards which are commonly foci of phobic reactions which would be appropriate, it is suggested, in the sense of having possessed genuine biological (i.e. survival) value in more primitive times.

Free-floating or general chronic anxiety is perhaps most commonly treated by medication. Describing such a state to one's general practitioner, at least in the recent past, would generate more often than not the production of a prescription of an anxiolytic or mildly tranquillizing preparation. Relaxation and meditation used as coping strategies and as means of dispersing anxiety have their advocates, as have other therapies such as acupuncture. To those patients who are able to respond moderately well or better to hypnosis, it offers a means of achieving some degree of voluntary or self-mediated control over these disabling feelings and thus gives a sense of self-mastery that is therapeutically a bonus.

Such continuous anxiety states are probably the tip of a much larger iceberg. Patients who complain of unremitting and unfocused anxiety, or of anxiety that attaches itself to virtually any and all normal activities, may be responding to a subliminal awareness of a major psychiatric disorder that is not yet manifest. Such complaints also present occasionally in 'borderline personalities'. In either case, hypnotherapy is unlikely to be of benefit.

A warning is in order here. Before attempting treatment by the methods described below, it is important to ensure that the anxiety complained of by the patient is not the covert expression of an underlying depression and that it does not represent the patient's perhaps numinous and premonitory awareness of the early stages of a disintegrative psychotic process. Similarly one must distinguish psychogenic anxiety from symptoms of physical disorders, whether intracranial organic pathology, endocrinal disturbances, food or food-additive sensitivities, intoxication and so on. It is also quite common to find that the condition of which the patient complains is a thoroughly normal reaction to a markedly threatening or stressful real-life situation that he may deny as significant, important or even uncomfortable. As always, differential diagnosis and the exclusion of organic and other pathology are essential preliminaries to treatment. Having satisfied oneself that the condition is indeed susceptible to hypnotic procedures and does not require other forms of treatment, one may proceed. It is worth remembering, however, that hypnotherapy for one or other symptom may proceed at the same time as organic or biochemical treatments.

TREATMENT STRATEGIES

The patient is first encouraged to identify his favourite and most happy memory as his 'private place'. As noted before, if (as sometimes occurs) a patient cannot recall ever having been happy, such a memory can usually be found through age regression. If this too draws a blank, then the therapist, in consultation with the patient, will have to create such a good place.

Induction is then carried out, followed by deepening. The latter is usually tailored to fit in with the patient's 'private place'. For example, if his 'private place' is a beach then one might use a path leading down a hill, steps cut in a cliff, or a stairway down to the beach. Once the patient is well established in his chosen scene, he is asked simply to spend a little time there, enjoying the feelings associated with or stimulated by it, whilst the therapist enhances these feelings with suggestions that utilize the patient's own chosen imagery of increasing feelings of well-being, peace and ease of body and mind, etc. so that he may enter as relaxed and tension-free a state as possible. The patient's attention is drawn to these feelings, with instructions to monitor his affective and physical state closely. Usually he will report that however profound the relaxation reached at this stage, some parts of his body are still somewhat tense. One might ask the patient to scan his body internally and to release any tensions that have persisted, and may add any imagery necessary to facilitate this.

For example, the 'private place' can be visualized initially as being shrouded in mist, this mist representing the tensions and perhaps preoccupying thoughts and worries experienced by the patient, with the sun gradually burning through and dispersing it, until all is clear, calm and warm. Another useful image, especially if the patient is visualizing himself sitting or lying by a stream or river, is to suggest that he has in his pocket slips of paper on which are written all the things that worry or upset him. He then takes these out one by one, reads them and throws them into the stream to be carried away. As the bits of paper are carried away, so he feels himself becoming free of the burden of his problem. (On occasion, this can backfire. One patient with whom this image was employed became distressed at the pollution of his favourite trout river, as described in chapter 6. Unfortunately, he had not responded to the instruction, noted as important in earlier chapters of this book, to change anything which is experienced as uncomfortable or distressing into an alternative form that is congenial.)

When the patient indicates that he has discharged all his worries, the scene is allowed to fade. It is replaced with a scene drawn from the patient's everyday life and suggestions are made to re-create the generalized anxiety of the presenting symptom. The patient uses either verbal or motor signals to indicate the onset of these feelings, and a low level of anxiety is maintained for a short while. This is then extinguished by suggestions of recovery of the feelings associated with the 'private place'.[49] If necessary the patient can be instructed to return to the 'private place' after a short period of experiencing his habitual anxiety, and to remain there until he is completely at ease again.

This cycle is repeated a number of times until it is well established and the patient has demonstrated his ability to extinguish anxiety quickly and without hesitation. He is then instructed to go through this process in regular daily sessions of self-hypnosis at home, with strong suggestions that this practice will result in the progressive extinction of anxiety for longer and longer periods in his everyday life. The session ends with a further period in which the patient spends time in his 'private place' to strengthen his relaxation and to give him a taste of how life will be as a consequence of the treatment, and he is advised to conclude each session of self-treatment in this way. The script might be on the following lines.

███████ Script 9.1

[The chosen induction has been carried out and the patient appears to be in a light trance.]

Good. Now I would like you to picture yourself standing at the top of a flight of steps. You look down them; notice that there are ten steps, with a lawn at the foot stretching away to a wall with a door in it. In a moment, I am going to ask you to walk slowly down the steps, and I will count them off one by one as you go down. As you walk down the steps, let yourself

feel that you are leaving the ordinary everyday world further
and further behind, so that it becomes more and more distant
and remote, as you feel yourself going deeper and deeper down
inside yourself, becoming more and more relaxed, detached
and comfortable, comfortable, detached and at ease. When you
reach the bottom step, you can let the steps and the ordinary
world fade away completely, and then go over to the door and
open it. When you go through it and close it behind you, you
will find yourself in that lovely old garden you told me about
and experiencing all the good feelings you remember and
associate with that garden, ease and peace of mind. [Pause]
Now, I would like you to begin walking step by step down
that flight of steps as I count. One ... two ... more and more
relaxed and detached. Three. ... Perhaps the noises from
outside this room are fading, and so you feel that you are
going really deep inside yourself. Four ... five. Pause there for a
moment and notice that the ordinary everyday world is
becoming quite distant. You are half-way down to that level of
comfort and peace that you can achieve today. Now go on. Six
... seven ... eight, more and more remote and detached. Only
two more steps to go until you step down on to that lawn.
Nine ... ten. Good. Stop there for a moment and let the stairs
and all the everyday world just fade away. [Pause] Good. Now
cross the lawn, noticing the feel of the turf under your feet,
and when you reach the door, open it and go through. Close it
behind you and notice that as you do so you close out any
troubles or distractions. Then turn around and find yourself in
that garden that is so special to you. Feel the soft warm
breeze, listen to the birdsong, notice the scent of the flowers,
the sunlight falling here and there, the colours [and so on, as
prescribed by the patient's prior account of the garden].
Notice how all your worries and fears, anxieties and tensions
are beginning to drop away, fade away, as you let the peace
and beauty of the garden soak into you. ... Let yourself re-
capture all the good feelings of the garden. ... For a little while
now, you will not hear my voice, but in the silence let yourself
absorb the peace, stillness and beauty of the garden, so that
when you hear my voice again, you will be completely at
ease, completely at peace. [Pause] Now I would like you to let
your mind roam around your body, and wherever you note

any tension or discomfort, let it go until you feel completely good, completely without any tension. *[Pause]* Good. Now let that picture fade from your mind, but keep hold of all the good feelings you have been experiencing. *[Pause]*

Whenever you go into the hypnotic state on your own by using the exercise I have taught you *[or 'shall teach you', as appropriate]*, go down those steps and through the door into your private garden. Recapture and absorb again all the peace and beauty of that place so that all the accumulated tensions that have built up since you last went there, all the anxieties and frustrations, fade away again until you are once more completely at peace in mind and body. When you come out of the trance again, you will go on feeling that relaxation, peace, ease and comfort, and each time you repeat the exercise and spend time in that garden, those good feelings will become stronger and will last longer, becoming more profound, so that your everyday life will become less tense and anxious, and the discomforts and fears you have felt will get less and less. You will find that the more frequently you spend time in your private place, the more those good feelings will begin to spread into your everyday life. *[Pause]*

Now I would like you to concentrate on the word: Peace. ... Peace. ... Peace. ... As you concentrate on that word, you might like to picture it written, or carved, or just concentrate on the sound of it. Peace. Each time you concentrate on that word, Peace, you will find yourself feeling just as you do in that garden, just as relaxed and at ease as in your special private place. Peace. Peace. From now on, whenever you find yourself becoming tense and anxious, or apprehensive and panicky, or feel yourself becoming angry and upset at nothing, or feeling any of the feelings which disturb you, you need only close your eyes for a moment and concentrate on the word Peace, and you will feel all the negative feelings ebb away, fade to nothing, so that once again you feel as you do in that garden, that special private place. Whatever you may be doing and wherever you may be, if you feel yourself getting wound up and the problems that have been spoiling your life coming back, you need only close your eyes and concentrate on the word <u>Peace</u>, and you will feel yourself relaxing and becoming at ease again in mind and body.

If it seems appropriate, the patient can then be taken back into the garden, to the door, and through it into one of the situations he has described in which the target anxiety is experienced. He is then asked to let the dysphoric feelings that are the target of treatment develop and to let the therapist know when he can vividly feel the same quality as he commonly does in that situation. He is then asked to concentrate on his key word and to note the diminution of anxiety. This can be repeated a number of times until the patient signals that he is finding it more difficult to arouse anxiety with that scene. He is then reminded to use the same technique in real life when this situation occurs and told that he will find the same calming effect following his focusing on the key word. He is then taken back once more into the garden, and then brought back to normal wakefulness.

Complaints of more or less sudden onsets of anxiety, apparently unrelated to any specific situations or stimuli, are encountered quite commonly. In some cases, a phobic stimulus not previously apparent to the patient can be identified. For instance, despite the disparity and variety of situations in which the patient has experienced the onset of panics one may find a common factor, such as exposure to other people.

A young man who complained of apparently completely random attacks of anxiety proved on detailed enquiry to experience these episodes whenever he expected to be addressed by another person. He had not been able to isolate this common factor, since sometimes the attacks occurred when he was alone. On those occasions it transpired that the telephone bell was the apparent trigger. His attention, and that of the doctors to whom he had previously described his problem, had focused on the fact that his attacks occurred equally frequently when alone at home, in the street, at work, in his favourite pub, at sport: virtually anywhere.

Generally, attacks of this nature do have some common factor or factors, but the reaction may occur in response to two or more quite separate and distinct stimuli or groups of stimuli. If that is the case, desensitization to all the relevant stimuli would probably be like killing the Hydra: as soon as one stimulus is extinguished, another would appear to take its place. A technique (such as a conditioned response of relaxation and calm to a 'key word') that enables the patient to manage and control the reaction whenever and wherever it appears would enable him to improve his everyday functioning, even if exploratory or analytically based therapy has to be employed simultaneously in order to deal with the underlying process that is being expressed and perhaps mediated by the symptom. In such cases, training or conditioning the patient to feel himself relaxed as soon as he attends to his key word is often very effective. On its own, however, without parallel endeavours to uncover the unconscious sources and significance of the problem, such an approach is likely to be of only temporary efficacy.

It is not uncommon for anxiety attacks to be an 'empty symptom' which has become self-perpetuating. The anxiety in such cases had its origin in some unresolved conflict, often originating in childhood or adolescence and emerging in adult life in response to some life stress or crisis or at a time when illness, post-operative malaise or some other weakening condition has reduced the patient's self-confidence, self-esteem and general emotional and physical stability. The underlying conflict or distress is not in itself sufficiently intense or potent to precipitate any difficulties until and unless the patient's personal strength is at a low ebb or other problems, often real-life ones, stretch his coping skills beyond their limit. The debilitating and disruptive effects of the symptom itself then become an additional stress.

In the case of an 'empty symptom', the habitual pattern will be reinforced and the symptom perpetuated by the patient's fear of it recurring. That is to say, the patient, having experienced several devastating panic attacks, becomes fearful and apprehensive about the anticipated next attack and this tension may overload his coping capacity, generating more symptoms. If such a pattern is interrupted by conditioned relaxation, he becomes more confident of being able to deal with any recurrence and the attacks will diminish and terminate without further investigation or treatment.

The strategy of choice would therefore be to provide the patient with a means of controlling any attacks of this nature by a training programme essentially the same as that described above, with perhaps additional emphasis on the use of a key word and its consequent reduction of tension, to be used any time he experiences a premonitory rise in anxiety (or general arousal).

Phobic reactions, whether in response to a single and clearly identified stimulus (e.g. spider phobia) or to more complex situations (e.g. agoraphobia) demand very careful and detailed elucidation first of the relevant stimulus or stimuli and then of the 'hierarchy': the increasing steps or gradations in stimulus leading up to the phobic episode. For instance, a patient complaining of panic at being outside his home will be able to describe a gradient of anxiety in response to a process that begins with, say, noting that it is time to go to work, tying his tie, donning an overcoat, picking up his briefcase, approaching the front door, opening it and so on, until once out in the street he experiences the full-blown panic.

The process of systematic desensitization is based on the elucidation of finely graded steps of this kind from the most innocuous on to the (initially) most anxiety-provoking stimulus. This 'hierarchy' is then used as the basis for planning the treatment strategy, which aims at extinguishing the anxiety response to each step in the hierarchy, tackling that which provokes the least anxiety first and then working upwards. This is often performed *in vivo*; once trained to respond to the therapist's presence with feelings of confidence, security and relaxation, the patient is then physically accompanied by the therapist through the steps in his hierarchy, pausing to implement an anxiety-management routine as soon as he experiences and reports a rise in his anxiety level. The patient progresses to the next step only when he reports full confidence in reducing the anxiety aroused by the previous one. Obviously, this is very expensive in terms of therapist time and effort, and as good and often rather better results can be obtained by practising such a programme in hypnosis.

Desensitization is quite commonly used *in vitro*, by simply imagining the movement through the hierarchy and using relaxation as the anxiety inhibitor. In recent years, the effectiveness of this procedure has been increasingly questioned. General opinion now seems to lean towards the finding that such imaginal exercises do not affect the patient's anxiety responses significantly, and similarly that more realistic exercises (using real rather than imagined stimuli) in the consulting room or clinic does not produce generalizations to the patient's life. The use of hypnosis, however, as the medium through which such imaginal exercises are carried out appears to make the inhibitory process more effective. It is suggested that the vividness and apparent reality of the stimulus, the more powerful affective reaction experienced by the patient and the reality (subjective as well as objective) of the relaxation response to a key word or other signal, makes the whole process an effective treatment.

Procedures for such a treatment programme must have become clear by this stage. One may use a key word, as in the previous script, or a word that has been chosen by the patient to trigger off an instantaneous return to the 'private place'; or one may use a physical stimulus, sometimes described as 'anchoring'. This is achieved by using a touch such as a hand on a shoulder or a clasp of one of the patient's hands, initiated by the therapist at the point in the exercise when the patient is signalling anxiety and the therapist suggests relaxation and, if necessary, a visit to the 'private place'.

The patient, once he has experienced this sequence a number of times, is instructed to use the same touch (by placing one hand on the opposite shoulder in imitation of the therapist's touch or by clasping one hand in the other) whenever he feels an increase of arousal, this gesture stimulating a return of relaxation. It must be remembered, as has been emphasized before, that any physical contact between therapist and patient needs to be carefully weighed, and if it is to be used, the patient must know of it in advance.

Phobic reactions to specific stimuli rarely exist on their own; almost always one finds more complex fears and confusions underlying them of which the patient is frequently quite unaware. In some instances the underlying process lies in an unresolved traumatic experience that may be quite easily and quickly exposed and dealt with.

A woman patient was referred to one of the authors because of a fear of going outside her home that had kept her totally house-bound for some nine months. She had had a period prior to this lasting some three years in which she had been able to leave her house only when accompanied by her husband, and this had progressively intensified until she was totally disabled from normal life. She responded well to hypnotic desensitization, but remained apprehensive as to its effects *in vivo*. After three sessions she was able to go a short distance away from her house on her own, but still could not bring herself to go into town to do the weekly shopping.

Age regression, using the panic feelings and their accompanying somatic symptoms as a guide, took her to an episode when she was three or four years old when she had been out with her mother and brother. A thunderstorm had blown up while they were in a park, and the mother, herself terrified, had drawn the children under a tree to wait for the rain to cease. The fear associated with this event through the combination of the thunder and lightning, with her awareness of her mother's panic expressed partly through anger at the children, emerged with considerable force with the patient's recall of this previously inaccessible memory. She was guided to clarify her perceptions of that event and especially to distinguish her mother's feelings from her own, and then brought back out of hypnosis. She then reported the realization that the feelings she experienced when about to leave her home exactly mirrored those she had rediscovered in the memory, and so was able to appreciate that they were 'second-hand' and displaced from their original source.

After this session she found herself able to go anywhere she wished with no more than some apprehension, which after a further two sessions faded completely, and she has since remained well and panic-free. Such a simple and easily resolved trauma is perhaps not particularly common, but is well worth looking for. Often, however, the underlying traumatic memory is more complex and involves more thorough-going treatment. This topic is of course dealt with in more detail in the section on analytically based hypnotherapy.

Self-hypnotic anxiety dispersal can be a valuable ancillary while other therapy is being carried out. Patients undergoing exploratory or dynamic therapy may experience at times considerable increase in their prevalent anxiety, and can be readily taught to use the 'private place' and anxiety discharge to calm themselves at bed-time or any other time when they need to be especially in charge of themselves and calm.

The same techniques can be usefully applied where the anxiety is wholly appropriate and yet unhelpful. For example, a child's fear of hypodermic needles is thoroughly appropriate but can be the source of intense suffering if such a procedure has to be carried out frequently, as in diabetes, kidney failure and many other conditions. Fear of dental treatment again is appropriate: avoidance reactions to imminent pain are altogether biologically natural. Reciprocal inhibition is useful in such cases, but it may be even more effective if anaesthesia for the relevant body part is also sought or the patient becomes able to remove himself subjectively from the whole situation and enjoy his 'private place' while unaware of the procedure being executed.

In preparation for labour, relaxation has been used for a very long time as a means of reducing anxiety and the physical tension associated with it. Most commonly hypnotic techniques are not explicitly used, but terms such as 'psychoprophylaxis' and 'neuromuscular disassociation' disguise skilfully designed hypnotic procedures, and it appears that the hypnotic character of such procedures is not recognized by their designers and practitioners.

Since the emphasis in hypnotic management of dental and other surgical procedures and of labour is on the control of pain more than on the management of anxiety, these topics are included in chapter 10.

10

PAIN

The treatment or management of pain is one of the oldest, if not
the oldest arena for the use of hypnotic techniques. The story of
Jacob Grimm's childhood experience of painless excision of a
tumour is related by Hilgard and LeBaron (1984, p.1). A less
dramatic episode of this kind was experienced by one of the
authors. His three-year-old son fell against the kitchen boiler one
day, scorching his buttocks. Clad only in a vest, he sought out his
father in the garden, and demanded: 'Daddy kiss it better.' Father
complied, whereupon the child ceased his tears and declared the
pain gone. The reddening of the skin faded visibly and was gone
after a few moments.

Numerous more formal accounts of the use of hypnoanaesthesia are to be found in the early literature, perhaps the
most well-known being the work reported by John Esdaile, who
whilst working in India in the mid-nineteenth century carried
out numerous major operations without chemical anaesthesia,
apparently without any pain being experienced by his patients.
Records apparently show, incidentally, that the survival rate
shown by his patients was better by a factor of ten than was
common at the time. His accounts were dismissed by his medical
colleagues in England on the grounds that his patients were
unsophisticated and primitive, despite the fact that they included
a number of British government officials. During the same period,
other surgeons are reported to have carried out demonstrations
in front of colleagues in which major surgery was carried out
without pain or distress on the part of the patient, but still
without these accounts being accorded either respect or recognition.

The authors own experiences show that today, well over a century after the first papers of substance on this topic, credence amongst surgeons generally remains rare: responses to suggestions of the introduction of hypnotic techniques in their field not infrequently echo the responses of their colleagues in the last century, and little more attention is paid today than then to the growing literature of reports of clinical trials in this field.

Without perhaps going so far as those who have suggested that hypnosis could replace chemical anaesthesia (especially in view of the fact that by no means all subjects will prove to be sufficiently able to use hypnosis to that degree), the use of hypnosis in the management of painful procedures is gaining ground. In dentistry especially its use in both Britain and elsewhere is spreading, while in obstetrics the technique is now widespread, although usually otherwise labelled and called relaxation or 'neuromuscular disassociation'. Hypnotic techniques are widely applied, without formal induction and without recognition of the nature of the activity. Distraction, displacement of attention and similar techniques are commonly employed in minor medical procedures such as the giving of injections and in painful treatments such as manipulation in physiotherapy.

However, formal and structured use of hypnosis by practitioners who are appropriately informed and experienced can increase the effects of self-induced analgesia and anaesthesia to the point where it becomes a major clinical tool.

As with all applications of hypnotic techniques, the modification of pain through this method occurs spontaneously and without formality. For instance, there have been many reports of soldiers in battle, or sports players in the heat of an important game, receiving serious injuries and remaining unaware of any injury or indeed of any pain until the immediate excitement and general high level of arousal have abated. Once the battle or skirmish is over or the game concluded and the subject notices his injury or has his attention drawn to it, pain is felt, usually instantly and severely. Until that point, however, whatever r eural signals were being generated had not penetrated to consciousness.

In the reverse direction, the application of some ritual that is expected and believed to produce relief from pain can be highly efficacious, especially with children. The parent who 'kisses it better' knows perfectly well that such a gesture, although it has no demonstrable physiological effect on the generation and transmission of neural signals, can be more effective than any common chemical analgesic preparation. The application of a plaster to a cut or graze has similar properties. It is a common experience for most of us that the pain that drove one to doctor or dentist tends to disappear once one is in the waiting room and confident of receiving help.

Distraction, too, is commonly used to avoid or obstruct perception of pain: a child may have his attention drawn to some toy or picture at the moment before the doctor inserts the needle into his arm, and if this is done skilfully and the child has not been so intent and anxious about what is about to happen that he is unable to attend to the distraction, he will be unaware that anything has been done to him. Of course, once he realizes he has been 'tricked' he is likely to protest that it does indeed hurt, but the pain was despite his protestations, actually outside consciousness at the moment of distraction.

The same sort of techniques and strategies can be used to establish anaesthesia for painful surgical and other procedures as in the control of chronic or recurrent pain from other causes. In this chapter the basic procedures common to most uses of hypnosis in the management of pain will be detailed first, followed by illustrations of the application of these strategies in various specific conditions.

HYPNOTIC ANAESTHESIA

In trance, whether attained spontaneously or by more or less formal induction, the sensorium can be controlled and its input limited. This is closely akin to the mechanism underlying certain conversion symptoms such as hysterical blindness and deafness, or the local anaesthetic states usually described as 'glove anaesthesia'. It can be relatively easy to establish hypnotic anaesthesia in the skin and deeper tissues, of much the same type as in the case of conversion involving anaesthesia, but interruption of sight or hearing appears to be much less readily induced through hypnosis. Furthermore, it is usually much easier to produce such anaesthesia in a peripheral body part than in the trunk or head, at least directly. It is a curious fact that although most subjects find it difficult or even quite impossible to reduce pain or sensitivity in a localized part of the trunk or in the head in response to direct suggestion with or without imagery. the same subjects may be able to produce total lack of sensation in a hand. They are then able to transfer the numbness to another body part and can, only by this means, reduce the pain in the head or the trunk.

There are exceptions to this general rule in that pain due to muscle tension, such as in the lower back, can often be reduced or eliminated by suggestions of relaxation and warmth, but this is of course essentially different from suggested analgesia or anaesthesia. Such lower-back pain stems from excessive and continued muscle tension and depends upon the maintenance of that tension for its continuation. Thus once the muscles concerned relax and their blood supply is enhanced by the vaso-dilation response to suggestions of warmth, the pain lessens and may disappear.

In contrast, the use of hypnotic anaesthesia requires the establishment of a block or interruption in the complex physical process initiated when tissue damage or stress generates signals eventually producing the cortical arousal interpreted as pain, the origin of which is subjectively recognized and located. The actual signals continue to occur after hypnoanaesthesia is established, at least to that point in the neural chain where the hypnotic suggestions have introduced an interruption or block; whereas in hypnotherapy of, for instance, tension pain in the head or lower back, the signals themselves lessen or are extinguished.

In general, if one wishes to reduce experienced pain and consequent distress arising from injury or illness in a part of the trunk, success is more commonly achieved by the induction of anaesthesia or analgesia in one hand and the transfer of the numbness to the target area than by attempting to deal directly with the target area. For example, in chronic pain due to spinal disc degeneration, one would suggest increasing numbness in one of the patient's hands, using imagery if necessary, until the subject reports a marked degree of anaesthesia. One may then check through touch, pinching of the skin or other stimuli that a sufficient degree of sensation loss has been achieved, and then place the hand over the area where the perceived pain is located and suggest that the numbness should migrate or spread from that hand into the area on which it rests until the pain is felt to have diminished to a tolerable level. This transferred analgesia may be similarly employed when a painful procedure is to be carried out on a body part that proves inadequately responsive to direct suggestion of anaesthesia.

In general, the degree to which an individual can tolerate a particular pain depends upon two main characteristics of the experienced sensation in addition to the obvious ones of intensity and duration: the site of the pain and its subjective dimensions in space. Most commonly the nearer the site of the pain is to the body centre the less tolerable it is, and the larger the area or volume of the body it appears to occupy the less tolerable it becomes.

Experiments using either ideo-motor signals or automatic writing have demonstrated that the subject does indeed remain aware of pain, but at a level of consciousness separated from and apparently out of touch with his central awareness. For example, having induced anaesthesia of one hand in a hypnotized subject, one may then make suggestions that the deeper levels of the subject's personality should communicate with the therapist in writing, but in such a way that this activity should remain outside the awareness or knowledge of the primary or central personality. One may then prick the subject's anaesthetized hand with a needle and he will not only then appear to be unaware of any sensations but will subsequently aver his ignorance of the event. When the hand is pricked, however, the subject will communicate his awareness of the pain by expressing this in writing.[10]

It follows that if suggestions are made that a particular pain should become totally blocked and that no pain at all should be felt whilst the cause of the pain remains unmodified, an internal conflict is created. At one level the pain is present and experienced, while at another it is denied. Such a conflict may prove intolerable to the subject or so stressful that sooner or later the block will break down and perception of pain will return to full consciousness. Nonetheless, in 'good hypnotic subjects' such blocking of all awareness of pain can be established.

At this point an important warning must be given. It is possible (with subjects who are able to use hypnosis really effectively) to block all pain sensations from a given area or body part. If some deterioration or increase in the pathology or trauma which produced the pain currently being suppressed should occur, the patient will be unaware of that change. This could be dangerous. It is therefore mandatory, except in the final phases of terminal illness, that the patient should be prepared for such changes. There are three principal ways of doing this. A part of the pain is allowed to remain and to reach consciousness so that any change in it is perceived; or a small area or volume of the relevant body part is left normally sensitive so that, again, any change is noted by the patient; or specific suggestions are made that, if there should be any change in the pain that is being blocked from awareness, that change will trigger off perception of the whole pain: that is the block will cease to function.

Rather than total blocking, therefore, a more effective approach to chronic or intractable pain or pain due to a continuing and unmodifiable cause is to suggest a continuing awareness of the pain, but in a more tolerable form or a more tolerable site. This approach can be illustrated by a case (treated by one of the authors) of extensive peripheral neuritis associated with liver disease, stemming from alcohol abuse. A woman with a long history of regular and excessive drinking was referred for help through hypnosis to control this. At the time of the first session, she had been admitted to hospital and a diagnosis of moderately advanced cirrhosis had been made. At that time she was unable even to hold a newspaper because of the unremitting hypersensitivity of her hands, and could not walk more than a few steps because of the pain in the soles of her feet.

This patient was trained under hypnosis to visualize the pain in her hands as a covering over her fingers and hands, represented by thin gloves. She then visualized herself rolling down these gloves from the wrist, until the only contact between her hands and the gloves was at the tips of her middle fingers. At that point her hands were, in accordance with the image, free of pain except for the tips of the middle fingers, which would continue to experience the same pain as before. This restricted area of pain was tolerable and did not interfere with the activities she wished to pursue. At the same time, the fact that she felt *some* pain avoided any internal conflict and she remained able to contain the pain in those areas alone: she had thus managed to reduce considerably the area affected by the pain and thereby the distress generated by it, making it easier to tolerate.

Another useful strategy in the management of continuous

pain is to transfer it to a part of the body where it is more bearable than in its original location. As noted earlier, pain in the trunk tends to be more subjectively distressing than pain in an extremity. Abdominal, back or chest pain, if transferred to a finger, will become less distressing and yet remain sufficiently in awareness that the cognitive dissonance mentioned above is avoided. It seems that spatial displacement is easier to accommodate cognitively than a logical contradiction. Further, the retention of some awareness of the pain enables one to ensure more confidently that any changes in it are perceived without delay or difficulty and appropriate action taken, when and if necessary.

An exception to this general rule is chronic pain stemming from conditions that do not require the kind of vigilance suggested above. For example, pain due to nerve pressure from degenerating intervertebral discs, pelvic displacement or the later stages of a terminal illness need not be monitored in this way. In such cases it would be legitimate to block awareness of pain totally and yet without danger, but in order to avoid the 'no pain – pain present' conflict, the most effective approach is commonly to set up a *temporary* block. Thus one might suggest that for a period of a few hours the patient will be completely free of pain, but that after that time the pain will gradually come back. This allows the contradiction to be tolerated: 'The pain is there but is blocked for the time being' seems to be a formula that does not arouse disturbing cognitive conflict.

███████████ Script 10.1

[Induction and deepening have been carried out. It is usually as well to produce at least one 'hypnotic phenomenon', such as arm levitation, as a preparation for or practice of the modification of sensory control that is being sought.]

I would like you now to turn your attention to your right hand. Notice how it feels very relaxed, limp and loose, and resting heavily on the arm of the chair. Notice the feeling of pressure where it rests and the feeling you get from the texture of the cloth cover of the chair. Now imagine how it would feel if I were to inject a nerve-block at your wrist

*[touching the skin at various points in a ring around the
wrist with the point of a pencil as you go on]*, so that as each
injection is given, you gradually lose all sensation in that
hand. First you will feel it going cold, and perhaps tingling a
little, and then, as it gets colder, so you will feel it become
numb, more and more numb. Soon it will have lost all
sensation and you cannot feel that hand at all. It will feel to
you as though all sensation stops at your wrist where the
nerve-block was injected. When you reach that point, let me
know.

*[When the patient indicates that he has lost touch with that
hand, you can check the depth of anaesthesia by pinching the
skin or pricking it lightly and asking him to report any
sensations and then, if necessary, adding further suggestions
of increasing numbness until the required degree of
insensitivity has been reached. Note that most patients
require time, rather than just additional suggestions, to allow
the loss of feeling to develop.]*

*[When the required stage has been reached, continue as
follows:]* Good.[51] Now place that hand over your right knee,
just over the part that gives you pain. I will help you.[52] Now
you can feel in your knee the weight of that hand resting on
it. Let the cold and numb feeling you have in that hand
gradually spread down through your knee, so that that knee
gradually goes cold and numb, cold and numb. When you can
no longer feel any pain in that knee, let me know. As that
knee gradually gets cold and goes numb, you will find that the
pain fades away until it has gone completely and you can no
longer feel it at all. When that happens, let me know.

If the anaesthesia is to be used for a painful procedure such as
perhaps venipuncture, incision of a boil or other surgery, then
obviously the suggestions of numbness and lack of all sensation
will precede the onset of pain. In such instances, an alternative
procedure to that detailed above may be more successful, since
before the surgical procedure being initiated there is little or no
sensation experienced in the relevant body part that can be

subjectively extinguished. One might substitute for the imagery in the script above an actual sensation produced by stroking the site that is to be the location of the impending procedure. Obviously, this technique can be employed only if the patient can and does accept physical contact in the area concerned without anxiety or other distress.

███████   Script 10.2

I am now going to touch your left arm and stroke it very lightly. You can feel that? Good. Now, as I go on stroking it gently and slowly, notice that you can gradually let the feeling of touch become fainter and fainter and quite soon you may find that you cannot feel me touching you at all. When that happens, let me know.

[When the patient indicates that sensation has been lost, continue as follows, while touching the arm more firmly.]

I am now going to touch you more strongly and you will feel the stroking sensations again because of that. Can you feel that? Good. Now again let the sensation fade until you cannot feel me touching you at all. Let me know when all sensation has gone. *[When the patient indicates loss of sensation, continue.]* Good. Now you have managed to lose all sensation in that part of your left arm, and you can feel nothing at all there.

[It is sometimes helpful to establish the boundary of the area of anaesthesia by touching the patient's arm in various spots, since this procedure reassures the patient – and the person who will carry out the planned surgical procedure – of the reality of anaesthesia in the delimited area.]

If a patient still finds it difficult to produce insensitivity, the process may be enhanced by having the hand and arm in a state of levitation before beginning suggestions of numbness. Since the patient has accepted the (unrealistic) weightlessness of his hand

and arm, the further change involving loss of sensation is more easily accepted, assisted, of course, by the fact that, as the hand is not in contact with anything, there are no tactile sensations to lose.

In some conditions which produce recurrent periods of pain, such as in the back and limbs through spinal problems or in the head through migraine, the pain itself may not be the best target for attention. In these cases one aims rather at treating the causes of pain, as was suggested earlier for pain stemming from muscular spasms. In such cases, relaxation of the spasm will be followed by reduction and even disappearance of the pain. The treatment of migraine by bio-feedback training to produce a rise in temperature of the hands and arms alone is often applied without recourse to formal hypnosis and is described in most texts on behaviour modification techniques. The same approach can be applied in hypnosis, either by direct suggestion or with the use of imagery such as immersion of the hands in hot water. It has been suggested that this procedure is effective through reducing the dilation of the cerebral vessels and the pressure in them as the result of the marked dilation in the blood vessels in the arms and hands. Be that as it may, patients who can produce appreciable temperature changes in their hands and arms do experience relief from the pain of migraine.

A special case relating to the management of pain is that of 'needle phobia' or fear of invasive, distressing and painful treatments that have to be carried out repeatedly. This is encountered principally in children with disorders such as leukaemia, renal failure, diabetes, etc. Where venipuncture or bone-marrow aspiration is permitted by the child but causes intense distress, analgesia or anaesthesia may be sufficient; but not uncommonly children become so distressed that the procedure may be difficult to carry out. The child may be so fearful and resistant as to make it well-nigh impossible even to get him to the hospital for the next treatment. In such cases desensitization should be added, together with distraction by thoroughly rehearsed recourse to a favourite place or activity. This topic is so well covered by Hilgard and LeBaron (1984) that no attempt will be made to detail appropriate techniques here, and the interested reader is referred to that excellent book.

Lower-back pain is endemic, at least in Western cultures.

Specialists in orthopaedics, physiotherapy or osteopathy will generally focus on the structural factors involved in the generation of such pain, pressure on nerve roots through narrowed intervertebral discs, bad posture and so on, but very commonly the problem is complicated by psychological factors. Such conditions often appear to be a form of protest against and means of avoidance of stressful life-situations, even when there is an undoubted physical source. There are often indications that the noxious quality of the sensations concerned may be exaggerated by such factors as depression of mood, anxiety about the cause of the pain and its prognosis, or totally unrelated areas of the patient's life such as the quality of his marital relationship, his employment prospects, or any other affectively loaded aspect of his life. The intensity of the pain, its noxious quality and its ability to interfere with activity is often clearly related to what the patient is doing or due to do at any given time.

In other cases the pain may strike without any relation to the patient's current life. As with all conditions for which one may consider hypnotic intervention, the complex and sometimes conflicting functional and motivational aspects of the pain and its perception must be assessed before treatment is undertaken.

If the pain has an important and perhaps useful or reward-producing function, all therapeutic endeavours are likely to be fruitless, however earnestly the patient seeks help. The part played by the pain in his life, the responses it evokes from his social network, and its role in the establishment and maintenance of the patient's self-image must be elucidated and included in the treatment strategy. Quite commonly, for example, pain, especially if disabling, may protect the patient from sexual demands or activities that are or have become aversive. Pain may serve as a self-punitive measure or a penance. Alternatively, it may serve as a punishment for a spouse, child or parent. In transactional analytic terms, the pain may be a 'wooden leg': 'I would be able to play the piano/cook the meals/win the marathon/get my degree/go to work if it were not for my back' (Berne, 1964). In any and all such cases symptomatic treatment, if successful at all in reducing the presenting pain, is likely to be followed by a new problem and will continue to generate further such elaboration, or repeated regression to the original complaint, until and unless the underlying dynamics are explored and changed.

Somewhat more cheerfully, however, symptomatic treatment does have its place. One of the authors, while attending a conference on hypnosis, was approached by a fellow-member for help one morning. This man had woken that day with lumbago and was bent double, unable to straighten and in considerable pain. He had been unable to reduce the causal muscle spasm and resulting pain through self-hypnosis. Perched uncomfortably on a metal chair, he was readily taken into trance and then into a summer meadow through which he ambled, enjoying the warmth of the sun on his back. Within two minutes, he indicated that the pain and stiffness were lessening. The trance was terminated, with suggestions that the feeling of warmth and relaxation would continue. He stood up completely upright, declared himself, joyfully, to be free of pain and remained so for the remainder of that day.

Such a treatment strategy is appropriate and effective in many cases where it is clear that the source or cause of the pain does not demand attention in its own right, where appropriate physical treatments are already being provided, and where there are no indications of significant underlying psychopathological processes. Arthritic and rheumatic pain, pain remaining after minor surgical procedures and the like can all be reduced or eliminated through relaxation, suggestion and imagery of situations and sensations that are experienced as soothing.

To illustrate this technique, the following script recounts the procedure employed with a patient who suffered from frequent very severe headaches and neck pain stemming, according to the orthopaedist and physiotherapist who had previously treated her, from shallow cervical joints that allowed some degree of displacement of the vertebrae in response to tension.

████████   Script 10.3

[It had already been established that warmth was helpful in alleviating the pain. Induction and deepening were carried out. The patient was then conducted to her 'favourite private place' and allowed to spend a short while enjoying the scene.]

You are now feeling quite comfortable and relaxed except that you are still aware of the pain in your head and neck. Is that right? [The patient indicated assent.] I would like you now to concentrate your attention on your hands. Imagine that you are placing them in a bowl of water that is just comfortably hot, and holding them there until they become really warm. Notice that as they warm up, you can feel an increase in the blood flow to and through them, so that they get warmer and warmer and somehow softer. When they are really warm and feel quite glowing, place them either side of your neck and then move them upwards so that they hold either side of your head, just where the pain is at its worst. Good [the patient actually moved her hands as directed]. Now notice that the warmth of your hands is gradually soaking and spreading into your neck. Now soaking into your head, and the blood flow in your neck and scalp is increasing so that both become warmer and warmer. Such a comforting and soothing feeling. As your neck gets warmer, so the tendons and muscles relax and ease, becoming soft and loose, and the flow of blood becomes easier and warmer, easier and warmer. Now as your hands hold your head, so the warmth spreads into your head, soothing away the pain bit by bit, warming and soothing, warming and soothing.

When the pain in your neck and head have eased completely and your neck and head feel only warm and comfortable, let your hands come down again. [Wait for the hands to return to a resting position, guiding them gently – with prior warning to the patient – if necessary.] Now let the normal feeling return to your hands, but let your head and neck still feel warm and comfortable, completely comfortable and free of all pain, so that they will remain so after you come back out of the trance. Good. Now let yourself gradually and slowly hold your head up again, without any strain or tension, just comfortably held clear of the back of the chair, slowly and gradually, without any strain, tension or discomfort. [The patient raises her head to a more erect posture and holds it there.]

Good. Now let yourself come back out of the trance in your own time, back to the ordinary waking state when you are

**ready, bringing with you the warm and comfortable feeling in
your head and neck. Completely free of pain and at ease.**

This patient, and others with similar problems treated in similar
ways, was able to use this technique in self-hypnosis after only one
training session and became able to abort 'attacks' of pain in this
way.

Management of pain in dental and other surgical procedures such as venipuncture involves not only the component of
pain and anticipated pain, but that of anxiety and even overt fear.
Induction of anaesthesia and demonstration of this can reassure
the patient to such a degree that the anxiety lessens, but more
commonly additional reassurance and anxiety dispersal must be
provided.

In most situations in which pain is experienced and is the
focus of hypnotic techniques, relaxation of the whole person is
appropriately and helpfully sought as part of the whole management of the experience. This is not the case, however, in labour,
where muscular activity is both necessary and inevitable. The
contractions of the uterus that lead to expulsion of the foetus must
therefore not be included in any suggestions of relaxation, and
should actually be reinforced. The technique advocated by Erna
Wright (1979) under the title 'neuromuscular disassociation' is
that of training the patient to contract some muscles while
relaxing the remainder. Most commonly this is practised by
raising one leg and arm while lying on the floor and making these
limbs rigid while relaxing the trunk and the opposing arm and leg.
The hypothesis involved is that this exercise enables the patient to
relax the skeletal musculature while experiencing uterine contractions, and at the beginning of the second stage of labour to
relax the pelvic floor and the vaginal musculature. In Wright's
training programme no overt induction of hypnosis is included,
although observation of patients undergoing this training leaves
no doubt concerning the dissociated and detached state achieved
through relaxation and concentration on the instructions and
commentary of the teacher.

The use of explicit hypnosis can facilitate both the
dissociation required to enable a parturient woman to relax all
muscles not involved in the process of delivery at any given

moment despite the involuntary contraction of others, and at the same time a reduction of discomfort and pain. Additionally, the anxiety and apprehension felt by many women before and during labour can be readily discharged in ways that have already been made clear in other contexts. It must be stated, however, that training in the use of hypnosis in labour should be provided only by practitioners with a background of obstetric training who are able to relate the techniques and images required to the anatomy and process of labour.

A SPECIAL CASE: TINNITUS

Related to pain, in the sense that it is a continuous and noxious experience, is the condition known as tinnitus. The subjective awareness of unpleasant noises in the head can be as stressful and disruptive of life as intense and continuous pain. There is little substantial literature on the treatment of this condition through hypnosis. Crasilneck and Hall (1985) report one study which suggests that some degree of control can be achieved in 'somnambulistic' patients, while Kroger (1977) notes a number of isolated case studies. The largest study reported (Marks, Onisiphorou and Karle, 1985) is of fourteen patients, of whom only one reported a decrease in perceived noise while a further five indicated improvement in terms of a more relaxed frame of mind and greater tolerance of the tinnitus, but without any change in loudness of the noise.

Tinnitus tends to affect people relatively late in life when, consequently, they are generally less susceptible to hypnotic techniques. Additionally, the condition appears to be related to obsessional and hypochondriacal personality traits. This makes suppression of the symptom or reduction in its noxious quality somewhat problematic in many cases because the complaint often becomes the focus of the patient's attention and quite commonly appears to become his main interest in life. General relaxation, discharge of tensions and frustrations can be beneficial, but reduction of the perceived noises is rarely achieved except in those patients who are especially good at hypnosis – presumably those described as 'somnambulistic' by Crasilneck and Hall.

With such a patient, it is well worth while attempting to attain control. Once it is established that the patient is indeed a 'good hypnotic subject', he is closely questioned as to the nature and qualities of the noises he perceives, and if possible these qualities are then related to some objective source of noise. For example, the tinnitus may resemble the sounds emitted by a VHF radio between stations, or by gas escaping from a cylinder, water flowing rapidly or some other commonplace sounds. This can then be visualized and suggestions made that either distance the noise source from the patient or reduce the emitted volume. Thus the volume control of the imagined radio may be turned down, or the tuning knob turned until a favoured piece of music is transmitted, or the tap on the gas cylinder turned off.

Alternatively, the patient may see himself as walking away from the source of noise. Another type of image may be employed to focus on the passage of the nerve signals mediating hearing in much the same form as described in an earlier passage concerning pain. The auditory nerve may be visualized as a multiple cable leading to an old-fashioned telephone switchboard in which all the jack-plugs are seen as inserted in their sockets. The plugs are then removed one at a time until the tinnitus is subjectively reduced. An array of electrical switches can serve the same purpose.

Such imagery does occasionally evoke improvement in the patient's experience. The main benefit for most patients, however, is to increase their stress tolerance through relaxation and ego-strengthening. It appears that the imagery, although not affecting the perceived noise, makes the experience less stressful.

PART III

TREATMENT STRATEGIES WITH CHILDREN

11

BASIC TECHNIQUES

INTRODUCTION

There are few important differences between hypnotherapy with
children and the techniques employed with adults. Naturally,
however, the language used is adapted to the child's vocabulary
and knowledge, whilst the imagery should be tailored to his
developmental level. Preparation is generally simpler, although
for ethical as well as practical reasons preparation of the parent or
parents is extremely important: as important for successful work
with children as is preparation of adult patients.

It is perhaps even more important with children than with
adults to ensure that the purpose of the interview is clearly
grasped by the patient. With older children, adolescents and
adults, there is probably less room for doubt, confusion or a
completely different idea of the reason why the interview is being
held, although from time to time one discovers that the patient has
been thinking on quite different lines from the therapist. With
children below the age of puberty it is vital to ensure that therapist
and patient have the same purpose clearly and explicitly in mind.

Work with children and adolescents is often more rewarding than that with adults because of children's readier acceptance
of the processes suggested and their more rapid and often more
complete involvement in the images used. The effects of a single
hypnotic session can be quite dramatic and heart-warming. Also,
children will often use self-hypnotic exercises whole-heartedly
and imaginatively and will experience pride in achieving self-
mastery through such work, without hesitation or self-
consciousness.

Language, techniques and images must be selected to
match the developmental level of the child. Where one may well

ask an adult or adolescent what he understands by the word 'hypnosis', the same question might be inappropriate with a child. With older children and adolescents, as with adults, it is important to clear away misinformation and misunderstanding and to allay anxieties, correct expectations and so on before embarking on the first steps of hypnotherapy. Such efforts, however, would be inadvisable with a child of, say, five or six and may even be counter-productive in that it may arouse anxiety or transmit the therapist's anxieties to the child himself. Children before the age of puberty tend generally, in any case, to be more readily submissive and reliant on adult control and direction (however self-willed they may appear on the surface or seem in their behaviour), so that a more authoritative approach is more readily accepted than by older children and adults.

As noted above, each step in the course of hypnotherapy with children should be adapted to the age and developmental stage of the child concerned. Some variations will obviously be determined by intellectual and educational status, vocabulary, cultural background and so on. In order to simplify presentation, preparation or introduction, techniques, scripts, induction and deepening methods, as well as the creation of treatment strategies and the choice of imagery, will be given in this chapter separately for several different age groups. Specific treatment strategies for the entire age range from early childhood to adolescence will be detailed in the next two chapters, and will be grouped within each chapter as closely as possible according to age.

CHILDREN UNDER SEVEN

Most authors suggest that hypnotic techniques in any formal sense cannot be used with children below the age of four. The Stanford Hypnotic Clinical Scale for Children, commonly used to assess the response of children to hypnotic procedures and suggestions, is standardized down to this age. Younger children will usually find it difficult to attend more than very briefly to any kind of formal induction, yet can be very responsive indeed to storytelling and the metaphors that can be conveyed in fairy-tales. Children who are particularly restless and overactive (whether inherently or because of arousal due to anxiety or distress) or who are depressed and withdrawn may have to be approached very indirectly, perhaps through play or physical contact. Such informal techniques are practised intuitively by those who are highly skilled and very sensitive in the management of small children, and hypnotic work with very young children cannot really be carried out without such intuitive awareness and creativity. Such skills cannot be readily laid out in words and can best be demonstrated or observed.

To use hypnotic techniques at all, a child must be old enough to listen to a story and optimally should have had some experience of this. The task then of catching his attention, holding it and eventually utilizing his absorption in a fantasy to modify his behaviour, affective state, pain (or whatever other therapeutic target one has in mind) becomes much easier to practise and to describe. Most children will be ready in this way by the age of four or thereabouts: by no means all will have learned to attend continuously for more than very brief spells, although some will be able to do so earlier.

It is important, before making any start on a session of hypnotherapy with a child, to survey the family vocabulary. For example, the phrase 'fairy-tales' will convey its conventional meaning in one family but be used in another to mean lies. If then you ask a child from a family where the latter is the case, if he enjoys fairy-tales, the answer might be misleading and the child become distressed because of the accusation he perceives in the question. It is vital to check with the parents or other care-takers particular words that may be intended (as indicated by the planned treatment programme) other than those of pretty well universal meaning and usage before beginning work with the child.

One of the authors, assuming from the apparent socio-cultural status of the family that they would use the phrase 'spend a penny' for passing urine, used that expression in a session with an enuretic child, only to have the child dissolve into giggles. It transpired that the family regarded this as a slightly rude term and discouraged its use in their children. One can, to be sure, usually escape from the effects of such bloomers, but they may spoil the session and thus make it much more difficult to continue work with a child.

An important choice that has to be made before beginning a session is whether or not one should have the parents present with the child. Generally the child will make a preference clear without a direct question, although occasionally it may be necessary or wise to ask. If the parents have been adequately briefed about the treatment plan and its rationale, they are rarely unhelpful or intrusive. We prefer to allow child and parents a wholly free choice and then, if the parents remain unobtrusive, it is often helpful to have them sit in the background. The child's attention can be successfully drawn away from them and then they are totally ignored. With very young children, one often finds that the child wishes to sit on the lap of a parent and reassure himself of their nearness and collaboration, approval and so on. In such situations, it is wise to include the parent in the whole process and utilize the parent's presence, actions and anything that the parent may contribute to the child's sensorium in just the way that incidental stimuli and actions are included in inductions and other processes with patients of any age.

For instance, the parent may be more or less unconsciously stroking the child's arm or leg as the child sits on a lap. Early on in the induction, and again later whenever appropriate, one would say:

While you walk in the magic wood with Mummy and your pussy, Tabitha, looking for the pool of magic water that will make your skin better, you can feel your mummy's hand gently stroking your arm, and you can notice how good that feels, how nice to feel her hand gently touching your arm.

Sometimes, in their anxiety for the treatment to work, parents may encourage or, more accurately, *nag* the child to pay attention. Naturally, one will have tried to reduce this by adequate preparation, but if it persists even this can be 'built into' the patter, and at the same time drop the parent a strong hint:

From time to time, you will hear your mummy joining in with me to help you listen to what I say, but bit by bit, she will speak less often, and then you will only hear my voice.

The introduction of a hypnotic session to modify pain with a child in this age group might be on the following lines.

Script 11.1   Storytelling

Do you like fairy-tales? Good. So do I. May I tell you one? If you listen really hard, perhaps you can actually be right in the story as though it were happening to you. It is a very happy story, and so you would enjoy being in it. Mummy will listen too, and if you want, she can be in it too. Would you like that? And is there anyone else you would like to be in it? Your dog, yes. What is your dog's name? Yes, let us have him in the story too. I think most people like to have their eyes shut when they are listening to a story, and perhaps you would like to shut your eyes too so that you can see what happens in the story. Now when you think very hard about something, so hard that you can see it and feel it, then it can help you to feel happy, or warm and comfortable, or it can make you laugh. The story I am going to tell you will do all those things and when you listen to it, and think about it happening to you, then the pain that is hurting you will just disappear and you won't feel it at all.

Now, once upon a time, there was a little girl, about the same age as you are. She lived ...

The suggestion of a treatment element is embedded in the prologue, without emphasis and without any didactic or directive tone but with clear suggestion of amelioration of the child's pain. The story that would follow would contain an image that relates directly to symptom relief. This might take the form of a situation in which the child in the story learns that stroking one finger with the other hand makes it magical and able to relieve pain, so that when that finger is subsequently applied over the area of pain, the hurt fades away.

Alternatively a story could be adapted to apply to temper tantrums and other behavioural difficulties, where an incident in the story illustrates the attainment of control over the target behaviour by the central figure. A script illustrating this approach will be found in chapter 13.

A great deal depends upon the child's understanding of the purpose of the interview. If this is clear, explicit and accepted by the child, one can be markedly more direct. For instance, one child, aged four-and-a-half, proved a particularly apt and co-operative subject. She had suffered from severe eczema since one week after birth. Throughout her life, no member of the family had had more than one hour's continuous sleep because of the disturbance created by her itching, the pain resulting from her scratching, and the high level of distress that she experienced and demonstrated in her behaviour. Since the second or third week of life, she had been on continuous multiple medication: cortico-steroids, antibiotics (to control the infections arising from her scratching) and sedatives, despite all of which she scratched violently (causing quite serious excoriation and bleeding), could sleep only fitfully, and was in continuous pain, irritation and distress. Having found conventional medication so ineffective, her parents sought help through all possible alternative routes, eventually seeking hypnotherapy. The dermatologist and paediatrician who had been looking after her agreed to this in sheer desperation.

At the first interview this little girl agreed, in a very adult manner, that she would like to learn how to stop the itching and make her skin better. Induction was begun using eye-fixation after very brief enquiry into her preferences and favourite stories. However, no result was obtained after more than ten minutes, but she agreed happily to try another way." She closed her eyes as instructed and pictured tied to her arm a huge red balloon, which grew so big that first her arm rose up in the air and then she was lifted up and could float away to fairy-land, carried by her balloon. On arrival she was greeted by her own special fairy and a kitten. The success of this manoeuvre was signalled by a broad smile. She then walked, escorted by her fairy and the kitten, to a clearing in the woods in the middle of which was a pool of magic water, which would make her skin better. She was told to place one hand in the water and then spread the water on to any part that was itching, and the itching would stop at the touch of the cool fresh water. Once all the itching was gone, and she was totally comfortable, she could then float back to the room in which the session had begun and open her eyes. Within a few minutes she opened her eyes, grinned broadly and told the therapist that the water had been so nice she had plunged into it and splashed around until all the itching stopped.

A brief form of self-induction was then described to her, with strong assurance that each time she went through this routine she would find herself in 'fairy-land' and would then be able to repeat the soothing and healing experience with the 'magic pool'. The self-induction was described as follows. Note that the 'magic key' to which reference is made is an Italian coin: any such object, unfamiliar and interesting to the child, may be employed.[54]

Script 11.2

Every evening before you go to bed, I would like you to spend a little time in fairy-land with your special fairy and your pussycat, so that you can soothe away the itching and hurting in your skin with the water in your magic pool and help your skin to grow better and better. What you will do is this.

You will make yourself really comfortable, and then hold up your magic key in one hand, and then stare at it very hard while you think about going to fairy-land. As you stare at it harder and harder, you will feel more and more that you want to close your eyes and the key will get heavier and heavier. When the key gets so heavy that it slips out of your fingers, your eyes will close and you will find yourself floating off to fairy-land, just as you did a little while ago. When you get to fairy-land, you will find your special fairy and your pussy waiting for you so that they can go with you to the magic pool.

When you have played in the magic pool and soothed away all the itching with the magic water, so that your skin feels really comfortable, you can then say goodbye to the fairy and the pussy and come back home. When you get back home, your eyes will open and you will feel very comfortable. Your skin will not be itching, and will feel really good, so you will be able to sleep comfortably and happily and sometimes have lovely dreams, and so you will not want to scratch during the night, and will not need to wake up.

In the course of the following week all medication, other than emulsifying oil for her bath, was discontinued. She stopped scratching, using the magic water instead whenever she itched. This continued well for the following year, after which contact was lost. Her mastery over her own condition was elaborated and enhanced in the second and third sessions of treatment by suggesting that she could use a special technique to suppress itching in everyday life, such as while at school, when she could not reasonably close her eyes and go to fairy-land. This was in the form of the suggestion that her hands, having been immersed each day in the magic pool, had acquired some magic themselves, so that if she simply placed a hand over an area that was itching, the itching would be soothed away. She accepted and practised this technique with total success.

Such co-operation may seem exceptional, especially in a child with an intensely distressing condition, yet many children of this age will accept in a most mature and practical way any suggestions or techniques that they believe to be hopeful. The key consists in part in the confidence and co-operation of the parents, in part in the confidence of the therapist, in part in the respect for the child's integrity and dignity expressed by the therapist, and in part in the explicit *collaboration* in treatment between child and therapist.

A necessary pre-condition is that the child has not become so depressed as to despair of any treatment attempts. Another is that the *parents* have not become resigned through despair, or progressed to rejection of the child, and that the relationship between the child and the parents has not developed in such a way as to include the disorder as an integral ingredient. Given these somewhat numinous qualifications, the child's co-operation or, better, collaboration can be readily enlisted when he or she understands the purpose of treatment and realizes the pleasant nature of the treatment planned. This often makes a sharp contrast to most medical interventions, of which the child may have had a surfeit.

A common experience in working with children of this age is that despite overt co-operation and willingness, they present quite intense but covert resistance and anxiety in response to induction. For example, as in the case of the child described above, a first induction using eye-fixation may be complied with very properly but without effect. Whatever is tried in the first attempt may seem to be followed conscientiously and without any overt resistance or difficulty, yet be wholly ineffectual. Sometimes, even if another induction is then attempted, this too will be resisted.

In contrast, resistance in other children of this age group will appear (misleadingly) to be very obvious, as shown for example in their eyes remaining stubbornly open despite repeated (and probably increasingly anxious) re-iterations by the therapist of suggestions of closure. Such children may actually be in a deep trance from quite early on in the induction, with their eyes remaining open throughout the period of trance.

One of the authors began an induction with a four-year-old using eye-fixation on a coin ('magic key') held by the child. This child, another subject in an early clinical trial of hypnosis in eczema, had been wriggling and rubbing herself continuously and without pause throughout the initial discussion with her and her parents. Once her eyes fixated the coin, all movements ceased. The therapist, aware of the parents' scepticism of the procedure, was perhaps over-anxious about the whole situation and did not notice the child's bodily stillness, or rather did not interpret it correctly. For something over twenty minutes suggestions about eye closure were continued until the (metaphorical) penny dropped (although the 500-lire coin did not!). Reviewing the session on video-tape disclosed very clearly that the child had entered a deep trance after only a few suggestions and a very short space of time, and had quite obviously become wholly unaware of the previously intolerable itching over her whole body.

Many younger children will insist on keeping their eyes open, apparently as a means of reassuring themselves, and this should be accepted. In such cases, eye-closure should be the subject of choice for the child rather than directly suggested. If a particular child appears to be following this pattern, one may prescribe the choice:

Your eyes are wide open. Perhaps they will stay like that, or perhaps they will close. Perhaps they will be open sometimes and closed sometimes. I wonder which it will be.

▬▬▬▬ INDUCTIONS

Eye-fixation on an object held by the child is one of the easiest and most successful approaches at this age. As discussed earlier, the authors like to use foreign coins that are unfamiliar to the child in appearance; weight and pattern and are therefore readily accepted by most young children as 'magic'. With some ceremony, they are given their special magic coin or key and asked to keep it very securely from then on, so that they can use it themselves at home to take them to their special place, where their pain, distress, itching or other difficulty can become better.

▬▬▬▬ Script 11.3   Eye-fixation – the 'magic key'[55]

Have you seen a coin like this before? No? Well, I am going to give you this very special coin. You must keep it very safely, because it is going to be your magic key so that you can go to fairy-land. In a minute, I am going to show you how to use it to go to fairy-land and have all the adventures that we have been talking about. When you go to fairy-land and meet your special fairy there, you will feel so much better, your pain will disappear and you will feel completely comfortable and happy and you will not notice any pain at all.

What you must do is to hold it up there *[raising the child's hand until the coin is slightly above a direct line of vision]* and look at it. Just hold your magic key up there, make yourself comfortable and stare at it really hard. That's it, good. Keep staring at it until your eyes get tired and want to shut. You will feel that magic key getting heavier and heavier and you will have to try awfully hard to hold the magic key up because it is getting so heavy, and your arm is getting heavier too. When your eyes close, the magic key will have got so heavy that it will slip through your fingers and fall down, but

don't worry about that because you will find it on your lap
when you open your eyes again. It will slip through your
fingers when your eyes close and then your arm will sink
down and you can be completely comfortable. When all that
happens, you will find yourself in fairy-land, and you will see
your special fairy standing there in front of you with the
rabbit you wanted, just waiting for you.

Your special fairy is there now, with the rabbit, waiting for
you, and when you close your eyes you will be able to see
them, and they will take you for a walk through fairy-land
so that you can do all the things you want to do, so that you
can feel better and forget all about the pain.

Fairy-tales are generally helpful and effective as inductions, in
part because of their reassuring familiarity. It is usually helpful to
enquire what the child's favourite tale may be and use that. The
story of Snow White is especially suitable, of course, not just
because of its history and general familiarity but because of the
eye-closure built into it at the moment when Snow White bites
into the apple. Virtually any of the traditional fairy-tales can be
modified and adapted to include therapeutic themes appropriate
to the child in question.

When asked what his favourite story is, the choice may be
of a television programme, which can be used equally well even if
the therapist is unfamiliar with it: the child himself may be
invited to relate a story from it, and this is then gradually taken
over by the therapist for appropriate modification. The child may
be invited to identify himself with a character in the story. This
latter, however, may be implied rather than stated and identification in this way is often even more powerful. The central
adventure will then be adapted to include a feature that creates
the right image for the change the child needs: diminution or
absence of pain, distress, anxiety and fear, itching and so on, or
whatever the target of therapy may be.

Towards the upper end of this age range, and occasionally
earlier, other approaches may be more acceptable, especially to
the child who denies any interest in stories and finds eye-fixation
uncongenial. An appeal to imagination is often the most effective

induction with those children who are appreciably apprehensive about more magical techniques.

████████████   Script 11.4   Balloon on water

Do you have a good imagination? No? Well, I wonder if you could imagine something so strongly that what you think about really seems to be happening. Shall we try? Good. Now, just imagine that there is a big tub of water there beside your chair. Yes, just where you could reach it.[56] On top of the water is a balloon. What colour would you like it to be? Red and yellow? Fine. So, imagine that on the water in that tub beside you is a big red and yellow balloon. Oh, you would like it to be blue as well. That's fine, good, a blue, yellow and red balloon floating on the water. Now, you had better put your hand on the balloon to stop it floating away up into the air. Yes, like that.[57] Hold it down or it will float away. Now, if you push it down a little way into the water, you can feel it pushing your hand up. Try that.[58] Good. Now let it up again a little way, but don't let it float away. You can bounce it a bit up and down on the water.[59] Yes, like that. That's good, that's very good. Now, imagine if the balloon were getting bigger and bigger, so that it gets harder and harder to hold it down. Perhaps it would be easier to imagine that if you closed your eyes. The balloon is ever so big and pushing up against your hand harder and harder. If you were to stop pushing it down, and just let your hand rest on top of it, that hand and arm would gradually float up into the air on top of the balloon.[60] Higher and higher, higher and higher, and as it floats up, you can see just how good you are at imagining things, and feel really pleased with yourself. Good. Now, if you like, you can let the balloon slip out from under your hand, and then your arm can just come down again, and you go on feeling so good, so comfortable, so good and comfortable.

The 'Touch, tingle, twitch and arm levitation' induction described in chapter 3 (Script 3.7) can also be used, especially in the more anxious and resistant child. The inductions listed here have been found by the authors to meet almost all contingencies and to be congenial to almost all children. Numerous alternative techniques are described by Gardner and Olness (1981), and readers interested in a wider range of approaches should refer to that book.

Formal deepening, other than by elaboration of the story used to carry the therapeutic image, is rarely necessary. Once the child has become involved in the images or story, the planned treatment strategy can be pursued.

Training in self-hypnosis is as vital with children as with patients of any age. Regular self-treatment is a vital ingredient in treating pain or other physical distress and in the management of habit disorders, emotional disturbances and indeed virtually any therapeutic course. Wherever possible, one would use the same induction for self-hypnosis as whatever technique was successful in the initial induction, but this is not essential. Once trance has been achieved and experienced, children will usually accept as their pathway into that state whatever the therapist suggests. Thus, for example, even if eye-fixation and a 'magic key' did not 'work' when first tried, it probably will work in self-hypnosis if the process is suggested to the child while in trance.

With younger children, it is sometimes helpful to suggest that the parents should assist the child in self-hypnosis. This may be no more than remaining present while the child enacts the prescribed routine, or it may involve more active participation. Judgement on this point will depend upon the child's preferences and the parents' need for involvement. After the age of five or six, as suggested by most writers, it may be wiser to make the whole process the child's exclusive responsibility, but on occasion the benefits in terms of the child–parent relationship may mean that the parents' contribution and participation is very valuable.

CHILDREN AGED SEVEN TO TWELVE

In general, inductions and further procedures with children in this age group are best done with the aid of phenomena such as arm levitation rather than fairy-tales. To be sure, many children of seven or eight still enjoy and will become absorbed in stories, and with such children this approach is likely to be the most acceptable. More commonly, however, this age group will respond better to a more adult approach. They are likely to understand an explanation of the purpose and methods of what is to be done and then follow an induction couched in rather more adult terms than younger children would be able to accept.

Eye-fixation, on a coin or a spot on the wall or an imaginary point between their eyebrows, is more easily accepted by older than younger children, since their attention span is somewhat longer. The balloon bouncing on a tub of water (Script 11.4 above) is generally well accepted, as is the 'Touch, tingle, twitch and arm levitation' procedure. Additional inductions suitable for this age group include the following, and may often be given a 'trial run' to familiarize the child with what to expect and what is expected of him.

Script 11.5   Magnets

Let's see how well you can imagine something. Hold your hands out in front of you [*arranging the child's arms so that they are held straight out in such a way that the hands, palms facing inwards, are about a foot apart*] like that. Good. Now, you know what a magnet is like, don't you? If you had a magnet in each hand, you would feel them pulling towards each other. Because they are a long way apart, you would not feel a very strong pull, but if you were to bring them a little nearer together, they would pull harder and harder until, when your hands get quite close, the pull would be so strong you would not be able to keep them apart any longer. Just imagine, then, that your hands are two magnets, pulling at each other, and then move them slowly nearer and nearer together. That's it. Now, feel the pull get stronger and stronger, stronger and stronger, getting really strong, until it gets too strong for you to hold your hands apart. There, you see how well you have imagined that. Now, let's do it again, but this time, perhaps you would like to shut your eyes to make the feeling even stronger. Good; that's very good. Now, keep your eyes shut, and imagine that the magnets are switched off, and your hands suddenly relax and come apart again. Good. Now just let yourself relax all over, just like your hands are relaxed and loose.

■■■■■■■   Script 11.6   Finger-lowering

May I show you something you can do with your hands? It
will help you to get into that special state of mind which you
can use to help you with *[whatever the treatment target is]*.
*[Arrange one hand so that the heel is resting on the arm of
the chair or whatever is convenient, the little finger curved
and resting its tip, the other fingers slightly curved but
raised.]* Now, notice that your little finger is resting on the
arm of the chair, but the others are held up in the air.
Imagine now that your fingers are getting heavier and
heavier, and getting more and more tired, so that they too
want to rest and not hold themselves up in the air. I wonder
which one will come down first? Perhaps this one *[touching it
lightly]* or this one *[touching another]*. No, it's that one.
Which will be next, I wonder? Good. Now only one is still
strong enough to hold up, and that finger too is getting
heavier and heavier. Good. Now think about your eyelids.
They are getting heavier and heavier too, and more and more
tired. Soon they too will be so heavy and tired that they will
sink down just like the fingers. Good. More and more tired,
heavier and heavier. Sinking down, just like the fingers. Good.
That's very good.

When using eye-fixation with the older children in this age group,
one would first have elicited a description of a happy time or place
in the child's life and, after successful induction, transfer to this
memory. The adult version of sinking deeper and deeper into
oneself is generally not as appropriate.

■■■■■■■   Script 11.7   The secret door

Let's see how you can go to that beach you were telling me
about. Just shut your eyes and think about a flight of steps.
You are standing at the top of a flight of steps, and you are
looking down them. There are ten steps and a little way
beyond the bottom is a wall with a door in it. What colour is
the door? Right. Now, in a moment, I am going to ask you to

walk very slowly down those steps. I will count them off as you go, and when you reach the bottom, you can go over to the door, open it and go through, and you will find yourself on that beach. You will be able to feel the sunshine on your body and the sand under your feet, and hear the waves splashing. It will be just as real as it was that time you told me about, and you will feel just as happy and comfortable in yourself as you were then. Now, take the first step: One ... two ... three.[61] You are leaving the ordinary world behind. Four ... Five ... halfway down the stairs, and soon you will be able to go through the door and be on the beach. Six ... seven ... eight ... nearly there now. Nine ... ten. Good. Now go over to the door. ... Open it and go through. Shut it behind you. Good. Now you are on the beach.

ADOLESCENTS

Techniques for induction in this age group are little if at all different from those used with adults. Many adolescents, however, despite overt interest and willingness, experience considerable anxiety about what they perceive as loss of control. One finds quite commonly that they will 'break out' of trance while an induction proceeds and wish to discuss what is happening or seek to reassure themselves that they can 'come out of it' when they choose. Naturally, this must be accepted and even approved before resuming and starting again more or less at the beginning. For the same reason it is wise to be highly permissive in style, with many iterations of the adolescent's control and direction of what is happening.

Ego-strengthening and arousal from trance are quite straightforward and different only in language from the techniques used with adults. Children quite commonly either keep their eyes open throughout the session or open them from time to time. They also frequently end the trance quite abruptly of their own accord. Many end the trance during the instructions for self-hypnosis: as the therapist describes how they will return from the trance to end their self-hypnosis sessions, they will follow the termination counting and open their eyes at that point.

The less formal response of children when compared with adults need not 'throw' the therapist. It is vital, however, to follow the child's lead even more closely than is the case with adults, and adapt continuously to the child's behaviour and actions. Thus, if the child terminates the trance prematurely, this must be accepted and incorporated in the procedure and at all times praised as a contribution to the child's mastery of the technique. For example, if a young child opens his eyes in the course of the session, the therapist can incorporate this in the script he is using at that moment.

You are leaving the ordinary world behind *[Script 11.7]* and *[the child opens his eyes]* you open your eyes to see how far down the steps you have gone and to make sure everything is as it was before you closed them.[62] Four ... five ... *[etc]*.

If the child's eyes open while the therapist is giving the instructions for self-arousal from self-hypnosis, this too can be incorporated very satisfactorily:

... three ... two, nearly there. ... One, eyes open, wide awake. That's very good. You see how well you can do it!

In a word, whatever happens can be incorporated as an integral part of the session. This is true of most things that occur with adults, but extends perhaps more widely with children. Unforeseen or intrusive events are disruptive to the child only if they 'throw' the therapist. Bold and confident management and the ability to 'think on one's feet' and make instantaneous changes in the script are all that is needed.

12

HABIT AND BEHAVIOUR DISORDERS

INTRODUCTION

The most common habit disorders for which treatment is sought in children are nocturnal enuresis, nail-biting and hair-pulling. We do not use the term 'habit disorders' for patterns of behaviour which however undesirable, and however much they may appear to be driven by habit, are more usefully and more accurately included in other categories of pathology such as obsessive-compulsive disorder, anxiety states, etc. For example, parents not infrequently ask for help with a child who habitually wakes during the night in some degree of distress, comes to his parents' bed and then either stays the rest of the night there or has to be returned more or less repeatedly to his own bed. Not infrequently, the child may then repeat the behaviour from time to time during the night. Patterns such as this are not to be regarded either as a problem located in the child (since any behaviour of this kind is actually a complex and reinforced interaction between parents and child), nor are they essentially *habitual* in character.

Many, though by no means all, undesirable habitual behaviours began life as symptoms of some disquiet, anxiety, or even fear. Occasionally one may be able to trace the original source and meaning of the pattern, and it is always important to establish whether or not the behaviour is now an 'empty habit' or whether it still expresses and relieves a continuing distress, conflict or other over-determined and unconsciously meaningful process. If the underlying problem is still active, then even if the child wishes to lose the behaviour and is wholly co-operative in exercises (however firmly rooted in well-tried learning theory strategies) to extinguish it, the behaviour will persist or will be replaced by another.

Differential diagnosis, in this sense, is usually successfully made by taking a careful history of the child's development, the evolution of the family and the onset and progress of the problem, and a detailed scrutiny of the current state of the child's personality and life. This chapter will describe various treatment strategies employing hypnosis, designed to extinguish habitual behaviours that have lost, or largely lost, their dynamic significance and pressure. In those cases where diagnostic assessment indicates that the behaviour concerned is still actively maintained by anxiety, insecurity or related emotional pressures and remains in psychoanalytic terminology 'over-determined', one should turn to analytically based techniques rather than those described in this chapter. Additionally, of course, depending on the formulation one has arrived at, it may be more desirable to use strategies which may for example include other members of the family in preference to individual therapy with or without hypnotic techniques.

As in the treatment of habit disorders in adults, one essential ingredient is to make the actions involved in the pattern vividly conscious. For example, a child who habitually, persistently, and extensively bites his nails is usually quite unaware of what he is doing until fairly late in the ritual, if then. The usual informal ways in which parents and others attempt to 'cure' the child of the habit is, of course, to make some remonstrance or apply 'negative reinforcement' (i.e. punishment) *after* the child has initiated the behaviour.

Learning theory indicates that the aversiveness of scolding or similar intervention by the parent will necessarily occur too late to affect the initiation of the problem behaviour, and then becomes associated with whatever the child is doing *at the time* of the intervention. In consequence, the child continues to begin to bite or nibble and then becomes anxious. This anxiety may occasionally abbreviate the period of time during which the child bites, but more commonly enhances the biting by setting up an additional pressure which the child endeavours to relieve *by* biting, and quite commonly adds further symptom behaviour in the form of 'nervous habits' as well as increased anxiety.

Most undesirable habits begin life as ways of discharging tension, rather on the lines of what is described by ethologists as 'displacement behaviour'. In animal behaviour, this refers to actions performed to discharge tension. For example a cat, when in a hostile confrontation with another cat, suddenly breaks off hostilities and washes its tail. This is, of course, a totally different concept from the psychoanalytic concept of 'displacement behaviour'. The analytic use of the phrase refers to the displacement of an affect and consequent action from one context to another: father, having been angered by his superior at work, finds fault with his wife on his return home; she in turn finds some reason to shout at the children, who then kick the dog. The anger and its expression cannot be vented on its real source because of the structure and nature of the relationship in which the interaction takes place, so it is diverted in a safer direction.

One usually finds that even though the originating dynamics of an undesirable habit are no longer present, the performance of the behaviour is still associated in some way with anxiety and its expression. The action is performed when anxiety rises, or when anxiety is experienced because effective distraction has lessened. A common complaint made by parents is that the child bites his nails or tugs at his hair while watching television or reading, and it generally appears then that the behaviour emerges because the child is then inactive and therefore not controlling his anxiety by distraction or engagement in some activity. Alternatively the presenting behaviour may occur in situations where the child experiences an increase in tension through self-consciousness, embarrassment, etc.

In other cases, the anxiety has become associated with the behaviour through the parents' endeavours to extinguish it. That is to say, the actions have become wholly 'empty habits' with little or no function in discharging tension, but each time the action is performed the child feels tension or anxiety because of the training he has received in terms of scolding or other negative actions contingent on his behaviour.

While the primary line of approach to habit disorders will be extinction of the habitual behaviour, the second main thrust of intervention will be directed to anxiety and tension discharge or, where appropriate, alternative and more effective ways of coping with arousing situations.

It is a truism in behaviour therapy that positive reinforcement is more powerful when accurately applied in behaviour control than is punishment. We therefore seek to apply rewards for non-performance of the target behaviour in such a way as to be automatic and dependent solely on the patient himself. This pattern is essentially the same as in the suggested programme for cessation of smoking (see chapter 7). That is, each time the child stops short of biting his nails, or whatever he wants to stop doing, he will experience good feelings. We also add the rewards of feelings of mastery, maturity, pride, pleasure in appearance (in the case especially of nails and hair), and whatever other reinforcements appear appropriate. The script below is directed at a habit many children (and adults) follow – picking and biting at the skin around the nails of the fingers – but can be adapted to any habitual actions.

██████ Script 12.1

[Induction and deepening have been carried out. If thought appropriate, the child can then spend some time in his 'private place' and then be asked to leave it again.]

Now you are feeling really good, relaxed and happy, just listening to my voice. Now we are going to do something that you do every day, but we are going to change it a little so that you find out what will happen when you don't pick at your fingers.

Imagine that you are at home, and you are watching television. What programme would you like to watch? Fine. There you are sitting in front of the television set, and *[whatever programme the child chose]* is just beginning. Perhaps you can hum the music that is playing? Good. Now notice that your hands are close together. The fingers of one hand are touching the fingers of the other and you can feel some rough skin on one of them, a little piece of skin sticking up, and it feels slightly irritating. Can you feel that? Good. One finger is just beginning to push against that little piece of skin so that you can feel it more and more clearly. The fingernail is just getting a good grip on that little piece of skin. Now your hands go rigid and hard, like two pieces of steel, absolutely rigid and hard so they can't move at all. Can you feel that?

Perhaps we shall have to wait for a moment or two while your hands go still harder. Like that? Good. You cannot bend your fingers or move them at all, but you can move your arms so that the hands move away from each other. Move the hands apart. Have you got them away from each other? Good. Now notice that as you move them still further apart you feel the hands relaxing again and going soft so that you can move the fingers again, and as that happens, you feel yourself going all relaxed and happy again, just the way you are in your special place. Can you feel that? Good.

Are you still watching television? Good. Now notice that your hands are coming together again, and you are beginning to find the little rough pieces of skin. Can you feel one? Good, but notice that when you push against that little piece of skin you feel all uncomfortable and tense. Can you feel a fingernail beginning to catch hold of that bit of skin? And that you are feeling really uncomfortable and awfully tense? Now let your hands turn to steel again, and notice just how uncomfortable you feel. So now move your arms apart again so that your hands are not touching any more, and you feel yourself becoming so comfortable again, relaxed and happy like in your special place, and your hands are going soft again, soft and able to move. Good.

Now stop watching television, and let the television set disappear. Instead, I want you to think about going forward in time, like Dr Who in the Tardis, going to a day two weeks ahead. You are suddenly two weeks older and you are looking at your hands. Can you see them? Good. Notice how nice they look, smooth and without little red sore places round the tips and the nails. They look really nice, and they feel really nice. Can you see how nice they look? And feel how comfortable they are? And feel how pleased you are with them? Good. That's really good.

From now on, you will spend a little while every day in your special place, and when you have had some fun there, I would like you to think about your hands and how nice they are getting, free from the little sore places and the rough skin, how nice they are looking without the marks of picking on them. And then I would like you to practise what we did just now, when you were watching television. Let your hands touch, find a bit of skin that you can catch with a nail and then let your hands turn to steel. You will find when you do that you feel really uncomfortable and tense until you move your arms apart so that your hands come apart and go back to normal, and then you will feel all good and comfortable and happy again, just as you do in your special place. And so you will simply not pick at your fingers. You won't have to try and stop yourself, the picking will just stop because you have taught yourself how to do that. And so in a very short time you will see your hands looking just as nice as they did when you went forward in time and looked at them, and then you will feel really proud and pleased with yourself because you now have nice hands.

◼ NOCTURNAL ENURESIS

Nocturnal enuresis is something of a special case. As with most of the conditions considered in this book, it is vital to make a careful diagnosis before embarking on treatment. Enuresis is conventionally classified as primary and secondary. Primary enuresis is considered to be *failure to achieve* nocturnal sphincter control, and is evidenced by the fact that the child has never been dry for more than a few nights at a time. Developmental delay is often thought to be one of the major factors in the aetiology of this condition, that is, the child's neurological development included some delay in the establishment of adequate neural control over the sphincters at the age at which the child was given some encouragement and training to avoid micturating in bed. Since the child was unable to respond at this stage, training was unsuccessful and probably abandoned, the mother resigning herself more or less successfully to wait indefinitely. On occasion, primary enuresis (usually in association with other habit problems) is found in families which are so chaotic and inconsistent as to make it very difficult for the children to acquire any consistent habits or skills.

   Secondary enuresis (i.e. bed-wetting that begins after the child has been continent at night for a substantial period) is generally considered to be a neurotic symptom, that is, a reaction to emotional distress or stress. It has been described as 'displaced weeping', and in some children quite clearly is of that nature. Anger, hostility, insecurity, frustration, depression and virtually any and all emotional problems may manifest themselves through this symptom. Many cases, however, show components of both primary and secondary conditions, especially since the enuresis itself commonly provokes or stimulates emotional stresses between mother and child and the child inevitably develops feelings of shame, inferiority and the like, however supportive and reassuring his parents may be.

If an underlying neurotic process is believed to be present, this must be approached in its own right through psychotherapy, play therapy, family therapy or other dynamic methods, with or without the use of hypnosis. Even in such cases, however, it is usually appropriate and very helpful to teach the child a method by which he can inhibit the symptom. Where the wetting plays an important part in the dynamic system of the family, it is unlikely to respond to the methods discussed here unless the family is concurrently engaged in therapy, since the determining pressures on the child would otherwise continue unabated and unacknowledged. One must also give careful consideration to any secondary gains from the symptom and eliminate these while at the same time substituting rewards of some kind for successful response to treatment.

Current fashionable approaches to this problem, usually on behaviour modification lines, emphasize heightening awareness of the occurrence of the target behaviour. For example the 'dry bed' technique, which requires the child to go to the lavatory repeatedly after retiring to bed, is designed to establish a strong 'mental set' focusing attention on bladder sensation and especially on the sensations of passing urine. Interestingly, while fashions in the treatment of enuresis wax and wane regularly, every approach seems to have the same degree of success when at its height of popularity. It seems unlikely that hypnotic methods offer any better prospects of symptom relief than other treatment methods, but they have the advantage that the 'treatment' is in the child's own hands rather than something that is *done to* him. Additionally, it works pretty well when other methods have proved unsuccessful.

Our approach is to reverse the pattern of most behavioural procedures and to ignore the problem behaviour as such, which by the time the child presents is usually fraught with anxiety anyway. We do this primarily by utilizing the fact that sleep is never total. It is now well known that even in deep general anaesthesia, patients are still often able to hear what is being said around them. The fact that a mother who will sleep through the noise of Concorde passing over the house will wake at the slightest whimper made by her child is equally well known. We therefore discuss situations like this with the child, and hope to stimulate him into recalling a similar experience on his own part, that is, waking to a stimulus which, were it not for its importance to him, would have been ignored and sleep maintained. We then suggest that he should give an identity to that part of him which evidently remains awake when the rest of him is asleep. If the child has a middle name, this can be employed to label the waking part-person. We then describe the plan, which is to instruct this part to be fully alert to bladder sensations so that he is ready to waken the sleeper when necessary and inform him of the need to rise and urinate in the right place.

The images used to arouse the rewarding feelings are drawn from past experiences the child can identify, such as the time he first mastered the skill of riding a bicycle, roller-skating, ice-skating, swimming or any activity or skill which is associated with joyful mastery. By eliciting these feelings and then associating them by direct suggestion with the achievement of the treatment aim, the child is strongly encouraged to think of himself as capable of mastering the problem and the actual treatment process itself becomes rewarding. That is to say, the initial training session and the subsequent self-hypnosis exercises in themselves give the child the feelings of mastery and pleasure.

While most children with nocturnal enuresis are extremely keen to overcome the problem and deny any reservations, there is almost always a secondary gain from the symptom. In consequence one finds that many children, however eagerly they assent to the use of this technique, somehow miss out their nightly session from time to time or, also very commonly, having achieved two or three dry nights in a row stop their exercises altogether and then express disappointment in the fact (as they see it) that the method did not work. It is therefore important to make the exercise itself rewarding as a counter-balance to the secondary gains of wetting, and to emphasize through strong suggestion that the pleasure, satisfaction and any other gains from becoming continent are desirable above anything else.

Script 12.2

[Hypnosis is induced, deepening carried out and ego-strengthening given.]

Now, Jimmy, I am going to talk to that special part of you which is awake when the rest of you is asleep. That part of you that we decided to call 'George'. Now, George, we both know that when Jimmy is fast asleep, you are actually still wide awake and know everything that is going on. I expect you have been trying for a long time to wake Jimmy when he needs to pass water, but could never get him to take any notice or to wake up. From now on, Jimmy is going to train himself to listen to you when you try to wake him up and so it is very important that you play the part of night watchman or sentry.

As from tonight, when you go to bed, I would like you to be very alert and keep a very close watch on your bladder. As soon as it is beginning to get full so that you know it is time to go to the lavatory and pass water,[63] you will nudge Jimmy and tell him to wake up, and go on telling him to wake up until he does. Then you will tell him why he has been woken, that is, that he needs to pass water and so has to go to the lavatory. You have to tell him that, because he will be pretty sleepy and will not know why he has been woken up until you tell him. Then you make sure he goes to the lavatory, passes water, and then gets back into bed and goes right back to sleep. You will be the sentry and make sure that Jimmy wakes up when it is necessary. Make sure, though, George, that when you go to bed, you know what you are looking out for. You are on the watch for the bladder filling up. You know what that feels like, so you can watch out for it.

Around bed-time, Jimmy is going to go through an exercise I
am going to teach him, in which he is going to remind you of
what you have to do, and he will also remind himself about
how he is going to wake up when you tell him to. He will do
this exercise every night until it is no longer necessary, so that
both you, George, and he, Jimmy, will be really ready and able
to do all this and so never wet the bed again.

Now I am going to talk to Jimmy again, but George, you
might like to listen, so that you know exactly what Jimmy is
going to do. Jimmy, this evening, and every evening from now
on, you will go into this special state of mind that you feel just
now. You will *[describe the self-hypnosis routine appropriate
for this child]*. Then, when you are really deep down, you can
go to your special place, that beach you told me about, and
play there for a little while. You might find some shells or
interesting bits of rope *[and whatever else the child described
when identifying his 'private place']*. When you have had
some really good fun, you can leave the beach again and talk
to George. Remind him of what he has to do: to stay alert like
a sentry, and watch out all the time for signs that the bladder
is filling up, so that he can wake you and tell you what you
need to do, that is, to get up, go to the lavatory and pass
water. Then you can come out of your relaxed state again,
still feeling all the good feelings you got in your special place
and feeling really good. Then you will get ready for bed, and
go to sleep, knowing that whenever you need to pass water,
George will wake you up, and you will go to the lavatory and
pass water there. And so, when you wake in the morning,
you will find that your bed is dry, and you will feel really
pleased and proud that you and George are taking control,
and that you are in charge. Even if occasionally George does
not wake you, and you find in the morning that your bed is
wet, you will know that you are gradually taking charge and
will soon be free of this problem. Before very long, you will
find that your bed is dry every morning, and you will then feel
really proud that you have mastered the problem all by
yourself, and then you will no longer have any worry about it.

Naturally, ego-strengthening should be added in more detail than this, and can be enhanced by referring to an experience the child has had in the past of mastering a difficulty and recalling the feelings of satisfaction and pride associated with it. This can sometimes be used as the 'private place' or in addition to it.

BAD DREAMS

It is often difficult to distinguish between disturbing dreams, nightmares and night terrors, and differential diagnosis, especially of night terrors, which more commonly have a neurological than a psychological basis, is vital. It is quite common to find that bad dreams, whether or not they actually rouse the child from sleep, are actually 'empty habits', the child having resolved the originating traumatic experience or feelings from which they stemmed, at least to a great extent. Once one is satisfied that more thoroughgoing and analytically based therapy is not required, dream control can be usually readily taught, and children thoroughly enjoy this.

The first point to make is the authorship of the dream. Once the child has related one or more dreams, go on rather like the following script, depending of course on the child's reply to the questions.

Script 12.3

Yes, that really was a horrid dream. Now tell me, who was dreaming it? You? Dear me! I wonder why you let yourself dream that? Would you not have preferred a different dream? Yes, of course you would! What would you like to dream instead? Yes, that sounds like a good one. So tell me why you didn't dream that instead? You didn't think you could choose? Well of course you can; after all, there is no-one there except you and you can choose whatever you like. No-one is making you dream that, and the only reason you had that horrid dream was because you didn't know you could change it and so you didn't try. Next time you get a bad dream, you can change it, because you know about that now. So if you dream that you are being chased by a horrible monster and you can't

run fast enough to get away from it, you can decide to have a
motorbike and ride away ever so fast. Or you can turn the
monster into a little cat that you can play with and cuddle.
Since you are doing the dreaming, you might as well have a
dream that you enjoy! So from now on, you are going to
choose. I think it would be a good idea to have a little practice
now. What would you like to dream about today? Good.
Would you like to dream that now? Right.

*[Now carry out an induction, then move on to starting the
dream. If you have negotiated with the child to practise
changing a bad dream into a good one, follow this through. It
would, however, be improper and potentially damaging to
attempt this without full prior agreement. Before beginning
on a bad dream, remind the child of the plan.]*

You are dreaming about being in a wood,[64] and it's dark and
rather scary, although you don't know why you are feeling
nervous. And now you know that there is a big, horrible
monster creeping up on you, so you try to run, but your legs
just won't move properly and you think the monster is going
to catch you. You are getting more and more frightened. So
you decide you are going to have a helicopter waiting for you:
look, there it is, so you quickly jump into it and fly up in the
air, safely away from the wood and the monster, and now you
can fly anywhere you want. You decide where you want to go
and the helicopter will take you there. Now you can enjoy
yourself and be happy and relaxed, and have a laugh about
that silly old monster you got away from so easily. Have you
done that? Good.

Now you know you can control your dreams and choose
what is to happen in them, and you will be able to do this any
time you want. But remember, unless you choose to change a
dream, it will go on by itself, so whenever a bad dream starts,
you will have to remind yourself it is a dream and that you
can make it into whatever you want.

■■■■■■   SLEEP PROBLEMS

Difficulties in getting to sleep or in regaining sleep after waking during the night invariably indicate stresses in the child's life that are beyond his coping mechanisms. It is therefore obviously necessary to explore these stresses and to address them in individual therapy, family therapy, or by making practical changes in the child's life such as advising teachers about appropriate standards for the child, dealing with bullying, or whatever may be the source of the stress. Concurrently with such actions, however, the problem of falling asleep can be tackled directly, in just the way that was described for adults.

13

PHYSICAL DISORDERS AND PAIN

Hypnosis offers several important contributions in the field of paediatric medicine. It is even more obvious with children than with adults that psychological factors, both affective and cognitive, play a major part in all physical disorders. It is usually rather difficult to establish the beginning of the common cycles that involve physical malfunction or disease and psychological processes, but we can make a rough-and-ready discrimination in practice between those disorders in which distress, anxiety and other psychological processes appear as a reaction to physical disease and those in which psychological processes appear to be significantly causal in the onset of physical pathology. Hypnotic techniques can be employed with considerable success in either case: in the treatment of the causal psychological disorders or distress or by reduction of the psychological sequelae of physical disease or the treatment applied.

The management of pain is a further area in which psychological techniques, and in particular hypnosis, can be of value in the treatment of the child. Finally, the management of terminal illnesses can include hypnotic techniques with considerable benefit.

It is generally accepted today that psychological factors enter into the incidence, course and prevalence of any and every physical illness, whatever the age of the patient. The attitudes, expectations, mood, personal adjustment and significant relationships of the individual all have a clear bearing both on the course of the illness and on compliance with treatment. In most medical and surgical circles this is now well accepted. Considerable care is taken, for example, with surgical patients to provide a sufficiently thorough and detailed preparation to maximize positive attitudes in the patient to the forthcoming procedure and its sequelae and to reduce anxiety both in anticipation and in the post-operative period. Such preparation has been well substantiated as having a major effect on rate of recovery, use of analgesic medication and so on. This was discussed in chapter 8, and applies as much to children as to older patients.

The application of psychological theories and techniques, and even more of hypnosis, to physical disorders and their treatment, however, goes well beyond the simple management of cognitive and affective components of illness and physical treatments. It is clear that anxiety stemming from ignorance, misinformation and misunderstandings tend to prolong illness and delay recovery from surgery, but the part played by both cognitive and affective processes in both ill-health and normal functioning is more complex. For example, the patient's motivation to maintain illness, the contingent environmental responses which may sustain, lengthen or abbreviate the illness, the patient's understanding of the disease process, and the effects of attitude, wish, confidence, and anxiety on the patient's somatic processes are now all seen as playing an important part in the progress of illness and the design of treatment programmes. Unconscious processes, beliefs, feelings and motives play an even more important part than conscious processes, although the recognition of this is probably less well developed in those professions dealing with the physical side of illness than in those whose primary concern is psychological and psychiatric.

The development of conversion states is a somewhat special cases. In some instances the symptom produced may have little or no foundation in physical pathology (and may even not correspond with anatomical facts, as in glove anaesthesias and some hysterical paralyses), but it will bear an extremely close and direct relationship to the individual's psychopathology. In particular, the significant aspects of this will be fantasies inaccessible to consciousness, fears, and needs. In children, the distinction between conversion states and other psychogenic physical disorders seems more blurred than it is in adults. In recent years, the diagnosis 'illness behaviour'[65] has gained prominence as a description of those states in which the symptoms of physical illness or malfunction appear to result almost solely from psychological factors but do not have the precision of the simple conversion state and lack the affective character of the latter.

The distinction between these two, however, is sometimes not very clear and may have more to do with a reluctance on the part of workers in child psychiatry to use the term 'hysteria' or its euphemisms. In 'illness behaviour', in contrast to a simple conversion, there is always an immediately preceding physical illness or injury. For example, distortions of posture or gait and loss of co-ordination nearly always occur after some physical injury, and it is often very difficult indeed to establish what if any physical causes for the condition are present or responsible for the symptoms.

If, as is generally accepted, psychological (both cognitive and affective) processes and states can negatively affect physical and physiological functions, it is highly probable that the converse is equally true. That is to say, where illness or malfunction of a physical origin exists, psychological factors can be enlisted to create a positive or health-directed effect on the course of the condition.

Hypnosis may be employed to mobilize such resources deliberately and therefore obtain greater effect and benefit. The clearest therapeutic examples of this approach are to be found in those conditions where psychological factors are most obviously implicated, such as asthma and eczema. We all take as a matter of course that the severity of these conditions fluctuates quite directly with the emotional state of the patient. One approach to their treatment, therefore, is to ameliorate the overall psychological state of the patient using individual psychotherapy, family therapy or any other approach that appears appropriate to the particular case. It is often difficult to discriminate between the psychological difficulties that precede the physical manifestations and those which are secondary to the physical symptoms and suffering. Nevertheless, treatment of the patient's conflicts, anxieties and disturbed relationships (and in the case of children especially, of the family) will usually be considered as important as the medical approach.

We can, however, take the application of psychological influence upon the physical rather further than this. Reference has already been made to Ewin's reports of the effect of imagery in hypnosis on the physiological effects of burns: imagery of coolness of the affected area of skin reduces inflammation, blistering, etc. The same approach can be very effective indeed in such conditions as eczema. A small clinical trial at Guy's Hospital by one of the authors (Karle, 1985) showed that children with eczema can learn to inhibit the sensation of itching and thereby reduce scratching, which not only traumatizes the skin but provokes infections, and to use imagery in self-hypnosis in such a way as to reduce the other overt symptoms of the condition.

For example, the first child to enter this study was four-and-a-half years old. (This case was described in some detail in chapter 11.) Not only did this child gain control over the intolerable itching she had experienced all her life, but the actual condition of her skin improved. This improvement was in part due to the fact that the skin was no longer excoriated extensively and deeply (and thus did not become regularly infected), but extended rather further. Over the next few months, she began to perspire on her hands, the production of sweat having been totally lacking until then. It appeared that the condition itself, not just the sensory symptoms, was beginning to change.

In all the cases treated in this study and so far in the clinical trial in progress at the time of writing at The Hospital for Sick Children, Great Ormond Street, the imagery used is derived directly from the child's own experience and wishes. Generally the approach is two-fold: imagery, often in the form of a fairy-story, is used to give the child control over itching sensations, while at the same time the imagery used is so designed as to facilitate improvement of the condition of the skin.

For example, if the eczema is exacerbated by cold and improved by moderate warmth and perhaps exposure to the sun, then sunbathing or bathing in warm water is built into the imagery used in the hypnotic and self-hypnotic sessions. The effects of this can be even more dramatic than in the case quoted above. One girl, aged fifteen, had marked patches of red and scaly skin on her face as well as over her body. In her first session she pictured herself lying on her favourite beach soaking up the summer sun. In the course of ten to fifteen minutes the patches on her face visibly lessened and disappeared completely by the end of the session, and a similar case of a woman of eighteen has already been mentioned.

Most children, however co-operative and well motivated, are commonly somewhat sceptical of the whole procedure until they experience the reality. Richard Lansdown (Chief Psychologist, Great Ormond Street) invented the 'magic finger' to this end. Having discussed the treatment plan with the child, he suggests identifying one of the child's fingers as the one to be made 'magic'. In hypnosis, a story is created for the child (often beginning with a favourite story identified by the child and then progressively modified to accommodate the 'magic finger') which results in one of his or her fingers acquiring magical power. He strokes the chosen finger three times at a point where this action fits into the story, and thus gives it the power to delete itching. The finger is then applied to any itching spot and the child experiences immediate cessation of the irritation. This is of course closely similar to the use of 'magic water', and other variants to suit the imagery of a particular child can be readily devised. Once the child has had this experience, the second stage of the treatment programme, the imagery related to the condition and development of the skin, will be better accepted.

With younger children imagery such as magic water applied to the skin having a healing affect need not be elaborated much further, since generally additional explanation about blood vessels in the skin or physiological processes will tend to confuse rather than clarify. With older children, however, suggestions about increased blood flow to the affected areas bringing nutriments and flushing away waste products and so feeding and purifying the skin, bringing about softening of the skin and stimulating sweating, should also be considered for inclusion.

Asthma can be approached in a similar way, substituting relief of feelings of tightness and choking and imagery of loosening and freer movement of the chest and lungs, with consequent freer air flow. Caution has to be exercised, however, in the application of hypnotic relaxation in some cases of asthma. In those cases where constriction of the bronchi is prominent, deep relaxation of the chest muscles can reduce respiration to the point of apnoea. A report was presented at one of the Workshops at the 9th International Congress of Hypnosis and Psychosomatic Medicine noting the occurrence of respiratory collapse in a number of such cases, suggesting that hypnosis should not be applied except where resuscitation equipment is readily available. Those cases where psychological factors are clearly in evidence plainly do not come within this category, although treatment should obviously not be undertaken without appropriate medical approval and even supervision.

Eczema tends to evoke feelings of desperation in the sufferer; the excoriation children inflict on themselves appears to stem from this feeling as much as from an attempt to gain relief from the itching. Asthma similarly produces such desperation, but with asthma there is also often intense fear. In both cases, the high level of arousal needs to be dispersed before the patient can gain maximum benefit from the treatment.

The treatment examples quoted in this and the previous two chapters may be regarded as paradigms of a very effective approach to all physical conditions in children. Naturally any treatment must be adapted to the particular characteristics of the condition from which the child suffers, and targets must be realistic. In all cases, however, a treatment combination of teaching control and so diminution of distressing or painful sensations, whilst also aiming to ameliorate the underlying condition through imagery, is perhaps the most effective contribution hypnosis can make to treatment.

The control of pain, whether resulting from physical pathology or from treatment procedures, is a particularly apt area for the application of hypnotherapy. Hilgard and LeBaron (1984) is the most thorough as well as the most sensitive account published to date of using hypnosis in the management of painful and distressing medical and surgical procedures with children. It will probably remain the primary reference work for this topic. Suffice it to say that children generally accept and use self-hypnotic procedures eagerly once they have experienced the effectiveness of these techniques. There are, of course, exceptions which can be very frustrating.

Children suffering chronic or life-threatening disorders, which either themselves involve more or less continuous discomfort, malaise and nausea or where the treatments involved produce such results, can be very resistant to endeavours to teach them techniques for controlling pain and discomfort. One must bear in mind that the illness and its associated experiences do not exist in psychological isolation but that the symptoms, sensations, and treatments received form part of an interactive universe which necessarily includes the child's family and their feelings, reactions and attitudes. The child's illness influences in particular the relationship between the patient and his or her parents. The resistance, and sometimes outright refusal, on the part of some children to employ such techniques commonly reflects the affective conflicts stemming from their illness experience.

For example, children suffering from renal failure often develop a highly conflictual relationship with their parents and with the world in general, especially if problems over growth and physical development become prominent. Such children often experience an intense need to place responsibility for their treatment and relief on their parents and medical attendants, and can be almost hostile to anyone who places emphasis on their potential for self-treatment. Their anger, resentment and sense of unfairness tend to stimulate markedly regressed behaviour and attitudes, sometimes with strong impulses towards death, which whether conscious or unconscious evoke resistance to treatment.

While this resistance is likely to impede physical treatments, and can certainly make the administration of these difficult, it can also impede the use of hypnotic techniques. If and when, however, these children can be led to discover the efficacy of hypnotic analgesia, for example in enabling them to undergo what had previously been painful procedures without pain, and the calming, reassuring effects of retreat to a 'private place', resistance is weakened and may then be penetrated.

For example, a boy of sixteen was referred for help through hypnosis· for the intolerable pain he experienced when physio-therapy for severe contractures was attempted. He had suffered from renal failure from early infancy and undergone two failed kidney transplants. A side effect of his repeated operations was the development of circulatory inadequacy in his limbs and contrac-tures of both arms and legs. Passive movement of his arms was possible although painful, but he screamed so violently and was so grossly distressed when his legs were touched that the physio-therapists found they were unable to proceed with the very necessary treatment. He was brought to his first session (intended to be simply a trial of hypnosis) in a wheelchair. The proposal to use hypnosis had been discussed with him by the nephrologist.

He opened the interview by saying: 'I don't think you'll be able to hypnotize me!' The first three attempts at induction were fruitless but he was willing to proceed further, albeit with a challenging grin. An assumed manner of casual confidence on the part of the therapist and the use at that point of an induction using distraction and confusion in a very low-key manner resulted in a shallow trance, sufficient to carry out a few challenges such as arm levitation and hand lock. He was still highly sceptical, but agreed that he must have been hypnotized.

The following week, he was seen with the physiotherapists. He entered trance quickly and found that the moderate pain induced by manipulation of his arms could be suppressed completely. When manipulation of his legs was begun he winced strongly and whimpered, but continued suggestions of relaxation and dissociation from pain enabled him to tolerate the procedure. The imagery used to facilitate this was that of electrical wiring, with junctions and switches located in the spine. He was taught to 'switch off' the nerves transmitting pain signals from his legs and hips. From time to time he lost this control, but was able to regain it on each occasion.

After some five or six sessions with the therapist present he became able to maintain trance and analgesia on his own, albeit with an occasional reminder from the physiotherapist treating him. His pride, when eventually he recovered the use of his legs, was heart-warming and stemmed in great measure from the fact that he had himself mastered the problem rather than having had it dealt with by either chemical analgesia or anaesthesia.

The imagery used for pain control in children depends, of course, on the patient's age and cognitive development. With the boy just described it was possible to use the same imagery one might use with an adult, that is, of electric wiring representing the nerves. With younger children, techniques such as the 'magic finger' or 'magic water' would be more appropriate, although given suitable illustration, more sophisticated images can often be used very successfully. For example, if the child is given a torch bulb or a simple buzzer or bell connected to a battery through a jack-plug, the demonstration of the light going out or the buzzer stopping when the jack-plug is pulled out can be used very effectively to engender the idea of a pain stopping when the nerve is disconnected.

Alternatively one might ask the child to go to his 'private place' and become wholly oblivious of the setting in which the painful procedure is to be carried out. The effect of this may be enhanced by including suggestions that the pain is on the other side of the door to the 'private place': the child therefore knows the pain is there but at a distance, and this seems to reduce the intensity of the cognitive dissonance involved.

Generally, in the treatment of physical disorders and injuries as much as in the management of pain, techniques are essentially the same as those used with adults. The language and imagery, however, are necessarily substantially different. It is as yet unusual for hypnosis to be considered as a normal or usual part of treatment in paediatrics, at least in the UK, and indeed it is occasionally suggested that hypnosis should not be used with children at all. In the Australian State of Tasmania it is illegal to hypnotize anyone under the age of eighteen. In view of the fact that response to hypnosis and the ability to use hypnotic processes is at it highest around ages ten to twelve, such attitudes are to be deplored: an important, effective and very economical aid to physical treatments is being ignored.

In summary, hypnosis can be applied in physical and psychosomatic disorders in children in three major ways. First, it can be very effective in reducing pain and discomfort, both those which stem from the disorder itself and those which arise from treatment. Secondly, hypnotic techniques can contribute substantially to the reduction of distress, anxiety and fear. Thirdly, hypnosis can be used in a more psychodynamic way, to enhance the child's will to recovery and to reduce the intensity and therefore the influence of conflicting drives and feelings. In addition, it may be employed to influence the physiological processes involved in the disorder, although this appears generally less effective in most cases than with adolescents and adults.

Gardner and Olness (1981) consider a wide range of specific conditions and discuss the use of hypnotic techniques in each, and reference should be made to that book for detailed guidance.

The management of terminal illness in children is an area of which the present authors have no personal experience. Both Gardner and Olness (1981) and Hilgard and LeBaron (1984) address themselves to this topic in detail. This topic will, therefore, not be attempted here.

14

ANXIETY AND DISORDERS OF MOOD

There is really very little specific to children in this topic, except as noted before in terms of the language and imagery used. It is again strongly emphasized that detailed differential diagnosis is vital before attempting treatment. For example, a boy of fifteen was referred because of depression of mood and educational failure. He had shown reasonable academic promise up to age twelve or so, and was then noted to become miserable, to withdraw from activities and games, and to apply himself less and less to his work. His parents became increasingly concerned about him and applied the correctives that seemed natural to them. He was sent to a 'crammer' to be coached, and so managed to gain a place at the school his parents wished him to attend, but his performance there continued to decline steadily.

His mood continued to worsen, and assessment and counselling were sought by the school. He scored no more than average on cognitive testing, and the conclusion was reached that his depression and educational underfunctioning stemmed from a negative reaction to the high expectations of the parents (both high-achieving professional people) and the pressures they applied to their son. It was therefore thought that the latter's recognition of his failure to meet their standards was the root of his apparent depression.

A detailed developmental and family history suggested, however, that this conclusion was erroneous. On the one hand, his academic performance had been well above average in the first six years or so of schooling, during which time he had been active, energetic and very much involved in sports. His academic performance up to age twelve did not match with a 'no more than average' general intellectual ability, nor was there any indication in his early years of failing to meet parental expectations. The current state he presented with was not consistent, either, with an endogenous depression of puberty. However, the family history included at least one member in every generation known to suffer from thyroid deficiency.

Appropriate investigation disclosed that this boy also had such a deficiency, of relatively minor degree but presumably having reached a pathological level when he passed through puberty. Treatment for this condition resulted in an almost magical change in mood, behaviour and work.

It would have been very easy to miss such a diagnosis and to begin work on his emotional state. In this family the temptation to embark on family therapy was very great (and probably would indeed have been helpful as an adjunct to the boy's hormone treatment). Had his hormone deficiency not been recognized, the treatment of choice would have focused on work with the family or with him individually, and would of course have proved minimally successful. Indeed, it could be argued that his condition and the family relationships could even have deteriorated as a result of the frustration that one could anticipate in response to the very probable continuation of his depression of mood and general underfunctioning.

Much as in cases of 'empty habits', elimination or extinction of 'empty symptoms' can often be achieved by imagery in hypnosis. It is relatively rare, however, for disorders of mood in children to be 'empty' and underlying stresses, conflicts and especially unconscious determinants need to be searched out before formulating a treatment plan.

Further determinants in terms of family dynamics must also be elucidated: the question of who is to be treated is an even more crucial one in work with children. Is it the child who has been presented as 'the patient', a sibling, one or both of the parents, or the family as a whole? If the identified 'patient' is a child before puberty, it is generally likely that treatment focusing solely on that child, and not taking account of the family changes that will also be necessary, has little chance of real success as a general rule.

As with all generalizations, there are exceptions: if one regards a family as a 'dynamic system', one anticipates that changing the functioning of a significant or relatively powerful subunit will evoke systemic modification. In some families, helping the 'index patient', one of the children, to gain control over rages or to become less anxious may introduce a sufficient change in family interactions for the system as a whole to change enough to create a more healthy pattern without further intervention. The question, therefore, of *whom* to treat remains complex.

Where the answer to this question includes other family members as well as the child presented as the patient, and strategies such as family therapy are chosen, work with the presenting child in individual sessions might still be helpful, although one must then be careful to ensure that the family therapy sessions are actively therapeutic and do not form simply a comfortable holding operation while the child is being 'put right'. These individual sessions could, of course, include hypnosis. This is especially so where the presenting symptom is one that interferes with the child's enjoyment of life, especially outside the family. Depression, anxiety, tetchiness, rages and all mood abnormalities interfere inevitably not only with the child's outlook on and enjoyment of life but also with his relationships, particularly with family and peers. In addition they tend to create secondary problems through, for instance, deleterious effects on school performance. This will, of course, enhance and widen the mood disturbances as well as contributing to lowered self-esteem and self-confidence.

For example, a boy of nine was referred for depression of mood with temper outbursts. He showed the common pattern of associated symptoms including reluctance in going to school in the morning, with anxiety, misery, intense fatigue and almost instantaneous tantrums at the end of the school day. He behaved extremely badly towards his younger brother on the way home from school and subsequently throughout the evening was rude to his parents, and most evenings would either retreat in temper or be sent in disgrace to his room, where he would then destroy one or other of his possessions. At school he claimed to be without any friends and to be the butt of general teasing and unfriend-liness. He denied jealousy of his popular, well-behaved and high-achieving brother, but the history and the family rela-tionships spoke otherwise.

Family therapy was proposed and accepted by the parents, the two boys being less positive. At the same time the boy himself was offered help individually, and he responded well to suggestions of using hypnosis to change the way he found himself reacting to a variety of situations. These were carefully chosen from those that he himself felt were spoiling his life. One of the problems he identified was the temper outbursts which occurred daily whenever he was asked to do something around the house. He quickly grasped the idea that such outbursts represented the release of pent-up tension, and that if the tensions he had accumulated during the day were somehow comfortably and safely discharged, the welling-up of rage that resulted in such a tantrum would not occur.

The image used in hypnosis was of steam in the boiler of an old steam engine. Pressure built up as the boiler was heated by the events of the day; specific events, such as being teased, were represented by an extra shovel of coal thrown into the furnace under the boiler. On arrival home he would go through a self-hypnosis routine and visualize the boiler, its safety valve screwed well down and the pressure inside approaching bursting point. He would then cautiously release a little steam from a valve, and progressively discharge steam from the boiler until it was simmering gently instead of shaking and bubbling. He would then drive the steam engine for a little while, releasing further steam through the whistle and generally enjoying an activity which used to be every boy's dream. When satisfied, he would leave the trance and join the family downstairs.

He reported the following week that he had been able to keep the pressure contained until evening through all but one day of the intervening period, and that this had made life easier at school as well as at home. He had spontaneously used the image without any formal induction to control outbursts at school, simply visualizing a discharge of steam from his engine's whistle when he felt he was about to lose his temper.

Over the next few weeks he reported continued improvement, especially in his relationships with the other boys in his class. This improvement was corroborated by the parents, who felt that their initial agreement to family therapy had been premature: things were already so much better that they felt it unnecessary to proceed. Enquiry a few months later disclosed continued satisfaction on the part of the parents with the way the family's life ran, and the index patient's relationships with both siblings and school companions had continued to be more satisfactory than in the past.

In all forms of therapy a problem which is relatively rarely discussed in print is that of linguistic differences between therapists and patients. It is all too easy for therapists of any professional background to become so habituated to the use of words in common parlance in their own profession and social circles, perhaps even with special and particular meanings common to their professional group or ideological persuasion, that they forget that some words in the world outside mean something different, sometimes subtly, sometimes markedly.

This is especially true when the patient concerned is of an educational and cultural background significantly different from that of the therapist, and of course even more marked when patient and therapist originate from different countries and cultures, and when the patient is a child. The problem also manifests itself, sometimes without being recognized, with adolescents whose peer-group language, which in any case changes more rapidly even than fashions in clothing, may not be familiar to the therapist.

Thus words such as 'anxiety', 'depression', 'grief', can lead to difficulties. A patient with quite patently severe anxiety may deny feeling anxious, and the therapist may be led to explore this denial, missing the point that 'anxiety' is simply not the word this patient would choose to express what he feels, and that he may have another word for it. Once that word is identified, the denial melts away. Before, therefore, endeavouring to work on mood disorders through words and images one needs to explore the patient's vocabulary, syntax and imagery: the means through which he understands his own affective experiences.

For example, the boy with the 'steam engine' was asked to describe exactly what he felt like when he was about to explode in a tantrum. Like most children he found this difficult, but with the aid of suggested images he expressed satisfaction with the picture of a steam boiler. Another image which may be equally effective is that of a dam with sluice gates. This can be elaborated, drawing pictures of the different stages of filling and discussing the consequent pressure on the dam wall.

Depression of mood is perhaps less easy to represent

pictorially than the pressure of anger or the tensions of anxiety. The image referred to earlier in connection with adults, of a heavy, dark fluid filling the individual and then being drained away, can be helpful with children, as can an image of all the worries or miseries the child is experiencing being written on pieces of paper which are got rid of in some way.

A boy of ten was referred for nocturnal enuresis and falling school performance. The youngest child (by ten years) of rather elderly parents, he had never been wholly dry at night. He had been gradually improving until some eight months before referral when his adult (and much-idolized) brother had died in mysterious circumstances while away from home.

Having agreed on hypnosis to help with bed-wetting, he chose an unusually adult scene for his 'private place': a wooded hillside where he would like to roam with his dog. The image then included the idea that he carried a number of heavy lumps in his pockets, which weighed him down. Having arrived at his favourite tree, he would sit and enjoy the view and, taking out these lumps one by one, he would let them roll down the hill.

At the end of the first session, when he left the trance, he began to weep. He said that this was because of his feelings about his brother, and it transpired that he had never been able to weep, except alone. He had held back his tears in front of his parents in order to spare them grief, this especially so because of the concern he felt for his mother's high blood pressure and his father's repeated minor heart attacks. At the second interview he described that when he went to his 'private place' each day, he decided what he needed to wear according to how he felt: on a bad day, he would wear an overcoat with large pockets to hold all the bad feelings, but on a good day, T-shirt and jeans were enough.

Children who speak of 'black moods' might be encouraged to use black paint smeared on themselves (in imagination!) to represent the mood, and then wash it off in the sea or in a stream. A child familiar with a stringed instrument might use the image of tuning it to restore harmony, or the idea of the instrument being not only out of tune but under excessive tension to represent anxiety, or with the strings slack to represent depression. Equally, the weather in the 'private place' can represent feelings and mood: rain giving way to sunshine, clouds or mist clearing, wind slackening, and so on.

It is not as a general rule necessary to elaborate the imagery of the 'private place' with children as much as with most adults. The capacity for fantasy tends to dull and even to atrophy as maturity develops, while most children are able to develop and become wholly absorbed in either their own, original fantasy world or fantasy elaboration of some real experience, or a story they have read, listened to or seen on television. The 'Narnia' tales of C.S. Lewis are a very fruitful source of material for those children familiar with them, and the better-known fairy-tales can also be employed with great benefit. Therapists with a talent for storytelling will need no prompting.

Most children have had experience of success and achievement however dull, unhappy, depressing and deprived their history. Learning to ride a bicycle is perhaps the most common such experience, and most children will find themselves able to recall the first time they achieved that mastery and balance, and to re-capture the feeling. Swimming, ice-skating, roller-skating, horse-riding, skiing, and many other activities which give a sense of balance, achievement and control can be employed using age regression, in order to create good feelings in the child. The sense of mastery is especially valuable in such an exercise, most of all for those children who have feelings of personal inadequacy, failure and the like.

Children with specific learning difficulties very commonly develop feelings of misery, self-undervaluation, stupidity and incompetence, which naturally tend to enhance the severity of their handicap and so set up a self-fulfilling cycle of failure. An informal experiment was performed by one of the authors on 100 consecutive patients, aged between eight and fourteen, referred for assessment of learning difficulties. In the course of the assessment, tests of reading and spelling were, of course, administered. When these were complete, each child was given a brief hypnotic induction and suggestions were made to enable them to recover feelings of competence and mastery and to bring these forward into the present time and place. While remaining in trance, each child was then given comparable tests of reading and spelling. In this way every child in the series improved on their initial scores in both reading and spelling by around six months in attainment age.

There is certainly no intention to suggest that specific learning problems could be treated through hypnosis, but the secondary handicaps most such children develop of depression about their adequacy, and a reaction of more or less intense anxiety when faced with print or pencil and paper, can certainly be reduced substantially by such techniques, enabling the children to employ their abilities more effectively in mastering the complex tasks of becoming literate.

In point of fact many children are wholly familiar with the use of imagination to alter mood, and use techniques such as this spontaneously. One girl remarked after her first experience of hetero-hypnosis: 'Oh, that's just like what I do when I get upset because of teasing! I just go away inside myself and then it doesn't hurt so much when the other girls get at me.' Many children become absorbed in fantasy, books or television to escape from anxiety and unhappiness, but the directed use of self-hypnosis to achieve recovery and re-establishment of positive affect, through age regression to an experience of achievement and mastery, is rather more positive than simply escape. It may be important with children who have developed a taste for escape, a strategy which revolves around avoiding or evading a problem by retreat into fantasy, to ensure that self-hypnosis does not develop into escapism but is employed in a more creative and outward-directed way.

Once again it may be necessary to iterate that hypnosis is not a therapy but a therapeutic medium or vehicle. This axiom is perhaps marginally less true with children than with adults, since the natural drive towards health is often less damaged in children than it is all too often in later years. That is to say, if the mood of the child can be lifted by the simplest techniques and exercises, this in itself will tend to improve the interactions between the child and the significant people in his life to such an extent as to make those interactions themselves effectively therapeutic.

This does not happen, however, with children who have developed well-established pathology. In such cases improvement in mood is likely to be relatively minor and short-lived so that secondary or reinforcing events are less likely to occur, or to occur sufficiently often for the maladaptive personality structures and interpersonal transactions to be affected significantly. The use of a fantasy world in hypnosis, however, enables the child to explore and experiment with alternative adaptive mechanisms and strategies, in much the same way as the sand-tray worlds often used in play therapy. As the child shares these exploratory experiments with the therapist, they provide highly potent material for analytic therapy.

No scripts have been provided in this chapter, but material will be readily available to all therapists from their own childhood memory, and a number of patterns or formats have been given in the earlier chapters on work with children (especially chapter 11) to guide the creation of original scripts. With children even more than with adults, however, it is important to adapt one's approach to the individual patient, to use all possible creativity in therapeutic imagery and metaphor, and to be fresh and spontaneous in presentation.

PART IV

HYPNOSIS IN ANALYTIC PSYCHOTHERAPY

15

BASIC CONCEPTS

The principal thrust of this book is quite explicitly practical and, as has already been stated, there is no intention to present and discuss complex theoretical issues. In the various approaches to the treatment of a number of conditions which have been described so far, there has been little need for major theoretical formulations and questions. The methods described are based largely upon learning theory and the general principles of behaviour therapy. There are, to be sure, appreciable variations in theory, terminology and methodology in the world of behaviour modification, but these tend to be relatively minor differences and adherents of any one approach can usually agree with those who follow another model on a fairly consistent common language, and hence a shared terminology.

The same is not true, however, of those psychotherapeutic theories and practices derived from psychoanalysis, and it is therefore more necessary in this field to detail the fundamental assumptions and presuppositions involved and to provide what amounts to a glossary of concepts before embarking on a description of treatment strategies.

In the course of scanning the literature on different schools of analytic psychotherapy, one might easily get the impression that there are as many theoretical models of personality as there are theoreticians and as many systems of psychotherapy as there are practitioners. Superficial similarities of language and terminology turn out on closer scrutiny to be misleading.

For example, one of the fundamental concepts of psychoanalysis is that of the 'transference'. Classically, this term is used to denote the relationship between patient and therapist that develops as the patient begins increasingly to project on to the therapist perceptions, feelings and attitudes which have nothing to do with the therapist as a real person nor derive in any way from the interactions that have overtly taken place between patient and therapist, but arise from the background of the patient's early life and experiences, usually of people who have played a significant part in his personal development.

In a very real sense, the patient–therapist 'dyad' becomes a stage on which the patient re-enacts formative experiences and reactions, and so brings directly into the interactions between the patient and the therapist the very processes by which his personality developed. However, the term is also used very loosely on occasion to identify the affective relationship between patient and therapist, without reference to the specific qualities and characteristics which the more strictly classical use of the term (for which it was coined) requires.

The gibe sometimes made against the self-analysis of Karen Horney illustrates this kind of loose usage: 'The difficulty with self-analysis is the counter-transference.' At the risk of being tediously explicit, we would point out that the point of this joke is not the way in which the therapist projects upon the patient those unresolved conflictual aspects of his own formative relationships (which is how Freud defined the term) but rather the affect (or affection) the therapist may develop for his patient.

In addition to the inconsistent use of the same words, schools of analytically based theories and therapies have multiplied since the emergence of psychoanalysis.

The original formulations of Freud and his immediate followers very quickly generated disputes and schism, which eventually led to fission in the original group of analysts. The history of the early evolution of the major schools (named after Jung, Adler, Horney, etc.) has been well chronicled elsewhere. New schools emerge from time to time and will no doubt continue to do so, while the older schools evolve and change in the pursuit of greater understanding and more effective treatment.

As a consequence of this proliferation the idiosyncratic use and interpretation of common terms such as 'unconscious', 'ego', 'psychodynamic', 'psychoanalytic', 'psychotherapy' has resulted in confusion, incomprehension and disagreement. The values assigned to these and many related terms appear to depend more upon political adherence than on scientific consistency of terminology. No two therapists will use any of these terms in an agreed way until they have formed a new school of their own, and then the agreement will last only until their new school begins to undergo the fission that appears to be the fate of all.

The parallel between psychoanalysis and the original schools of theory and practice subsumed under that umbrella term on the one hand, and religious systems and institutions on the other, has been elegantly and learnedly described by Ernest Gellner (1985). Had Gellner extended his brief to include the schools of theory that have multiplied in the last few decades, rather than limiting himself largely to Freud's own (and mostly earlier) writings, the parallel would have been closer still. Yet one element of the comparison would have eluded inclusion: it is relatively easy to define the common denominating beliefs of all religious institutions which claim title to the label 'Christian'. Similarly, the unifying dogma held by all those groups included in the title 'Islam' would be relatively easy to identify. Yet to define and map in detail the common ground of psychoanalytic therapeutic models and practices is likely to prove impossible.

For instance, probably all psychoanalysts and psychotherapists of whatever persuasion would agree that a substantial and potent part of what it is to be human is in normal circumstances outside or beyond the reach of an individual's conscious mental processes, i.e., is *unconscious*. Yet there are schools of psychotherapy which do not mean '*unconscious*' when they use that word. For example, a less than thorough reading of texts in rational emotive therapy or cognitive therapy suggests that adherents of those schools do indeed accept the concept of inaccessible areas of thought, memory and affect; but more careful scrutiny, especially in terms of practice, suggests that the classical concept of repression and consequent *inaccessibility* of such repressed material is not used to mean what it was originally intended to mean or, worse, what it conveys to the average reader.

Furthermore, the intrinsic self-contradiction in Freud's original formulations of the term 'unconscious' (e.g. in both the original and the second *Lectures in Psychoanalysis* and in *The Psychopathology of Everyday Life*) appears to have been explicitly elucidated only as late as 1982 by John Beahrs (Beahrs, 1982).

The concepts of 'co-consciousness' and of one-way communication between ego and id and between ego and superego can be seen as implicit from Freud onwards. That is to say, material present in the ego is communicated to the id and to the superego (or is automatically transmitted to those functions), but the content of the latter two is inaccessible to the first.

As Beahrs pointed out very elegantly, the 'unconscious' is not *unconscious* in that it is self-aware, and the term is used to indicate the fact that the content of the 'unconscious' is literally inaccessible to the ego under normal circumstances. Freud himself clearly meant and consistently used his terminology to mean what, and only what, he intended it to mean. The thrust of this argument is to emphasize the importance of using language and terminology which will be understood in the same way by all our readers. Despite these caveats and criticisms, however, the authors' commitment to analytic therapy is undiminished.

THE ROLE OF HYPNOSIS IN ANALYTIC PSYCHOTHERAPY

Classical analysis, however, of whatever school, is not a practical approach to the treatment of the vast majority of patients who present either in the National Health Service or indeed in private practice in the UK. Apart from the dearth of qualified practitioners, the NHS will never provide the resources for such treatment for large numbers of patients, and the majority of people are unable to afford either the time or the financial cost involved in private analysis. For a long time, therefore, there has been a search for shorter, quicker and easier routes to therapy. 'Short-term' or 'brief' psychotherapies have been put forward and developed into schools or sects, and the search for short-cuts has included hypnotic theory and practice.

Insight, that is, a full understanding of one's own thinking, feeling, relating, and reacting, includes not simply a cognitive grasp of the components and determining processes of one's inner and outer behaviour, but a fully emotionally coloured awareness of the quiddity of these processes. This concept is perhaps one of the few which are common to the various theoretical schools, and is usually seen as the philosopher's stone of therapy. Insight, it seems to be believed, will transmute symptoms into health, understanding into personal change, and developmental arrest into personal growth. The proponents of brief psychotherapies appear undeterred by the experience which most psychotherapists have had: the patient whose sudden and dramatic insight in one interview promised marked changes which proved to have evaporated by the following week.

It is all too easy to poke fun at the inconsistencies, contradictions and conflicts within the world of analytic theory, yet no matter how much or how valid the criticism levelled against any or all such schools, there is no sign of an alternative approach which will enable us to provide effective help for the ever-increasing numbers of people who ask for it. Investigations of the efficacy of analytic psychotherapy using the methodology of conventional medical research frequently fail to justify continued use of analytically based techniques for the treatment of psychological and psychosomatic disorders.

At the same time, however, the experience of both practitioners and patients defies abandonment of such approaches: the benefits reported by many patients treated with such methods cannot be ignored. More recent research, fortunately adopting more appropriate methodology, shows that these methods are indeed efficacious. It is, however, generally recognized that analytic approaches are effective with or appropriate for only a proportion of patients asking for therapy. Nevertheless we cannot, in all good sense, abandon techniques which evoke such good results simply because they do so only with selected patients.

This subject and these techniques will not and should not go away. Many of the schools into which psychoanalytic theory has splintered are seeking to achieve more thoroughgoing and validated understanding of human personality and its development in both health and disorder and to evolve more effective methods of treatment. The following three chapters are written with this in mind and assert that hypnotic techniques can make a valuable contribution to any analytically based therapy.

To make the processes and techniques which are to be presented in the following chapters comprehensible, the underlying theoretical concepts must be made explicit and a terminology defined. To be sure, hypnotic techniques can be (and indeed very often are) used in any form of psychotherapy, and it has been argued by many writers since Mitchell (1914) that Freud's explicit rejection and abandonment of formal hypnosis marked the transition between his endeavours to use the techniques he had learned at the Salpêtrière and his use of hypnotic techniques as we know them today in the guise of free association. Characteristics of the hypnotic state may be observed in the behaviour of the analysand employing free association and may equally be noted in patients undergoing other forms of dynamic psychotherapy, especially those which aim directly at breaking through the ego-defences and achieving access to unconscious material.

The principles of hypnotic techniques, however, are not linked to any one specific theoretical school. It is possible to advocate the use of hypnosis in insight-orientated psychotherapy generally without specifying any particular theoretical orientation other than a belief in the value of recovering or uncovering 'lost' or 'repressed' memories, especially of traumatic experiences. Hartland (1971) repeatedly advocates the use of 'uncovering techniques' without going into any detail and without indicating what is to be done with or to the resulting 'uncovered' material.

In the view of the present authors, the approach implied by his recommendation is both unprofessional and untherapeutic. The use of uncovering techniques, that is, gaining access to repressed material, must always be followed by further therapeutic work to deal with and resolve the conflicts and affect which led to repression in the first place. We therefore intend to propose as common or inclusive a minimum theoretical base for the application of the techniques which follow as can be devised.

An ingredient of virtually every form of psychotherapy deriving from analytic theory is that recovery of previously inaccessible (i.e. repressed) thoughts, feelings, impulses and memories is not simply important, but essential to the therapeutic process. Such recovery is generally seen as the prelude to further work. Insight, the Holy Grail of analysis and analytic therapies, does not generally occur simply as a result of breaching the barrier of repression and returning to consciousness memories, impulses and feelings which have been thus barred, but is achieved by the 'working through' of the material so recovered. In most therapies there is considerable emphasis on this integration of newly recovered material into the total awareness of the individual if an insight, once achieved, is to give birth to effective and lasting changes.

Understanding of the process that leads to insight and hence change must be based on a model of personality and psychopathology, and the following very fundamental model is intended to have enough in common with the most widely accepted and practised theories for it to be accommodated within the models espoused by the majority of clinicians and thereby ease the marriage of the reader's pre-existing theoretical stance and practice with the techniques we describe.

A fundamental assumption in what follows is that human beings differ at birth in ways that are significant and potent for their subsequent development. A writer, whose name is sadly untraceable, employed the phrase 'constitutional mush' to describe the multiplicity of constitutional factors (often un-identifiable individually) which are assumed to be responsible for those characteristics of the individual which cannot be accounted for in terms of his known life-experience. At the risk of incurring similar criticism we shall assume that the individual differences which may be observed in the new-born such as in reactivity, sensitivity to stimuli, characteristic patterns of reaction to arousal, passivity or phlegm on the one hand and activity and affectivity on the other, are essentially due to an inherent, constitutional and fundamentally unlearned datum. These inherent and congenital differences must stem from physiological differences, which in some cases appear to be genetically determined. We are thus born with significant temperamental differences.

These differences include the direction or valency of reaction observed in infants. Observation of new-born infants, and infants during the first few weeks and months of life, suggests strongly that individuals differ from birth in the direction or valency of their affective reactions as well as in their threshold for and strength of reaction. Some babies react positively to stimulation: with attention, apparent interest, pleasure and acceptance; while others, apparently not differentiated from their peers in any other way, react with apparent apprehension, fear, displeasure and withdrawal or avoidance. By these differences we define the term 'valency'.

It appears that the pattern of response to stimuli originating outside the individual is at least partially congenitally determined, and if this is so, subsequent reactions will also be to some extent pre-set. For example, it would follow from this viewpoint that a child whose congenital reaction-pattern is one of fear and withdrawal will react to emotionally neutral events as though they were emotionally negative, and therefore perceive them as ego-dystonic or dysphoric. This response could then also apply (as analytic therapy often reveals to have been the case) to events which an outside observer might reasonably expect to be experientially positive, stress-reducing, impulse-satisfying, or otherwise pleasurable.

To illustrate this concept, let us take the example of suckling. Listening to or observing breast-feeding mothers, it is occasionally apparent that this activity, which from its fundamental nature should be pleasurable to the infant, can be wholly dysphoric for a wide range of reasons. At the simplest level, cracked nipples or other painful conditions in the mother may cause the latter to experience and show signs of pain at breast feeding which will be communicated to the child. The infant's behaviour may then become restless, frustrated and angry, or alternatively passive, withdrawn and apparently miserable.

A mother who has no such physical problems but who is ambivalent or negative about breast-feeding or about the baby itself (for whatever reasons: whether inherent to the mother's own psychopathology, or to the circumstances of conception, to her experiences during the birth, her life situation at the time, etc.) may visibly evoke negative reactions during feeding from her child, these reactions in turn being shaped by the child's temperamental characteristics.

These reactions, demonstrated by the child, will themselves be seen to stimulate reactions in the mother, and in this way the framework and essential affective character of the mother–child relationship begins to develop and elaborate. It must be noted that the temperamental character of the child, the independent attitudes, expectations, needs and emotional resources of the mother, and the affective setting in which these early interactions take place are interwoven in a complex network. A child with, for example, an introversive temperament whose reactivity is of negative valency, suckled by a mother who is positive and warm about motherhood and who is rearing the child in a supportive, secure and warm life-situation, will develop very differently from a comparable child reared by a mother who resents the child's birth, who experienced a traumatic labour and who is unsupported and un-nurtured herself. In the same way, a child of warm, positive and extroversive temperament, reared by a resentful or ambivalent mother, will develop quite differently in this situation from an infant with a less outward-directed temperament or with a lower threshold for stress.

The fundamental datum of endowed temperament is therefore developed and modified in its expression by the earliest experiences of the infant, especially by those which have major affective impact through the fulfilment of basic needs and the experience of pleasure or pain. This is necessarily an interactive process, in which the child is as much actor as recipient. This latter point is important, since the experience of producing responses from others is central to the developing self-image of the infant.

We can see these early events producing three principal results. First, they steer the development of the mother–child relationship (the basic template of future relationships as well as the major influence on the child's early development). Secondly, they shape the development and expression of the child's affective reactivity. Thirdly, they lay down the framework of the child's self-image, especially his perception of the effect he sees himself as having on the outside world and the persons in it and his experience and perception of himself as withdrawing from or moving out to the world.

These processes can be observed in three main ways: by observing mothers with their children (a requisite in the training of psychoanalysts, but sadly not in all training in therapy); by listening to mothers (which largely only those therapists who work with children generally have the opportunity to do at length); and (rather indirectly) in analytic therapy.

The earliest theorizing on early personality development emerged from the analysis of adults, and it has been suggested from time to time that such theories should not be considered to have universal application since the observations on which they were based were taken from adults in analysis and therefore neurotic; but these theories have since been well validated by direct observation of normal infants.

We can see these early events creating a number of determinants for future personality development:

1.   a mental or cognitive 'set': a framework strongly influencing, even if not determining, the cognitive formulation or interpretation which the individual will apply to subsequent experiences;

2.   an internal emotional state or persistent mood and hence continuing subjective colouration of experience;

3.   a template for reactions in the future which shapes the pattern of automatic responses to relational events, that is, events occurring in a relationship (what Berne and the transactional analysts would describe as 'transactions').

Even earlier events such as the experience of birth itself have been claimed by many writers as significant in these terms. Recall of the birth-experience, in hypnotically-induced regressed states, has been claimed to be accompanied by cognitive, affective and relational insights which have proved effective in relieving neurotic or other maladaptive patterns in adult patients.

For example, one of the authors saw a video recording at the 9th International Congress of the International Society of Hypnosis of a therapy interview with a young woman suffering from depression of mood and grossly low self-esteem. After induction and deepening, she was asked to allow herself to go back through her life following the thread, as it were, of the depressed affect of which she was complaining, and to regress in this way until she was back at the experience in which she first felt that particular mood.

After some time she began to describe strong and increasing feelings of being squeezed, of being suffocated, and considerable pain. She began writhing about in her chair, pushing outwards with her hands and gasping for breath. Suddenly she appeared to go limp and began to shudder, saying she felt dreadfully cold. She then began to weep, sobbing that she felt rejected and unwanted, and that she could feel she was hated. The therapist intervened with a number of questions, the answers to which clarified that the experience the young woman was having was that of her birth.

After interpretative suggestions had effectively eased the patient's distress, the trance was ended and her experience discussed with the patient. It transpired that the patient's birth had indeed been resented by her mother, who was at that time unmarried and unsupported, having been rejected by the father of the baby as soon as she had told him of the pregnancy. The implication drawn from the session was that the child had felt the mother's anxiety, anger, rejection and other negative affects as being directed at her during and immediately after the delivery.

This affective tone or 'set' appeared to have formed the framework of her outlook on the world around her and of her self-image. That is to say she saw herself, in an unarticulated and amorphic way, as to blame for the suffering and general negative affect that she had experienced at birth, and this guilt-feeling had infused and shaped her subsequent development. The therapeutic intervention made was designed to enable her to re-evaluate the experience, to re-interpret the origin, meaning and direction of the affect, and in this way to change her self-image. This session was visibly a powerfully moving experience for the patient. There was a very marked catharsis or affective discharge, and the therapist reported that major changes in mood, general mental state and behaviour followed and were maintained and consolidated at later interviews.

It might well be argued that material emerging in sessions such as the one just described, especially if dating from pre-verbal stages of the patient's development, are more aptly described as fantasy than as recall. Just as Freud was uncertain for some time as to whether his patients' reports of sexual approaches by their fathers should be regarded as historical fact or as too improbable, we also may be uncertain as to the historicity of such re-enactments of the experience of birth. The question is certainly accessible to experimental investigation, but the answer is probably irrelevant for the use of such techniques in therapy. Whether historically true or not, interviews such as these act as potent metaphors through which the patient simultaneously perceives and communicates an important truth: that the feelings of guilt, worthlessness, rejection and hostility originated from outside the self and only later became incorporated or introjected.

A fundamental concept of all analytically-based therapeutic models is that some especially potent experiences, whether brief and traumatic, repetitive, or continuous and painful, are repressed, blocked from consciousness, and that the repressed 'complexes' (the complex constellations of cognition and affect) exert a determining influence on mood, behaviour, apperception and relationships into and through adult life. Pathological, that is, maladaptive, effects may result in the emergence and maintenance of neurotic symptoms. These are generally considered to be determined by more than one complex, although occasionally a symptom may be produced by and represent a single traumatic experience.

The next fundamental concept in analytic therapies is that the recovery or disclosure ('uncovering' in some texts on hypnotherapy) of such traumatizing events, and their restoration to consciousness, is a means by which the effects, in terms of symptoms, can be reduced or eliminated.

It was, of course, the fact that the patients whom Freud treated with such techniques relapsed or produced alternative symptoms which led to his supposed abandonment of hypnotic techniques. Restoration to consciousness of causative traumata, and the abreaction which commonly accompanies such a manoeuvre, can occasionally have a major therapeutic effect. In and of itself, however, it is unlikely to undo the manifold and complex consequences of years of interactions, relationships, and the development of self-image which have taken place since the experience of the traumatic event and its repression. Not only is it unlikely that the complex consequences of such trauma should be dissolved 'at a stroke', but in clinical experience such 'instant cure' is rarely observed except in the most superficial and short-lived ways.

The more complicated and profound process of gaining 'insight', which involves affective as well as cognitive recognition of intra-psychic associations, was sought by Freud as a more potent and far-reaching procedure effecting more profound and therefore long-lived changes in intra-psychic organization. Insight is considered to involve not simply the recovery of repressed material (memories, affect, etc.) but, more importantly, an understanding of the inter-relationships between the previously repressed material, the pathogenic processes, the symptoms produced, and the personality as a whole. This understanding needs to be more than cognitive: a very common experience in the practice of any therapist is the expression by a patient of a coherent intellectual formulation of his problem and its aetiology, but without any affective component, therefore lacking impact and having no effect on the patient's total state or symptoms.

This could, of course, be predicted from the axiom that no experience has an appreciable effect on the functioning or development of an individual except to the extent that it has emotional force or power (this, in behaviourist terms, would be interpreted in terms of contingent reinforcements). Consequently, for a learned pattern to be changed, modified or eliminated, the alternative or contrary experience must have at least equal impact. In a pattern that has been practised or rehearsed over a period of years and during that time has received, by its very nature, repeated reinforcement, the emotional force with which the patient experiences the re-cognition and therefore re-interpretation must be that much greater, and greater in particular than the affective power of the original experiences.

Therapies directed at personality modification, symptom removal and the establishment of adaptive in place of maladaptive patterns of behaviour (both covert or intra-psychic, and overt or inter-personal), which work through the achievement of insight, need therefore to function within an emotionally charged framework. The attachment of patient to therapist, of which the transference is a central and especially powerful part, provides such a setting. The classic process central to psychoanalysis of 'analysing the transference' is a means by which the fundamentally characteristic patterns in which the patient reacts, feels, apperceives and relates (particularly to significant others in his formative years) are evoked, elaborated and encouraged in the relationship with the therapist and then made the focus or locus of the search for insight. This process is potent and effectual *because* it takes place within a highly charged inter-personal relationship, hence allowing the patient access to the original immediacy and intensity of the feelings.

At this point, the term 'unconscious' must be examined. The implication this word carries is that the content of that part of the human mind so identified lacks consciousness, an implication which is wholly untenable, however necessary it may appear logically. It is arguable whether it was ever intended that the term 'unconscious' should be used in this way, rather than to indicate that the content of this part of the mind is not accessible to some other part or parts of the same mind.

For example, experiments on subliminal perception have demonstrated that signals or even complex messages affect the behaviour of individuals who honestly insist that they did not perceive those messages (Dixon, 1981). It is evident that perception and comprehension of those messages did take place, but at a different level of consciousness. Beahrs (1982) proposes an alternative model and suggests the concept of several separate 'lines of consciousness' co-existing within the individual. In addition he suggests that one or more of these 'lines of consciousness' may be aware of each other, but the central consciousness of the individual (perhaps most simply designated by Freud's term 'ego') is not aware of the existence and certainly not of the content of these 'co-conscious' parts of his own mind. Bliss (1986) suggests that self-hypnotic dissociation splits consciousness into similarly separate 'lines', albeit without the one-way communication that Beahrs believes to be necessary for the explanation of human behaviour and pathology.

The influence of unconscious presuppositions, beliefs and attitudes is illustrated by the commonplace experience that a single event witnessed by several observers will be reported in a different way by each observer. For example, the BBC showed an experiment on television demonstrating this. A brief playlet was performed in front of a studio audience, the latter being questioned one at a time immediately afterwards. The members of the audience differed on the number of actors, their gender and colour, the activities in which the actors were engaged and, most significantly, who did what to whom. The play showed a brief act of violence as its climax: some members of the audience were quite certain that the aggressor was white and the victim black, while the remainder were equally certain of the reverse. When all the audience had reported their perceptions, a video recording of the play was shown. In the final discussion, it was quite clear that all of the audience (and no doubt most of the audience watching the programme) believed that the videotape they were subsequently shown of the play had been doctored.

We see and hear, it is commonly said, what we expect to see and hear. More accurately, one could posit that what we believe we receive through our eyes and ears has been edited by omission, addition and distortion, and that this processing takes place outside the reach of our central consciousness or 'ego'.

Furthermore, what we do (externally in observable behaviour or internally in thought and feeling) is equally shaped by processes of which we are not centrally aware.

The potential for maladaptation inherent in this editorial processing is infinite. We see it in every interaction between individuals; in the relationships between individuals and groups or institutions; between groups; between institutions; and even between nations. We see it most clearly and specifically in patients. In this sense, therefore, we regard psychotherapy as the process whereby the individual becomes able to perceive his environment more directly and with less distortion, to perceive his own intrapsychic processes with less censorship and, in addition, to be more clearly and more consciously aware of his own editorial processing and censorship.

This is necessarily no more than the most cursory summary of the essential elements common to most dynamic and insight-orientated therapies, and is obviously not to be regarded as any kind of comprehensive statement. Indeed, it could be anticipated that adherents of *any* particular school of theory will reject what has been proposed, since in endeavouring to find the common ground for many conflicting formulations we have probably stepped on the corns of all.

We will, however, attempt to summarize the theoretical basis for the psychodynamic therapeutic strategies to be described in the following chapters in the following propositions. It must be borne in mind that these propositions apply to 'active' neurotic processes and to their treatment, in contrast to the 'empty habits' and their extinction described in earlier parts of this book, especially in chapters 7 and 12.

1. Both adaptive and maladaptive personality characteristics and patterns derive from the life-experiences of the individual.

2. The apperception or subjective interpretation of these experiences on the part of the individual is shaped in part by his temperamental character or predispositions in the first instance. As life proceeds, so previous experiences and their effects on the individual exert a determining effect on subsequent experiences and result in a cumulative shaping effect on his apperceptive 'set'.

3. The power inherent in any experience to influence development depends upon the emotional impact of that experience: this may be either in terms of the intensity of the affect aroused, or of the repetitiveness and frequency of either the same or closely related experiences.

4. Maladaptive as well as adaptive patterns tend to generate self-reinforcement. That is to say, once a pattern (which may be a 'symptom' of neurotic disorder, or equally well may be an effective and satisfying social skill) has been established, it will tend to evoke responses from other people that act as contingent reinforcers. For example, in the case of maladaptive patterns such as depressive and intra-punitive reactions, disappointment, betrayal, rejection and similar transactions between the patient and those around him will either occur in response to his own behaviour or will be perceived as present even in the most well-intentioned actions on the part of those with whom he interacts. A.A. Milne described an archetypal instance of this in the character of Eeyore. (The opposite, as applying to adaptive behaviours, is self-evident.)

5. Most commonly, the experiences from which both adaptive and maladaptive patterns stem become inaccessible to the central consciousness of the individual. Many of the most important of these occurred in the pre-verbal phases of the individual's development and cannot therefore be formulated and directly recalled in verbal terms. In addition, many are charged with ego-dystonic and dysphoric affect, which led to repression. These considerations are particularly true with the earliest adaptive processes and in neurotic conditions.

6. To effect lasting changes in such established and self-reinforcing patterns, the root memories that have been repressed must be returned to consciousness and such a return or recovery must include the relevant affect. This can be achieved only within an emotionally potent relationship which includes the transference, that is, the therapeutic relationship must be the medium in which the formative relational experiences of the patient are re-enacted in the therapy.

7. Hypnotic techniques can be employed to facilitate access to material and processes normally inaccessible to the individual's 'ego', by providing strategies which by-pass 'ego-defence mechanisms' such as repression, displacement, reaction-formation, intellectualization and rationalization.

It is hoped that this formulation can be accepted as a definition of the basis on which the treatment strategies to be described in the following chapters can be understood, even if it does not constitute an adequate and acceptable minimum statement of the psychoanalytic approach to therapy.

16

UNCOVERING TECHNIQUES

It is common to find, in the personal memory of a patient, gaps that are differentiated from the gaps we all have in that they appear to be relevant to the problem or condition for which treatment is sought. Sometimes this is apparent to the patient, who feels strongly that an important event took place at a particular time or in a particular setting yet is unable to 'lay hands on' the memory. More often, it is the therapist who comes to believe that material that is relevant in some way is blocked from consciousness, and that recovery of this material would forward the course of therapy.

On occasion it may be clear from the outset, or from early on in treatment, that such a repressed portion of experience is central to the patient's condition. Phobic reactions, especially if monophobic, may appear from quite early in exploratory therapy to have been generated by and to reflect a single major traumatic experience, although most usually in the context of more generalized anxiety or insecurity. In such cases, one may regard the symptom as a re-enactment of the original experience in a disguised and displaced form.

For example, a woman who was referred for an intractable and increasing agoraphobia presented as an otherwise well-integrated and well-functioning person. Happily married, mother of two children who were themselves well adjusted, she had quite suddenly begun to experience severe attacks of panic when away from her home, both at work and when shopping. Initially, these episodes had occurred only when she was alone, but as they increased in frequency and severity they began to occur even when she was accompanied by her husband. At the time of referral she was virtually house-bound, although able to tolerate going in the car with her husband.

There was no previous history of anxiety or other psychopathology, although she described herself as a somewhat shy person. She responded well to hypnotic induction, and quickly learned to use self-hypnosis to reduce her by then chronic anxiety and to apply it effectively in a programme of systematic desensitization. Within three weeks, she had recovered some of the lost ground: she became able to go shopping as long as her husband accompanied her, and could go alone a short distance out of her house.

At the same time as carrying out a programme of symptom management on these lines, we talked more generally about her personal history. Her childhood had been happy in the early years, but the separation of her parents when she was about six years old had rather changed this, and her account of her later years was tinged with a little insecurity and generalized anxiety, although she did not appear to have developed any symptoms or to have been handicapped in her life to any appreciable extent, that is, no psychopathology seemed to have been evident. Without either the patient or the therapist having any specific expectations, we agreed to undertake some exploration under hypnosis and to see if any specific topics, situations or events were causally and meaningfully related to her current problem. The technique used was that of age regression, using an affect bridge. (The details of these procedures are described below.)

After a short while, the patient said that she felt herself to be about six years old, on her way home from school. It was rather dark and it was raining, and then there was a thunderstorm. At this point she became increasingly agitated and began to behave very like a frightened small child. She was then given reassurance, asked to return to the present day and brought out of the trance, having been given suggestions of leaving the anxiety and fear behind her.

Discussing this experience once back to normal consciousness, the patient found that she now had access to memories of that period in her childhood that had previously been unavailable. Her experience of being caught in a thunderstorm had occurred in the context of considerable anxiety about her parents, home, personal security, etc., and had occasioned her intense terror. She believed that the memory of this event and of its context had been completely inaccessible until this point, but the experience in hypnosis had been wholly real and she felt that she *recognized* the event. The feelings she had experienced were identical to those she felt when seized with panic at going out of her home. The following week, she reported that she had been able to do the family's shopping on her own; she had felt apprehensive and somewhat tense, but had not experienced any panic.

Treatment was discontinued after one further session, which was made up of no more than some ego-strengthening and discussion of the fact that she would take some time to get used to her renewed freedom. Her principal feeling at this time was pride in her achievement. A follow-up meeting a year later showed that the improvement had been maintained and that the increased confidence and self-esteem that accompanied it had enabled her to take a job managing a staff agency, without anxiety and with immense confidence and enjoyment.

Sometimes, in the course of exploratory therapy, it becomes patent that an area of experience has been unconsciously edited: some aspects or portions of the memory have been differentially repressed and the place, context or time of the lacunae can be identified more or less confidently by the patient. It is then possible to use age regression to a specified time and/or place, or to a specific situation which is the focus of the memory loss.

In other cases, a picture may emerge of the patient's past in which it is clear that the affect involved has been 'lost' or changed. It may perhaps appear that the patient's denial of stress or distress related to an event, situation or relationship is the product of a differential repression: the content is accessible, the affect is not. Alternatively the overt or consciously recalled affect associated with an event may appear clearly inappropriate, and incongruent with the overall formulation or hypothesis that has been developed in the course of therapy to this point. Again age regression, with an identified 'target' in the form of the suspect event or situation, may disclose the repressed affect, and it is believed that the re-combination of this with its appropriate content will precipitate a change in the patient's adjustment, self-image, and especially in his understanding of his own condition and processes.

An illustration of this is the case of a man in his early thirties referred after a series of nearly successful suicide attempts. Anti-depressant medication had had little or no effect. He presented as angrily depressed, the first interview being filled with expressions of self-contempt and hatred for the world and his fellow-humans. He gave vent to lengthy tirades against a world in which the cruelties and injustices seen on the television news each day could take place. He wanted no part in such a world. At the same time, he expressed total contempt for himself and described himself as a failure. In fact, he was a highly respected and successful member of a learned profession, had recently published a best-selling novel whilst his second novel, still uncompleted, had been sold in several countries, and the film rights were being eagerly sought. He had an intact marriage, and two children whom he loved.

From his history it emerged that he had been adopted in early infancy. He insisted that this had no bearing on his problems, since he had totally accepted his adoption and regarded his adoptive parents as his parents. He was quite unaware of the considerable but heavily disguised ambivalence in his attitudes to and relationship with his parents, and seemed genuinely unaware of this ambivalence in his relationship with his wife also. Assertions of contentment with his adoptive status rang hollow.

Although he proved totally resistant to any exploratory work in this area, he agreed that it could be helpful to use hypnosis to seek the roots of his feelings of inadequacy and depression. We used an affect bridge, starting with a recent event in his professional setting when he had been almost overwhelmed by feelings of inadequacy.

In response to the instruction to go back to the first time he had had this feeling, he showed increasing distress and then he reported himself as sitting in a pushchair, aged under two, with his mother standing above him. He described how another woman approached and made admiring remarks about him to his mother. The latter explained that he was adopted, whereupon the other woman simply turned and walked away. At this point, the patient burst into tears and sobbed bitterly for a considerable period.

Once out of hypnosis again, the patient seemed quite shaken and very subdued. He said that he realized that there was a level of feeling about his adoption which was wholly new to him, yet he felt he recognized. In the interviews that followed, he appeared to have much more direct access to affect generally, especially negative affect, and to perceive his relationships and attitudes more clearly than before. Eight sessions after the one described, we ended his treatment. Follow-up over the next five years showed the improvement to be maintained. He had no further episodes of depression, no suicidal impulses, wishes or even thoughts. He was working well in his professional role and had completed the book he had been working on. This had become a best-seller; his next book followed suit and all in all he felt life was good.

It is, of course, very satisfying when such dramatic events occur and are followed by symptom relief. More commonly, though, however dramatic the recovery of memory in the hypnotic session, much work remains to be done. The removal of repression, even of a central event, and the acquisition of insight do not necessarily produce as great a shift in personality organization as to constitute successful or sufficient treatment; usually, much more work needs to be done to integrate the recovered memories, explore their ramifications, make further connections with the present, thereby adding other insights and discoveries, and additionally to work through the recovered memories and their affect.

It is relatively rare for a single trauma to be so potent that its retrieval from repression will in itself precipitate sufficient change in the patient's life. In neurotic conditions it is more common for the repressed memories, fantasies, impulses or affect to be less directly causal: such conditions are relatively rarely the product of a single or even repeated trauma. Nevertheless, one feature common to all psychodynamic therapies is the search for repressed material. Commonly the retrieval of such material can lead to a Gestalt insight that significantly alters the pattern of functioning of the personality.

A twenty-eight-year-old woman, referred herself to one of the authors for therapy. A well-qualified nurse pursuing a successful career, she presented as very positive, attractive and outgoing. She gave as her reason for asking for help the fact that she had fallen in love and wished to marry, but felt she could not do so as things were. She had a very full sexual life, but had found throughout her adult years that she recoiled from sexual activity with any man for whom she felt affection. She could have intercourse only with men for whom she had no particular emotional attachment. This clearly presented her with an insoluble dilemma.

In the course of her analytically orientated therapy she described a childhood disturbed by warfare between her parents which had culminated in their separation when she was in her teens. A triggering factor in the separation appeared to have been the increasingly overt sexual interest the father had demonstrated in the patient and her sister, who was one year younger. During the succeeding few years, the patient had been required by her mother to visit her father weekly to collect from him the maintenance payments ordered by the court. During these visits, which the patient regarded with a mixture of pleasure and fear, her father got her to do the housework in his flat, including making the bed, and developed the custom of teasing her very provocatively during this activity.

She was vividly aware, even at a distance of nearly ten years, of the mixture of excitement, erotic arousal and a feeling of pride on the one hand, and fear, disgust and revulsion on the other. She felt ashamed that despite her now pretty open recognition of the nature of this interaction, she found herself even now, well on into adult years, unable to terminate these visits, although she had reduced their frequency, or to change the form they took. It seemed impossible, however, to bring the relationship between this pattern and her presenting problem to consciousness. Curiously, there was nothing in the transference that reflected this ambivalence: she showed neither seductiveness and erotic provocation nor anxiety and revulsion in the therapeutic relationship.

We were able, however, to explore and expose the feelings she experienced more vividly in the hypnotic state than otherwise. In the course of reviewing one of her visits to her father's flat during her teens she 'jumped' suddenly, and without any suggestions having been made to this effect, to an experience of only a few days earlier, when she had gone to bed with her fiancé and found herself intensely revulsed by his love-play. The connection was at last perceived. The patient was now able to recognize in a more profound way than had been possible for her before this experiential event the incest ambivalence and anxiety that had shaped her sexual behaviour. We had agreed on a set number of twenty interviews at the outset, and this session occurred at the fourteenth. On completion of the contract the patient was looking forward without anxiety to her approaching marriage, although she said that she had not yet put her new-found freedom to the test.

Less seriously, it could be suggested that some element of the transference that had been concealed successfully in the course of therapy was revealed two years later, when the therapist received a birth announcement from the patient, who had married her fiancé shortly after completing treatment. On this card was written: 'This is all due to you!'

In other cases one may arrive at a formulation that stands upon the concept that a single traumatic experience, or period of such experience, may set up a 'conditioned reflex' with some degree of generalization and that this constitutes a maladaptive pattern which in turn generates a spreading or widening area of maladaptive elements, culminating in the condition for which help is being sought. For example, experience of neglect or even physical abuse in childhood may stimulate the emergence of passivity and submissiveness, so that the child presents as a 'victim type', evoking persecutory behaviour from both peers and adults. These experiences enhance and generalize the internal pattern, with a probable end product of chronic depressive personality traits. The anger at ill-treatment becomes increasingly turned inwards on the self. It is often extremely difficult to detach the appropriate or natural anger and rage felt by the patient from its perverted object (the patient himself), because of the guilt aroused by attempts to explore its original focus, and the fear associated with any insight that dawns.

Re-living one or more of the originating experiences, usually, of course, occurring in the context of parent–child interactions, may allow the therapist to 'freeze' the experience at the point where the patient's rage is still natural and before it is turned inwards, and then focus on the *process* by which it became perverted. This in turn may then allow the individual to discover the same pattern in current as well as other childhood experiences and free himself from the conditioned response of submission, suppressed affect and depression.

In summary, we would suggest that re-evoking experiences relevant to the presenting state of the patient and significantly causal in it is an integral part of all therapies which use exploration and aim at insight. Hypnosis can offer those patients with sufficient hypnotic talent a quicker, more immediate, sometimes more profound route to such insight. The impression given when such an approach is used is that the hypnotic dissociation makes it possible for either the content or the affect, or both, of relevant memories to by-pass ego-defences.

TECHNIQUES

The terms 'age regression' and 'affect bridge' have already been used. The former is probably familiar to readers in its sense of the experience of going backward through one's life and *re-experiencing* rather than remembering earlier events. The process and some of its features were described in an earlier chapter, in the form in which it may be demonstrated in experimental or teaching settings.

In endeavouring to recover elements of an earlier and important experience, or indeed an entire experience that has been repressed and made inaccessible to normal consciousness, we must have some way of directing attention and awareness to the relevant point in time. In a case where the experience is known, and it is the affect we are hoping to disclose, we know where to go: to the original experience. In other cases the therapist may have deduced the context, even the nature, of the relevant event or of the period in the patient's life during which a traumatizing experience is likely to have occurred, even though the patient himself is not aware of this. More commonly, however, the search is essentially 'blind' in that neither the patient nor the therapist knows when the incident took place, in what setting, or what it contained. Even if the therapist has a pretty shrewd idea of what is being sought, he may not have sufficient confidence simply to direct the patient to what he, the therapist, thinks is the target: few of us would be so confident.

The 'affect bridge' is the technique by which the patient is guided to discover the relevant point in his life, the source of trauma and its consequences. The underlying hypothesis for this method is that the affect the patient currently experiences inappropriately, in the context of any symptom he may manifest, reflects the affect related or bound to the causal or archetypal experience.

The present-day affect is therefore regarded as the proximal end of a link between symptom and cause, and the affect itself is therefore used to guide the patient's retrogressive movement in hypnosis through his previous life experiences to its distal end, the formative or archetypal trauma. Thus the patient is first asked to re-evoke a recent occasion on which his symptom has been manifest or especially intense, then to focus on the affect he is experiencing, and then to allow himself to go back to earlier times in his life, holding the affect he has recovered firmly in mind, until he reaches the first time he ever experienced that affect.

Quite commonly, the patient will initially report events of which he has at least some memory, often not very remote from the present, and has to be exhorted to allow himself to go 'further back', seeking the first experience of that affect. Not infrequently this process has to be repeated a number of times, as the regression takes place in steps and may involve many different occasions and experiences before the earliest one is reached.

In using age regression, one must of course have techniques and a plan for handling the experience when it emerges. The recovery of a traumatic event from repression is in itself potentially highly traumatic, and at the very least intensely distressing and disturbing, and must not be undertaken without preparation both of the patient and of the therapist. If a major trauma is suspected or even moderately likely, one should take the precaution of creating some space or distance between the patient and the event.

This can be done by asking the patient to see the event as on a television screen, with his life represented perhaps by the tape in a video recorder which will be played under his control through the television set. With such an image, the patient can if necessary retain a firmer and more vivid grasp on the fact that the event is in the past, not the present, and that he can stop the experience he is observing should he need to do so. In this way the 'hidden observer', as this phenomenon has been described, is more clearly in charge of the event and not simply observing, and remains in touch with the fact that in the present he is actually in the therapist's room and not wholly in the scene that is being 'replayed'.

A common reaction to effective and well-aimed age regression is a more or less massive abreaction. From Freud onwards, the value of abreaction has been questioned and remains questionable. The release and discharge of long-dammed affect can have a thoroughly cathartic effect and may be followed by lessening or even disappearance of symptoms, but such improvement tends to be short-lived if further work is not done on the material disclosed.

When using this technique, the therapist must be prepared to witness and manage what can be intense and quite frightening reactions on the part of the patient. He must also be prepared to provide confident, strong and reassuring control over the process and to make suggestions that will enable the patient to survive the experience without further damage, and to use it constructively. On occasion, the affect experienced by the patient is so overwhelming that therapeutic intervention cannot be carried out, and the patient has to be led to withdraw from the experience with partial or even complete amnesia. Complete withdrawal is rarely necessary and it is usually sufficient to suggest that the patient should forget whatever part of the memory he cannot cope with, with the result that a large part of the retrieved memory often remains accessible and the remainder is likely to emerge spontaneously during the following few days, as and when the patient can tolerate it.

Before embarking on such an uncovering process the therapist must have a plan of intended action, which he is likely to have negotiated with the patient. Is it intended, for example, to explore in order to identify a root experience which is known to be blocked from consciousness, the 'working-through' of which is to be done without hypnosis? Alternatively, is the intention to attempt a resolution of a trauma by means of ego state therapy (see chapter 18)? Or, perhaps, is some other technique of restructuring of the experience intended to follow its disclosure? The fact is that age regression with successful disclosure of a relevant and affectively potent memory that was previously repressed or dissociated is not in and of itself likely to be therapeutically effective or beneficial, and is no more than a means of obtaining access to material that then needs working through or other management. It should not, therefore, be employed until and unless it is positively indicated and an appropriate treatment strategy has been devised.

The depth of trance and dissociation achieved by some patients make it on occasion laborious and time-consuming to insist on speech. In such instances, a very useful technique is that of using signals to facilitate the patient's replies to questions. In trance, it is a considerable effort to speak and many patients, especially if the trance is deep, will give up the effort; it is just too complicated and arduous. Additionally, such signalling appears to offer a direct communication channel for the more deeply buried or 'unconscious' parts of the mind, which can use such channels quite independently of the censorship of the 'ego', just as automatic writing by-passes conscious control and direction.

The technical term used is 'ideo-motor signals'. It is wise to discuss the use of signalling with the patient and obtain his agreement before induction is carried out. Before embarking on age regression, but with the patient in trance, he is then asked to raise specific fingers to signal 'yes', 'no', and 'I do not want to talk about that'. Conventionally, the index finger of one hand is identified as 'yes', the little finger of the same hand as 'no' and the thumb as 'I do not want to talk about that'. It is useful to make the first question 'Are you clear about how to answer questions using your fingers?' The second step may be to ask something on the lines of 'Are the deeper, more hidden parts of your mind willing to answer questions that may help to resolve the difficulties you are having?' Such a signalling system does, of course, demand that all questions must be framed in ways that can be answered 'yes' or 'no', a limitation which challenges the therapist's ingenuity while somewhat restricting the information the patient can communicate.

The difference between conscious-voluntary movements and the typical ideo-motor movements of deep trance stimulated by deeper levels of the personality is unmistakable: the former are normal, smooth, voluntary and well co-ordinated and occur promptly when a question is asked; the latter appear after considerable delay (as much as ten or even fifteen seconds after the question), are slow, unco-ordinated and jerky, and will be reported by the patient subsequently as occurring without his will and sometimes giving unexpected replies, even contrary to his wishes.

It is generally a good idea to suggest, when introducing the signalling system, that the patient can at any time use speech to amplify or modify answers, or to communicate anything he wishes, in addition to the finger signals. A special use of such signals is in a form of ego state therapy where the therapist can be left in ignorance of the content of the whole process of age regression, the point or experience reached and the resolution achieved by the patient, the latter simply indicating what stage in the process he has reached. This is detailed in chapter 18.

Script 16.1   Age regression to known period

[Induction has been carried out, and the trance deepened to at least a medium level; 'somnambulistic' trance, or something approaching that, may be needed for age regression in some patients. Ego-strengthening and suggestions outlining the work to be done and its anticipated benefits are given.]

In a little while I am going to ask you to go backwards in time, so that you feel yourself getting younger and smaller, going back to a time much earlier in your life. You will be able to go back and experience again things that happened to you as vividly as can be, so that they will seem to you to be happening here and now. You will feel as you did when an event first occurred, and you will know all you knew then. But now you will be able to understand it with your adult mind, and so will have a much clearer grasp. When you come back to the present day again, you will remember all you experienced, except that if there is any part of it that you are not ready to cope with, you will be able to forget that again, and not remember it until you are ready to do so.

You are going to go back to when you were four years old, so that you can experience once again what you felt at that age. When you feel yourself to be four years old again, you will tell me by raising one hand, and then you will be able to answer my questions from your four-year-old self.

Imagine now that you are looking at a large clock. You can see the second hand moving one second at a time. Now it stops. Now let the second hand begin to move backwards, and it is going backwards faster and faster, until it is spinning round so fast you can see the minute hand now moving backwards too. Time is going backwards and you are going backwards in time. Faster and faster. Now it is going so fast that you can see the hour hand moving backwards, faster and faster, faster and faster. You are now going backwards in time so fast that even the hour hand is spinning into a faint blur. You are getting younger and younger, younger and younger. You are going back to being four years old, four years old, back to being four years old. You will let me know when you are four years old by raising your 'yes' finger. [Continue with appropriate additions until the patient signals that he has arrived at the target age.]

Good. Now tell me where you are.[66] What can you see? Who else is there? What can you hear? What are you doing? What do you feel? What is happening?[67] [When the replies to questions indicate that the patient has reached the 'target' experience, this is allowed to proceed. When appropriate, the experience is terminated, the patient reassured, and brought back to the present.]

Now let that scene fade from your mind. You will remember as much as you feel you can cope with. Let the scene fade away, and let all the feelings you are experiencing fade away. Relax. Let your mind and body relax and become at ease. Relax. Relax completely. Good. Now, go to your private place, and let yourself be filled with all the good feelings of peace, tranquillity and ease of body and mind that you know are there. [Add whatever detail of the 'private place' may be helpful.] Good. Now let yourself come forward in time again, back to the present day. Let yourself come back to the present, sitting in my office. Let a picture form in your mind of what you saw just before you closed your eyes: the pictures on the wall opposite you, myself sitting to one side [etc.]. Good. Now let yourself gradually return to the waking state, and when you are ready, let your eyes open so that you become fully awake, alert and refreshed. Bring with you, as you waken, all the good feelings of your private place, so that when your eyes open and you are fully alert again, you will still feel relaxed and at peace.

Script 16.2   Age regression by affect bridge

[This is to be used when a symptom or affective response such as panic, sudden feelings of inadequacy, etc., are at issue, and the originating experience or experiences are unknown.]

[Induction, deepening, ego-strengthening and all other preparatory work, including the setting up of ideo-motor signals, if desired, have been carried out.]

I would like you now to let yourself go back in time to that moment you were telling me about when you began to feel so terribly afraid. Go back to last Wednesday, when you were just putting your coat on to go out when you felt a panic beginning, and wanted to hide away. When you are there, standing just inside your front door last Wednesday and feeling the panic beginning, your 'yes' finger will lift. Let yourself go back, just a little way, through time. Good. Now let the scene fade from your mind, but hold on to all the feelings you are experiencing. Hold on to those feelings, and now let yourself go back through time, back through your life, following those feelings back to a much earlier time in your life. Go back, back through your life following those feelings, right back to the very first time you felt those feelings, and when you are back there, back to the very first time you experienced those feelings, your 'yes' finger will lift.

[Continue with short pauses, repeating the instructions to go back to the first time of feeling those feelings, until the signal is given. At the point when the patient reaches the recent episode of panic, this will be noticeable in his posture, facial expression, etc. When he reaches the older, perhaps even original experience of these feelings, this too is likely to be

clearly evident: the patient may weep, cringe, hold his hands up as though to guard against a blow, and show any or all of the behaviour of a frightened child. The patient may be questioned about the timing, location, content, affective character, etc., of the experience, either by being asked to describe verbally what is happening, or through direct questions to be answered by ideo-motor signals. The session is then terminated in much the same way as in Script 16.1, or by using one of a variety of techniques, detailed in chapters 17 and 18, designed to resolve the trauma in a constructive way.]

Script 16.3 The television screen

[The patient is in trance. Preparatory ego-strengthening referring to the work to be done has been carried out, and the patient may have spent some time in his 'private place'.]

Now let everything fade from your mind, so that you are thinking of nothing, absolutely nothing, except my voice. Just listening to what I say, feeling completely at peace, completely comfortable. I would like you now to imagine that you are looking at a television screen. There is no picture showing yet, just the black and white 'snow' that you see when there is no signal. Beside the television set is a video recorder. When you can see the television and the recorder clearly, your 'yes' finger will lift. Good. Now lean forward and switch on the recorder so that it can start playing the story of what happened to you when you were three years old and *[whatever is appropriate]* so that you can see it on the television screen, happening just as it did all those years ago. When the picture forms on the screen, your 'yes' finger will lift. As you see the story happening on the screen, you will be able to tell me what happens and what you are feeling. *[When the finger lifts:]* Good. Now tell me what you see.

Other techniques or images will no doubt suggest themselves to other therapists. The authors have used images such as going through dark passages in which pictures hang on the walls representing scenes from the patient's earlier life, so that as he walks down the passage he comes to one scene after another. A very useful image (which is used commonly for tracing a happy memory to use as the 'private place') has already been described: the photograph álbum (Script 6.6). Again, as the patient leafs through the album, starting at the present and the front of the book, he recalls earlier and earlier events until the target period is reached.

It hardly needs re-iterating, but emphasis must always be placed on the fact that recovery of a repressed memory or of repressed affect is not enough to effect relief of the problem in any but a very few cases. Psychotherapy is much more than 'uncovering', and the latter is only the first step in a process of re-working the uncovered material in such a way as to reduce traumatic impact, resolve conflicting feelings and attitudes, and above all to work through the manifold and complex ways in which such traumata have become woven into the life of the patient and, indeed, the very structure of his personality. One must not forget, either, the importance of working through the ways in which the patient inevitably projects into the therapeutic relationship (which tends to become very intense, and very quickly so, with the use of hypnosis) the structure and content of past relationships: the transference. The use of 'uncovering techniques' is therefore no more than a process whereby material is made accessible to therapeutic work: it should not be regarded as therapy in and of itself, even though on occasion it appears to be enough. This will be the case only with intact, well-integrated and well-structured personalities, who are generally unlikely to present as patients.

17

TREATMENT STRATEGIES

GENERAL CONSIDERATIONS

There is more than a little overlap between conditions stemming from a single major trauma or series of major traumata and those that reflect the effects of a pathogenic environment. Pathological characteristics and behaviour, as well as symptoms, whether behavioural, affective, or both (as is more usually the case), may be regarded as patterns of reaction that have been learned and reinforced, either by external events or by their own affective contingencies internal to the individual.

For example, the young woman patient described in the previous chapter, who flatteringly attributed the birth of her first child to the therapist, could be regarded as demonstrating the intrusion of a learned pattern of conflicting reactions that were archaic and out of place into her current life situation. Thus one would suggest that the concurrence of personal liking, affection and love on the one hand, and erotic attraction on the other, re-evoked in her the affectively hazardous experience of the combination of such emotions in relation to her father: hazardous because of the influence of the incest taboo and the associated feelings of rivalry towards and therefore threat from her mother. Her recoil from sexual contact with a man towards whom she felt affection as well as erotic attraction can be seen as a re-enactment of the incestuous situation and affect which was so vividly (and realistically) in the air in her family and in her childhood. This re-enactment, however, would be regarded as archaic and out-of-date, and additionally as inappropriate or out of place in that the man concerned was not, of course, her father, so that the incest taboo need not apply, nor would there be any rivalry with her mother. Despite its displacement, however, the reaction itself remained potent and was in fact self-reinforcing.

This last aspect needs elaboration. It is well known that belief in superstitious conventions tends to be maintained by the beliefs themselves. For instance, if it is predicated that walking under ladders will precipitate a misadventure, then one avoids walking under them and so sees the absence of misadventures as confirming the belief. Such mishaps as do occur will be ascribed to other causes, and the individual will consider himself lucky to have avoided further accidents that would have happened had he been thoughtless about ladders. Comedians find this a productive seam.

The patient described, having avoided intercourse with all men whom she liked or loved, successfully shielded herself from either the discovery that disaster would not strike if she did consummate such a relationship, or the more probable discovery that disaster would strike in such a case in the form of unsuccessful or unsatisfactory coitus. This, after all, would be highly probable if she accepted coitus while in a state of high anxiety, apprehension and expectation of disaster. The reaction remained, therefore, intact and its continued existence ensured its further continuation.

In the case of traumatically originated reactions, such as many phobic states, the same reinforcement applies. The agoraphobic patient knows all too well that avoiding going out precludes the experience of panic attacks (a positive reinforcement) and knows equally well from such experiences as he does permit that going out, especially unaccompanied, does precipitate such attacks and all the accompanying distress (negative or aversive consequences).

Neurotic patterns, whether originating in particular traumatic experiences or in damaging relationships and environments, share the characteristic that the meaning of the neurotic reaction is at best obscure, and more commonly quite unknown and impenetrable. All forms of therapy based on psychoanalytic theories aim at disclosing and unravelling the meaning of the symptoms, that is, enabling the patient to gain experiential insight, in the sense not just of cognitive grasp, abstract understanding and so on but a full emotional and intellectual experience of the reality of the essential link between past experience and current symptoms.

Classical analytic techniques depend generally on the invasion of the originating relationships into the relationship between therapist and patient: the establishment of the transference. The therapeutic process involves detailed exploration, within the transference, of the mechanisms of projection and displacement and therefore of their origins. The pathogenic elements and processes in the patient's formative years may be directly reflected in and expressed by the symptoms displayed and are sought in the reactions of the patient to the therapist, where they can be analysed with an immediacy that is unobtainable when exploring behaviour outside the consulting room and appointment time. The fact that the actual person who is the focus of the transferential projection is the same person who provokes and supports the patient in understanding the relationship and its origins gives the process additional power.

The fulcrum of therapeutic change is the analysis of the transference. The affective reactions of a patient speaking with the therapist about events and persons outside the consulting room are far less powerful, and therefore much more easily controlled or diluted or can be denied much more readily, than those taking place at the time they are observed and analysed: what psychoanalysts speak of as the 'here-and-now'.

Hypnosis can be used to bridge the gap between the 'here-and-now' level of affect and the 'there-and-then' content. It should be noted at this early point, however, that using hypnosis as an adjunct to analytic therapy certainly does not replace analysis of the transference and does not lessen the need for that stage of therapy to be performed with rigour. Using hypnotic techniques to intensify access to past experiences should not result in conducting the analysis outside the transference. Transference occurs quite independently of the use of hypnosis, and will need to be resolved before treatment is complete.

The use of techniques such as age regression or an affect bridge can make clear to the patient the link between his current experiences and the roots or archaic models and patterns on which they are based. Insight may, and quite commonly does, occur almost instantaneously as the patient finds himself precipitated from a recent event in which his maladaptive reactions were manifested to an experience much earlier in life which he had 'forgotten', or not recognized as related, or from which the affect had been lost or changed.

For example, the woman suffering from agoraphobia described in the previous chapter instantly recognized the relationship between her childhood memory of the thunderstorm and her current problems. This recognition was, and usually is, of the form: 'Yes, of course – that's what it means, that's where it comes from.' The proof of the pudding is, as always, in the eating: if significant experiential changes follow the achievement of insight, the relationship between the allegedly causal experience and current pathology or maladaptation is supported.

One could then argue that the treatment strategy concerned need be no more than recovery by the methods described in the preceding chapter of relevant and presumably causal traumata, leaving the rest to the patient's insight, drive to health, new satisfactions, liberation from stress, freedom from the distresses of symptoms, and so on. Very occasionally, this does seem enough. If the patient's personality is fundamentally intact without major damage or deficit, and equipped with adequate and flexible adaptive mechanisms; and if the patient is at the same time in a life-situation that is not severely depriving or damaging, then effective and lasting symptom relief may well be gained through only a very few sessions conducted on 'uncovering' lines.

If, however, the patient has undergone deprivation or privation (in terms of the basic needs of infancy and childhood), has experienced severe or repeated traumata and has therefore been severely damaged or developed rigid maladaptive personality structures, the effects of such uncovering will be at best very limited. More work will need to be done, and one will generally find that the contribution of explicitly hypnotic techniques is small compared with more conventional psychotherapeutic input. It is therefore important to emphasize the inadequacies and even dangers of hypnotherapeutic techniques in the hands of practitioners who lack a sound training and thorough experience in appropriate models of psychotherapeutic treatment. The results of failure to work through the uncovered material and what emerges as a consequence will range from short-lived improvement in the patient's overall state and symptoms to deterioration and even disintegration of his psychic adaptive strategies, and may at worst precipitate total disintegration of his personality structure.

Further, the recovery of repressed material is not uncommonly accompanied or followed by emotional discharge or 'abreaction' which, if not handled appropriately and effectively, can leave the patient in a rather worse state than before.

This is especially true if the relationship with the therapist has not developed enough trust and strength and if either the therapist or the patient, or both, has not already formulated a framework within which the uncovered material may be understood and handled. In such a case, the patient is likely to feel that he has been exposed by the therapist to excessively distressing or even damaging experiences which he cannot accommodate. He would experience this as an assault and a betrayal of the confidence placed in the therapist by the act of commitment to treatment. To be sure, if material the patient is as yet not ready to accommodate in consciousness is revealed by such exploratory work, amnesia is likely to follow ending of the trance, but he will remember very vividly the distressing affect he experienced in the trance and, rightly, blame the therapist for his premature exposure to such affect.

It is therefore mandatory for exploratory work of this kind in hypnosis to be undertaken only when a sufficiently detailed formulation of the nature and structure of the patient's condition has been made, and the basis for it therefore understood. Either the patient or the therapist should know in outline what they are looking for (i.e. what kind of event or memory), why the search is being made (i.e. how it fits into the framework of therapy), and how any relevant and powerful discoveries are to be handled.

The only safe exception to this general rule is with well-integrated patients who already have substantial insight and self-knowledge, whose own inner resources can be relied upon to cope with any new material, and who have such external resources in the form of close relationships that any stresses resulting from the hypnotic process can be contained and resolved. This is rare: if they had such strengths and resources they would be unlikely to be patients. Such a situation is more probable outside the clinical setting with a colleague in the context of teaching or training.

TREATMENT STRATEGIES

One of the simplest and perhaps most elegant treatment strategies in this field is the explicit use of the adult personality of the patient as the hidden but potentially active observer of the recovered material being experienced by the patient's earlier or child self. The observing adult self can be either passive or active: alert but essentially a bystander, or actively intervening in the process.

For example, a case reported by a participant at one of the Workshops run by the authors was that of a middle-aged woman who was referred because her increasing intolerance of closed doors had extended even to the door of the refrigerator. She found herself panicking whenever she came across a closed door of any kind. In the course of therapy, the therapist had satisfied himself that the origins of this lay much further back than the patient's account of the onset of the problem. Age regression led to an experience that had occurred (or was believed to have occurred) in early childhood, when the little girl had discovered the door of her room apparently locked when she tried to leave the room during the night. In hypnosis the patient re-lived this event with intense fear. While still in the regressed state she was asked to move forward in time rapidly so that the opening of the door by her mother followed quickly on the heels of this discovery, so that the patient could observe herself to be safely released from the room. The condensation of the two experiences, of being locked in and of being able to leave, into one highlighted the dissociation of these two events which had occurred in the patient's unconscious memory and effectively dissolved it.

Had the therapist known of the event and simply explained to the patient that since she was no longer in that childhood room she must have got out of it, it is unlikely that much symptom relief would have followed although, to be sure, pointing out such obvious facts can sometimes have quite major effects. Such an approach, utilizing the possibility of condensing subjective time and thereby re-associating dissociated experiences, can be employed when it appears that the event was traumatizing because of its isolation.

For example, a child admitted to hospital may experience quite severe reactions to separation from the mother including, of course, complex fantasies and feelings about the mother's reasons for and feelings about the separation. This memory, complete with its own affect, may be sufficiently traumatic in itself or occur within an affective framework that potentiates it (such as an ambivalent mother, severe anxiety in the mother, etc.) that it becomes detached from the continuum of the child's experience and eventually encapsulated and separate. It is therefore then unaffected by subsequent events, such as reunion with the mother.

One may argue that such experiences are very common and are not followed invariably by psychopathology in later years. However, it would perhaps be helpful to regard such experiences as potential and hidden booby-traps that can be activated by certain more or less specific stimuli: rather like the magnetic mines used by navies which are quite harmless until a sufficiently large steel object approaches within a specified distance, at which point they arm themselves and explode.

Many people have undergone such difficult experiences in childhood and nonetheless function perfectly well. Only when a later event of sufficient and related affective impact occurs does a problem arise. This could be, for example, discovery of a spouse's infidelity, marital separation, bereavement, or any other event that echoes or resonates with the original traumatic experience and in doing so stimulates the earlier affective response. This later re-stimulation (or, in the jargon, 're-cathexis') may result in the emergence of a symptom which in form will represent the significant aspects of the child's experience and will symbolically communicate the child ego-state.

For example, an individual who has reacted excessively to the discovery of infidelity on the part of their spouse may be understood to be re-enacting the reactions experienced in the circumstances of a separation in early childhood or infancy which was understood at the time as a betrayal. The patient might demonstrate the stages typical of such an experience (rage, resignation, apathy: the so-called anaclitic depression) and be unable, in his regressed and withdrawn state, to take effective and adaptive action. In such a case, recovering the repressed memory of the earlier experience and re-integrating it with the continuum of the patient's life and memory will have the effect of loosening its hold on present-day behaviour and affect.

The actual technique involved would be the use of an

affect bridge from the recent event, with age regression to the experience which formed its point of origin. The patient would be asked to report or describe what he is experiencing in the regressed state, and then might be asked to come forward in time, reporting periodically, until an event is identified which can be used to resolve the distressing aspects of the focal experience. Throughout this process the patient is observing what his child self experiences, so that in his adult self he gradually understands the event concerned in a way that the child, lacking both years and an objective perspective, was not able to do. In this way the patient can then integrate the newly recovered material into the context of his known personal history, family framework, etc.

Apart from guiding the patient's subjective movement through time, the therapist has nothing more to do until and unless any residual distress needs to be dissipated before articulating the association revealed by the episode, terminating the trance and then returning the patient to normal alertness. It may be necessary, especially if the distress is great, to emphasize to the 'child' the pertinent facts of the resolving event, for example, in the case of the patient with the fear of closed doors, pointing out that the door *was* opened by mother who then gave comfort and reassurance and who clearly had not disappeared for ever. In the case of the betrayed husband or wife, it might be necessary to articulate more specifically the subjective link made by the child between being separated from mother and the reaction experienced on the one hand, and the re-enactment implicit in the current (adult) situation.

More work, however, needs to be done without hypnosis to tease out and deal with the usually very mixed affect and attitudes following from the event which formed the genesis or template of the symptom or complaint. It is highly probable that much of this material will have been repressed or displaced, and therefore persists to the present day. In a case such as that of the betrayed spouse showing a re-enactment of anaclitic depression, the effects of the childhood experience will inevitably have affected family relationships, self-image and in particular the child's ability to trust. The re-discovery of the original trauma may indeed throw light upon some aspects of the present-day state of the patient and constitute an effective insight, but the ramifications of the effects of the original trauma may themselves have to be explored and resolved before he can come to terms with the present-day situation and resolve it.

In the technique described above, the patient's adult self is no more than an observer and does not intervene in the scene or scenes being reviewed. An alternative to this relatively passive role is sometimes of especial value: the patient's adult self is to enter the traumatizing scene and provide the child self with the succour and comfort it needs. This may sound a little theatrical and fanciful, but it can be a very powerful subjective experience.

A woman patient who had been sexually abused by her father at the age of six could recall the event clearly and related it at her first session with one of the authors. She related also that she had freed herself from his grasp and immediately told her mother, who had scolded her severely for telling 'filthy lies' and sent her to her room as a punishment. When she was subsequently molested both by a neighbour and again by her father, these events went unreported; her mother had said: 'Daddies don't do things like that!' and the patient could therefore not tell her mother anything of this kind without further punishment being inevitable.

In hypnosis she was asked to go back to the original scene, visualizing it on a television screen. As she related what was happening, when she reached the point of running upstairs to her bedroom after being berated by her mother, she was instructed to enter the scene in her adult self, meet her child self on the stairs and pick her up in her arms to comfort her. At this point, without explicit instructions, the screen faded away. Further suggestions were made concerning the child's need for explanation, acceptance and reassurance of her own innocence. The patient subsequently reported a massive change in her feelings concerning her responsibility for the event, the pervasive guilt she had felt, and in her perceptions of her mother.

In subsequent sessions, this patient's access to other memories showed a substantial widening, and a great deal of material that had previously been unknown emerged without the use of hypnosis. This included both events and affect, especially in relation to her mother, which was then worked through largely without the use of hypnosis, although the same technique was employed from time to time to clarify and resolve similar experiences.

The introduction of the patient's adult self into such scenes is a very effective device for managing the distressing affect of such experiences. However, it goes rather beyond this: the adult's *understanding* of the event can be given to the child self. This re-interpretation appears to re-structure more than the single event portrayed and 'resonates' to later experiences patterned on the formative experience. The patient actually appears to achieve insight into a much wider range of life-situations than the single event reviewed.

The use of age regression as a setting for therapeutic action extends somewhat further still in the form of 'ego state therapy' which, because of its considerable complexity, is discussed in the next chapter.

18

DISSOCIATION, MULTIPLE PERSONALITY AND EGO STATE THERAPY

DISSOCIATED STATES AND MULTIPLE PERSONALITY

The two standard texts on diagnosis, *The Diagnostic and Statistical Manual of Mental Disorders* (DSM-III, 1980) and the *International Classification of Diseases* (ICD, 1977) both include the diagnosis 'multiple personality'. The criteria given in the former are as precise for this as for any other psychiatric diagnosis, but the condition is by no means generally accepted as real by psychiatrists and psychologists in Britain. DSM-III (p.258) states that the condition is 'probably extremely rare' and the literature reporting such cases, with certain exceptions, supports this suggestion.

These exceptions include Bliss (1986) and Beahrs (1982). This is, of course, not surprising since these authors address themselves specifically to this condition. Bliss, for example, quotes evidence suggesting that as many as one in ten psychiatric admissions represent cases of 'multiple personality', although diagnosed otherwise. British reports are noted largely for their absence, although interest in the subject is growing.

The concept of a secondary personality co-existing with an individual's primary personality is nonetheless common. Expressions such as 'I wasn't myself last night' or 'I didn't feel myself' or 'That wasn't me at all' indicate an informal awareness of behaviour (both overt and covert or internal) which is out of character and inconsistent with the 'normal' personality of the individual. Under the stimulus of abnormally high stress, or the influence of alcohol or other drugs, atypical behaviour is common enough and may also include amnesia for a period of time.

The fact that claims of 'split' personality occur most commonly as the grounds for pleas of reduced responsibility for criminal acts (usually brutal) tends to arouse the suspicions of the general public, as well as of psychiatrists and psychologists, that the condition is a fiction created to enable offenders to escape due punishment rather than a genuine state in which the individual concerned was in plain fact 'not himself' for a time. Such suspicions have been confirmed on occasions when adequate investigation disclosed deliberate masquerading on the part of violent criminals.

A multiple rapist/murderer was made the subject of a television programme some years ago. He had convinced a number of eminent psychologists and psychiatrists of the reality of his dual personality: as a pillar of the community, good husband and father on the one hand and a deliberate and particularly sadistic monster on the other. The case was disclosed to be a calculated deception only through subtle experiment by Martin Orne. Up to that time, the man concerned had apparently responded very well to hypnotic induction and performed to the total satisfaction of those experts who had examined him, his alleged 'alternate personality' (in the now current terminology) emerging only in hypnosis, with the primary personality seemingly totally unaware of the alternate.

Dr Orne brilliantly showed up the flaws in the apparently genuine hypnotic state of the subject who, while seemingly hypnotized, did not demonstrate the characteristics of 'trance logic' and followed normal logic in his behaviour rather than the former. This exposure of pretence was subsequently confirmed by the discovery that the man concerned had an extensive library on hypnosis and psychopathology from which, fortunately, he had failed to gain as thorough a grasp of the characteristics of the hypnotic state and the syndrome of multiple personality as would have made his case flawless.

Fictionalized accounts such as those given in the film *The Three Faces of Eve* and in *Sybil* (Schreiber, 1974), although they purport to be accurate accounts of real cases, tend to be too dramatic to be taken as seriously as perhaps they might. Additionally, the suggestions made in *Sybil* that the patient was found to have sixteen alternate personalities (and cases reported in the more serious work by Bliss that are alleged to have possessed as many as fifty) reduces their credibility still further.

Instances such as the murderer mentioned above serve, of

course, to confirm public and professional scepticism. After all, what better defence against responsibility for one's own acts or omissions could there be than to say, with full conviction, 'It wasn't me!'

Rare though the condition may be and sceptical though most professionals are, it is recognized in some quarters (including, of course, the American Medical Association and the committee which gave birth to the ICD) and evidence is accumulating to suggest that it may occur more frequently than has been assumed until recently. The possibility that dissociated part-personalities may occur in a variety of conditions and forms should be borne in mind in making the diagnosis.

In a less obvious way, the concept of multiple personality occurs in psychological and psychiatric thinking in other forms. The fundamental model of personality underlying transactional analysis is an example. 'That is your Adult speaking' and 'That was your Child playing up' suggest explicitly that behaviour can be produced by a separate part of the personality which is in some way outside or separate from the central and conscious will of the individual. Fugal states in the absence of an epileptic process or alcohol intoxication, followed by amnesia, are most commonly interpreted as hysterical. They may equally well be regarded as instances of such extreme dissociation as to result in temporary dominance of the individual by a separate aspect of the personality, with detachment from the control (or even consciousness) of the central personality.

Both Beahrs and Bliss suggest that hypnosis should be employed to induce the dissociation of the central personality which must take place before the alternate personality (or personalities) can emerge and be engaged in conversation. For a diagnosis of multiple personality to be made with confidence, more evidence than that arising from such interviews is needed. In particular, there must be substantial evidence that the patient has a history of episodes in which he acted under a different name and in ways that would be inconsistent with his normal personality; and in addition that he is amnesic (in his primary personality) for those episodes. As a general rule, the use of hypnosis to display the alternate personality is appropriate only to confirm the condition which has already been indicated by the history of the patient.

Bliss suggests that such behaviour, together with a wide range of apparently psychotic states, should be regarded as the product of self-induced hypnotic states. He draws a parallel between hypnotically induced dissociation, dissociated behaviour and amnesias on the one hand and a wide range of psychiatric disorders on the other, and suggests that treatment based on this hypothesis is more successful in relieving disorders of behaviour and affect than other forms of therapy.

Beahrs proposes a model of personality which depends upon the concept of 'co-consciousness' (see chapter 15). This embodies the idea that consciousness proceeds on a number of essentially separate 'lines'. The degree of separation varies both consistently (some lines are consistently more dissociated or separated than others) and in the course of time (a given line may become more dissociated for a time or less so at another time).

Central to this model is the concept of a central line of consciousness – the 'directorate' – which as a general rule is the focus of the individual's conscious awareness and directs his overt behaviour. In many ways this is close to the classical Freudian concept of the 'ego'. Beahrs suggests that some at least of these co-existing 'lines of consciousness' possess the characteristics of an integrated or whole personality, cognition, conation, affect, memory, and self-awareness, and that these characteristics have become separated from the central consciousness in that the content of this separate 'line' (or personality) is inaccessible to the ego, while at the same time the nature and content of the latter *is* accessible to the alternate personality. An important consideration is whether the separate personality possesses the characteristics of an independent personality: cognition, conation, affect, memory, and a sense of its discrete identity separate and distinct from the primary personality.

Although Beahrs and Bliss differ in their explanations of the mechanisms involved, the phenomena they describe are similar and may be identical. (They also resemble more commonly accepted concepts of repression and hysterical dissociation.) It is generally considered that these dissociated conditions arise as the result of traumata in childhood, commonly in the form of severe sexual abuse, and that the dissociation serves an adaptive function in protecting the individual from the memory and associations of the traumatizing experiences. The essential point, however, lies in the idea that such repressed or dissociated aspects of the primary personality constitute an independently functioning personality within the same body. The orthodox concepts of repression and of hysterical dissociation do not, however, imply so wholesale a process as to result in a more or less complete personality (possessing the characteristics noted above) being hived off into an internal limbo where it continues to exist and from which at specific moments it may emerge into overt activity through displacing the central personality.

The incidence of genuine cases of this kind remains unknown and, as indicated by DSM-III, is probably very small. It seems probable, however, that patients who demonstrate less extreme dissociation are rather more numerous, and that secondary personalities which are less integrated and less complete than in a full-blown 'multiple' are seen, although not always recognized. It is suggested, however, that the concept of such dissociated personalities can be usefully applied in treatment through hypnosis, in cases where dissociation and repression are prominently present but there are no alternate personalities.

▆▆▆▆▆▆▆ EGO STATE THERAPY

Aside from debate on the reality of such states, the question persists as to whether the model is of therapeutic value. That is to say, if a patient is regarded and treated *as though* he were a case of multiple personality, can he be treated more efficiently or more effectively than through the application of another model? Without committing themselves to the fervent advocacy of this approach shown by some, the present authors would give a cautious and qualified assent. Dissociation enables some individuals to tolerate and survive traumata that might otherwise damage them even more. It is possible to employ the characteristics of dissociative processes within therapy to enable some patients to 'handle' experiences that otherwise would be inaccessible or unmanageable. That is to say, dissociative processes can help patients to cope with specific experiences with which other strategies have proved unsuccessful and can be used adaptively in therapy even though they generally serve (in the long run) maladaptively when mobilized to cope with intolerable stress outside the control and guidance of therapy.

A case report may clarify this concept. A woman aged twenty was referred by her general practitioner because of her occasionally rather strange behaviour (this case is reported in Karle, 1984). The referral letter was curiously vague about the nature of this behaviour, but referred to the girl having made an unmistakable 'pass' at the doctor. The first interview was conducted with some difficulty since the patient was quite severely deaf and consistently refused to use the hearing aid prescribed for her. Once she agreed to wear headphones from an amplifier, conversation became somewhat easier. She expressed anxiety about some strange experiences: chiefly, finding in her wardrobe various garments which she did not recognize and which she felt she would not wear under any circumstances: transparent blouses, skirts slit to the top of the thigh and the like. With every appearance of veracity, she denied that she ever roamed around the town at night dressed in such garments, as her GP had reported. She gave a somewhat odd impression of innocence and naivety, expressing interest only in classical literature and quiet home pursuits, seeming content to spend her life quietly vegetating in a genteel way.

With some reluctance, she agreed to the use of hypnosis. When a satisfactory trance had been achieved, the therapist asked if there were things in her life of which she was normally unaware but which were responsible for the unexplained events that had just been discussed. While apparently remaining in trance, the patient began to speak in a quite different way: her voice changed from its demure and quiet tone to a somewhat raucous and coarse one. Her vocabulary changed equally, and the therapist gained the impression that the rather fey and unreal girl with whom he had just been talking had been replaced by a vivid and vigorous individual of totally different personality. Incidentally, and interestingly, this 'personality' did not require the use of an amplifier to hear the therapist's voice.

One might regard such a case explicitly as an instance of dual personality, although a formulation of dissociation and repression of sexual and aggressive impulses would serve just as successfully to explain the state of this patient. As far as she herself was concerned, the experience she had in this interview was of another and previously unknown personality existing apparently within herself, but with no contact or communication with herself. She was frightened by feeling her body seemingly taken over by another person and horrified by the thoughts, feelings and impulses she had heard expressed through her own mouth.

The secondary or alternate personality clearly represented and embodied the unacceptable aspects of the self. It is arguable whether such a personification of unacceptable cognitive, affective and conative characteristics is significantly different from 'simple' repression or whether its assumed character, of an independent but co-existing identity, should be accepted as a reality serving the same ego-protecting functions. This question, however, though intrinsically interesting and important theoretically, is less relevant in the present context than the question of whether a formulation of multiple personality is more or less useful than any other in planning treatment. This question is easier to answer, since it depends upon empirical evidence.

With this patient the manifestation of an alternate personality was ostensibly accepted by the therapist: 'she' was interviewed exactly as she would have been had the patient presented with this personality, but with the added dimension of the therapist's awareness of the observing primary personality. In a sense the interview had to be conducted rather like family therapy, where a therapist, when addressing one member of the group, frames his comments or questions in the light of the fact that he is being heard by the whole group and not simply that member whom he is currently addressing.

A prominent feature of the secondary personality was her intense and hostile contempt for the primary, whom she regarded as a feeble nonentity, a 'wimp', who had to be 'got out of the way' as a preliminary to taking over full and uninterrupted control of the shared body. Some six or seven interviews were conducted with the secondary personality whilst the primary 'listened in', the content of these sessions then being discussed with the primary. The latter reported at each interview finding herself in increasing contact with the secondary in the time between her appointments with the therapist. The primary was able to form a co-operative relationship with the alternate which enabled the primary personality, especially in the light of the therapist's interpretations and the influence of his uncritical acceptance, to perceive positive characteristics in the alternate.

This appeared to facilitate a process whereby the primary

gradually came to regard the alternate less and less as an alien personality and to recognize her progressively as an essential part of herself. The highly polarized extremes personalized in this way gradually integrated. They began to communicate with each other and in so doing, each became able to moderate her unipolarity until the differences between them became insignificant and the 'split' simply faded away.

Such a strategy, whether regarded as a device, as a metaphor, or as a realistic recognition of an existential reality, can be applied even where the split is not reified as it was by this patient. For example, therapists of several schools will use the formula of 'the child inside' or of 'incorporated parent figures', while transactional analysts unhesitatingly refer to re-cathected ego states in one of the three categories of Parent, Adult and Child. The Gestalt technique known as 'the empty chair' or that of 'introducing the child', in which the relevant part-personalities are to be imagined as occupying another chair and then engaged in dialogue by the patient, is also similar. The dissociated aspects of the personality are personalized and then engaged by the patient through his taking alternate chairs to 'speak' for each part of himself. He then endeavours, with the guidance of the therapist, to resolve the dissociation and its determining affect.

Identifying the dissociated parts of the personality *as* another person (or persons) allows a colloquy to take place through which the individual may allow himself to tolerate, then accept, and finally to integrate the experiences, affect, drives and so on that had been dissociated.

Dissociation, whether iatrogenic or spontaneous and perhaps contemporaneous with the pathogenic processes underlying the presenting problems, can be utilized powerfully in this way. By treating the patient's supposed alternates as separate, one can communicate with them explicitly and guide the patient into resolving the dissociation: first by getting to know and befriend the alternate, then by providing the cognitive and affective input the alternate appears to require, and finally by absorbing the alternate(s) into the primary. Since dissociated personalities are notoriously difficult to handle, this technique offers a useful alternative approach to longer-term and often less successful means of resolving the 'split'.

An example of this approach will be found reported in

detail by one of the authors (Karle, 1986; 1987b) in which a woman of forty-three with a life-long history of depression following extensive sexual abuse in childhood was treated in part through this approach. Her early experiences included the first incident of sexual abuse by her father (see chapters 15 and 17 for other aspects of the treatment of this patient). She had immediately told her mother, who had scolded her for telling filthy lies, saying: 'Daddies don't do things like that', and sent her to her room as a punishment. This betrayal by her mother seemed markedly more traumatic to the patient than the sexual interference by her father, which although distressing and disturbing did not carry the terrifying implications of abandonment by her primary protector (her mother) or denial of the reality of her experience and feelings about it.

In the course of working on this first experience, the therapist used the expression 'Little Mary' to identify that part of the adult patient which had become fixated developmentally at the time of this event. The therapist interpreted that the 'child' part ('Little Mary') of the patient was still trying to convince her mother of her innocence, and to convey to her mother her need for protection and for comfort (this was patent in the transference). The patient took this literally, and began to speak of 'Little Mary' as an independent entity.

Before long she reported periods of amnesia in which, as she discovered from members of her family, she behaved abnormally and strangely. She also began to bring to her interviews pages of childishly scrawled messages about Mummy. It was agreed to give 'Little Mary' an opportunity to talk with the therapist, and several such interviews were held (using hypnosis to facilitate emergence of the supposed alternate personality) in which the patient gave a very convincing performance as a six-year-old child. The patient then agreed to attempt the re-integration of the two parts of herself: child and adult.

She was asked to return in hypnosis to the time her father had molested her sexually, and simultaneously to observe the scene as her adult self. The scene was played out without the therapist intervening, up to the point at which the child was ordered to her room. At this moment, the therapist asked the patient to enter the scene in her adult self, meet her child self on the stairs, pick her up, comfort and reassure her, and generally to act as she would towards any child in such a situation. She was to continue in this fashion until the child was wholly reassured and at peace, and then to return to the present day.

The patient reported successful performance of the task in terms of the child's restored equanimity. Perhaps more important was the feeling that she could recognize in her adult self that her child self (or herself at the time of the event) was in fact innocent: her belief that she herself was 'filthy' had been substantially modified in the course of this session.

The patient was very taken with this formulation, and before long quite spontaneously produced a third 'personality', which appeared to date from a major trauma at age twenty and 'took over' from time to time. A number of interviews were held in which 'Big Mary' was allowed to emerge. She expressed intense feelings of depression and strong suicidal wishes. 'Big Mary' (as distinct from the adult 'Mrs X') demanded attention, both at interviews and outside, and 'acted out' in various ways, on one occasion leading to emergency admission to a psychiatric unit where she gave her maiden name (she did not marry until she was twenty-three), totally disorientated and believing the date to be 1963 instead of 1986. Again re-integration was suggested, and was achieved in a single somewhat protracted interview. Within a few days a fourth 'personality' emerged, dating from the age of ten. This proved to be the final one: once this part-person had been comforted, reassured and re-integrated, the patient began to accept full responsibility for herself and to recognize her internal integrity.

This patient did not fulfil the criteria for a diagnosis of multiple personality in that the 'alternates' emerged only during treatment and had not previously made themselves manifest. There was considerable evidence to suggest that many of the earlier 'breakdowns' the patient had experienced, and for which she had been repeatedly hospitalized, might have been due to the emergence of alternate personalities, but this proved impossible to substantiate. Furthermore, the link between the use of the concept of the 'child inside' in therapy and the emergence of the first alternate seemed too close to be other than causal. Nonetheless, the use of the 'alternate personalities' as a device enabling this patient to deal with her contradictory feelings about, and to bring the affective character of the relevant ego states into open confrontation with, her adult ego proved effective.

Ego state therapy can be regarded in three distinct but related forms. On the one hand Edelstien (1981, pp. 70ff.), following the work of John and Helen Watkins (1979) presents this approach in the therapy of the dissociated part-personality, as though the part-personality or alternate were an individual patient. Alternatively we may construe it as confrontation between the part-personality or re-cathected ego state and the adult or contemporary personality of the patient, and attempt a guided *rapprochement* between them as in the cases quoted above.

A third formulation may also be of interest. The concept of the 'hidden observer' has been current in theories of hypnosis for some years. With this approach, the therapist suggests that the traumatic events dating from an earlier time in the patient's life, re-evoked while he is in hypnosis, are experienced at one level by the patient's regressed ego in a direct and participatory way. At another level, the dissociated adult ego of the patient remains as it were *outside* the hypnotic state and observes the events in a detached and objective way. This 'hidden observer' is not only aware of what the patient is doing and experiencing but is, equally, observing the actions and words of the therapist. Even when the patient appears to be wholly involved in whatever is going on in the session, and may be displaying intense affective reactions, the 'observer' remains unaffected and dispassionate.

In this way, it is hoped that the reality-testing functions and greater maturity of the adult patient may be applied to the event or events that were unmanageable, intolerably distressing and disruptive to the patient when they occurred (and therefore led to dissociation and repression), thereby creating a re-interpretation which is less ego-dystonic.

It must be borne in mind that the 'hidden observer' observes more than the events within the patient himself: it is also intensely aware of the therapist and his behaviour. Casual actions that the therapist may believe to have been unnoticed by the patient (yawning, scratching, etc.) will often be remarked upon by him after such a session and are likely to have been perceived as indicating a lack of concern, consideration or sympathy on the part of the therapist.

This concept is by no means limited to the theories and practices of hypnotherapy. Most psychotherapists are aware that what they say and do, their facial expressions, body language and so on are all being monitored in great detail by the patient, whatever else may be happening in the interview. Most therapists too are vividly aware that their comments and interpretations are not addressed solely to the conscious part of the presenting person but also to aspects or part-selves of the patient often not directly accessible and not within the consciousness of the patient himself. That is to say, in offering a comment or interpretation one is likely to bear in mind that what one says is heard not only by the patient's overt personality but also by regressed or fixated part-selves that may never emerge overtly but are nonetheless perceptible in disguised and subtle aspects of his total behaviour.

These part-selves may be in the form of immature patterns of cognition or of archaic affective reactions, or may be seen as introjected parent-figures and other incorporated significant figures or past foci of earlier identifications. The process we identify as ego state therapy proceeds by making the dialogue between therapist and part-self overt and explicit, even though this may run the risk of inducing an iatrogenic multiple personality, as occurred in the case described above.

Edelstien suggests that these part-personalities become established when the individual is exposed to intolerable stress, and serve to protect him from the stressful experience by isolating the memory (in the form of an entire ego state) outside the consciousness of the central personality. This explanation is generally accepted in different terminology as the basis for the establishment of dissociated states, including the syndrome of multiple personality.

In addition, however, he suggests that the part-self 'believes' it has a continuing current function which was, of course, its reason for emergence or creation: to protect the central self from further trauma. This function will, however, have become obsolete as the individual developed. Edelstien's advocacy of ego state therapy therefore focuses on using direct dialogue with the dissociated part-self to create awareness in that part-self of the change in the patient's life circumstances which have made the protective function out-of-date, inappropriate or unrealistic (even, as is often the case, counter-productive). He endeavours to enlist the goodwill of the part-self in such a way as to divert the functioning of that self into adaptive and constructive channels.

This process is mediated by asking the hypnotized patient to permit the part-self to come into the open and communicate directly with the therapist. The procedure does not commit either patient or therapist to the concept of multiple personality. There is, however, a strong possibility that a patient with an hysterical personality structure (itself highly probable in a patient with whom this procedure is workable) will pick up obvious clues in the language of this method and produce the syndrome subsequently.

An alternative approach that uses the patient's contemporary personality to communicate with the dissociated part-self has already been discussed in its various forms and need not, therefore, be elaborated at length. The patient is asked to go back to the period in his life from which the problem dates, possibly from a significantly traumatic event. This is identified through what is known about the aetiology of the patient's condition, the age from which it is considered the underlying problem was originated (as for example through a major trauma), or by an affect bridge (see chapter 16). The event or experience which is believed to be formative is identified and entered, and the adult self of the patient is then asked to intervene in such a way as to reduce the distress, anxiety, guilt, or other negative affect experienced by the child-self.

An unusual and elegant form of this approach was demonstrated by Professor Graham Burrows (University of Melbourne) at a Workshop in 1982. The subject was asked, while in hypnosis, if there were problems in her everyday life that interfered with her enjoyment and success. She signalled that this was so. She was then asked if these problems stemmed from events earlier in her life, to which she again signalled assent. In reply to further questions, she signalled that she did not wish to discuss either the problems or their origins. She was then asked to allow herself to go back to one of the events from which her current problems had developed.

The subject's posture gradually became more and more tense and her facial expression showed signs of distress. She was then instructed to use all her adult knowledge, understanding, wisdom and warmth to help her child self to understand the event she was experiencing and to comfort and reassure this child self. She was then asked to signal when her child self had been wholly reassured and comforted, and was at peace. After a short while, the subject's posture and facial expression gradually relaxed until at last a pleased and relaxed smile appeared. She was then brought out of hypnosis. She remained unwilling to discuss the content of what she had experienced but expressed confidence in her feeling that she had now resolved and freed herself from a problem that had indeed been a source of some difficulty to her until then.

Such procedures may seem more than a little theatrical, even tinged with the shade of Mesmer, to therapists reared in more traditional and orthodox models of treatment. It is interesting to note, however, that a contemporary and follower of Mesmer, Charles d'Eslon, physician to the King of France, wrote in 1780: 'If the medicine of imagination is best, why should we not practise the medicine of imagination?' This sentiment should not be too readily dismissed: a procedure or technique is of value to the degree to which it works. Further, few of us would hold that the formulations of whatever theoretical school holds our allegiance are literally true, but rather that those formulations and models are of the nature of allegories.

In the final analysis, or if not there, then in the penultimate, mental processes will be understood in electrical and chemical terms and not in terms of ego, id, and superego, drives, repressions, defences and the like. Psychoanalytic terms and models are at a substantial remove from the fundamental reality of intrapsychic processes and have the character of symbolic representations rather than of literality. The concepts and processes of ego state therapy seem no more bizarre today than did free association to our colleagues of four or five decades ago, or any of the more recently developed theories, models, and techniques such as Gestalt therapy or body work do to their contemporary critics.

For clinicians and practitioners whose business it is to alleviate human distress, the important question is whether this model, that of multiple part-selves and their treatment through ego state therapy, is pragmatically justified and whether it can lead to further and more intimate understanding of personality, and especially to more effective therapy.

Neither question can be answered confidently in the present state of knowledge, because hitherto the available data is composed only of individual and anecdotal case studies. Nonetheless, the techniques concerned appear to result in significant adaptive change in those patients whose cases have been reported.

The concepts inherent in such a model of therapy can be translated into other terms. We may regard the part-selves and their subjective universe as reified or personified representations of basic ego-defences. Utilizing these personifications as protagonists in an internal dialogue, or in a dialogue with the therapist, enables the patient's 'central self'/ego to observe and sometimes participate in a dramatization of its own defensive processes, bringing into awareness, through the medium of this metaphorical representation aspects of the personality normally outside the reach of consciousness.

This opens the way to some degree of direct restructuring of the personality, even though this is performed in symbolic operations. The archaic, fixated and immature defences are exposed to the ego and its reality-testing in their personalized forms. The unmet needs which they represent or the traumata from which they developed are symbolically dealt with: the unmet needs are fulfilled, the traumata recognized as being past and over, the related affects discharged, and the psychic energy bound up in the now obsolete defences is released.

We would argue that the differences between this approach or methodology and more orthodox and traditional techniques and procedures lie more in the language and symbolism employed both in the therapeutic process and to describe it than in their fundamental characteristics. Furthermore, what evidence has been obtained suggests that ego state therapy operates more quickly than more orthodox techniques without losing anything in profundity. It is true that such approaches can be used only with some patients, but this is true of all therapeutic methods.

What we need now (although no more in this area than in any other in the field of analytic theory and therapy) is further research, especially into long-term structural changes in patients treated by this method.

19

OTHER USES OF HYPNOSIS

The overall purpose of this book is to give the newcomer to formal uses of hypnosis a working guide to the basic techniques he will find most useful in the treatment of the more common disorders. At the same time it is not intended to be a substitute for *in vivo* training, and anyone intending to use these techniques *de novo* is urged to familiarize himself with the practice of such methods by undertaking further training in workshops or other settings rather than applying them immediately with patients. In the light of this intention to provide a beginner's guide, we have not attempted to include the full range of conditions in which hypnosis may be helpful. We have not attempted either to include all currently practised methods, but limited ourselves to those likely to be of the most general use. Reference should be made to the books listed in the bibliography for information on conditions and problems not dealt with here.

However, a number of conditions and problems may present clinically, in addition to those presented and discussed in earlier chapters in detail, and some brief notes on these may be helpful here, together with description of some non-therapeutic methods or applications (in the strictest interpretation of that term) of hypnosis. These latter include the use of hypnotic methods in the management of exam nerves, stage fright and similar states, and in forensic work.

ADDICTIONS

It has been reported that hypnosis is a useful ancillary treatment in the management of withdrawal from addictive substances (Burrows and Dennerstein, 1980; Crasilneck and Hall, 1985;

Hartland, 1971; Kroger, 1977). The ability which can be developed through self-hypnosis to control both physical and affective reactions points to an obvious application in programmes whereby addicted persons are freed from dependency on drugs of any kind. It seems unlikely, however, that hypnotic techniques alone would be effective in these cases except for the most whole-mindedly motivated patient.

Control of the behavioural aspects of drug abuse, in combination with control of the affective aspects of the dependency, can be approached in some cases with considerable success. The programme described in some detail in chapter 7 for assisting people to stop smoking can be applied very satisfactorily to excessive and habitual drinking, as long as the patient is adequately motivated. The authors have used this approach with habitual drinkers, but have no experience of applying such techniques with other forms of substance abuse. It is improbable that severe or long-standing cases of drug dependency will respond satisfactorily to this approach.

There are two major difficulties with this group of patients. The first is that a varying degree of cognitive, intellectual and cerebral loss or damage results from the prolonged use of some toxic substances (including, of course, alcohol) and these may seriously affect the ability of the individual to apply these methods, and indeed his willingness to do so. Secondly, the personality changes that follow substance abuse in some cases make consistent and committed practice of the necessary exercises problematic.

Patients who have abused intoxicating substances heavily and over a long period have commonly lost and can be unable to generate sufficient consistent motivation, and if appreciable cognitive losses have also resulted their concentration and application are likely to be inadequate to the task of effectively practising self-hypnotic exercises. At the same time, hypnotic processes may be very helpful as an adjunct to other forms of treatment to reduce distress, discomfort and other unpleasant aspects of arousal as well as increasing self-esteem and self-confidence.

PSYCHOSEXUAL DISORDERS

Anxiety is prominent in all cases of psychosexual dysfunctions. 'Performance anxiety' in the case of psychogenic impotence, and unconscious conflicts concerning sexual activity in vaginismus, are among the clearest manifestations of anxiety as a contributory if not major causal factor in these dysfunctions. Reduction of anxiety will be of value in connection with any treatment programme.

In addition, creating associations between the confident and pleasant feelings of the 'private place' and pictured memories of successful and satisfying sexual activity in the past (perhaps using age regression) or images concerning successful sexual activity in the future can be used with considerable confidence in less severe cases.

One must, however, be aware of the role of underlying neurotic processes in establishing sexual dysfunctions. Treatment methods which are essentially behavioural, such as that briefly sketched above, will founder if continuing unconscious conflicts and anxieties are left untouched. Once again we re-iterate the importance of careful diagnosis. One of the authors was consulted by a couple whose marriage of ten years' standing had remained unconsummated. They had resigned themselves to this state of affairs, and had applied to adopt a child. The adoption agency had referred them for assessment, since it was felt that the asexual character of their relationship could present problems for them as parents. They had never sought help for their inability to complete the sexual act, which apparently stemmed from the husband's detumescence at the moment they attempted intromission.

They accepted the offer of treatment, which was made independently of the question of their suitability as adopters, and responded well. The fourth interview was attended by the husband alone: his wife had been admitted to a psychiatric unit a few days earlier, on the day after they had successfully consummated their marriage. The fact that the failure to consummate had been attributed to the husband's impotence had directed attention away from the wife's intense but heavily concealed sexual anxieties. Intra-psychic conflicts may sometimes be so severe that in-depth psychotherapy is required to resolve the symptoms (Sharff, 1982).

Where the dysfunction is secondary (consequent upon some traumatic event occurring after the patient had already experienced satisfactory sexual activity for some time), sexual arousal and its physical concomitants may be obtained in hypnosis through either age regression or fantasy, with substantial benefits to the patient's confidence and optimism.

In all cases presenting as sexual dysfunction, the relationship between the patient and his or her sexual partner must be carefully investigated. Such a problem is never located exclusively in one member of the sexual pair, and treatment of one partner only cannot be more than partially successful.

HABIT SPASMS

Tics are notoriously resistant to most forms of therapy. It is common for such habitual spasms to increase in frequency and intensity with increased anxiety, so that anxiety reduction by hypnotic methods can be helpful in reducing the symptoms, although rarely sufficient to extinguish them altogether.

More success is obtained generally with those spasms which can be reproduced voluntarily. In such cases, the techniques of 'paradoxical intention' and 'mass practice' can be enhanced through carrying out the exercises with the patient in hypnosis and with additional ego-strengthening and post-hypnotic suggestions of improvement.

The technique known as paradoxical intention is carried out by asking the patient to reproduce the tic or other action to order. At intervals in the course of the session a signal, agreed upon in advance with the patient, is given by the therapist, the patient then immediately producing the symptom. As the exercise proceeds, the patient finds it progressively more difficult to produce the action to order, and as the programme proceeds, the involuntarily produced symptoms decline in intensity and frequency (see Rimm and Masters, 1979, for a detailed exposition of this and related techniques). This programme works well with the compulsive 'whooping' which sometimes continues after a child has suffered from whooping cough long after the infection has subsided.

Mass practice, as its title implies, consists of many

repetitions of the symptom at short intervals through the session, and at specific and repeated times between sessions. The effect is closely similar to that of paradoxical intention in that the patient finds it increasingly difficult to produce the symptom in the course of the exercise, with similar reduction in intensity and frequency outside the treatment sessions.

Tics which cannot be reproduced voluntarily, such as those affecting isolated muscle groups not identified by limb or other gross movements, are highly resistant, although, as suggested above, reduction of overall tension can be helpful. This applies equally to blepharospasm and to Gilles de la Tourette syndrome, and work is usually more usefully put into improving the patient's self-esteem than directly into modifying the tic.

Treatment through displacement can sometimes, however, be moderately successful in such conditions. This is done by asking the patient to identify a muscle spasm that would be discreet (that is, not observable or identifiable by onlookers) and would not interfere with necessary functions such as, for example, clenching the fingers of one hand. The patient is instructed to imagine the nerve impulses that generate the tic migrating into the left hand, and simultaneously to clench this hand as soon as he feels his habitual spasm beginning. Once this is well established and the involuntary spasm no longer occurs in its original site, the new form of the symptom can be tackled. It may, however, be wiser to leave the new version of the symptom intact if this is acceptable to the patient, since there is a distinct possibility that extinguishing the displaced spasm may result in a reappearance of the original symptom.

Some patients with Gilles de la Tourette syndrome spontaneously develop such displacement techniques, and try to convert their involuntary movements into deliberate and apparently appropriate behaviour. For example, involuntary movements of the legs may be elaborated into adjustments of stance, or similar movements of the arms extended into such actions as attending to the patient's hair.

In all cases, exploratory work, whether done by orthodox interviewing or by uncovering techniques in hypnosis, is strongly advocated since both the accompanying tensions and the symptom itself will have psychological significance (either primary or secondary) and may well be associated with secondary gains.

Clearly, if the problem is largely psychogenic it is important that this be revealed and resolved if treatment is to be effective.

GENERAL USES

The employment of hypnotic methods in the reduction of anxiety and tension and to the amelioration of mood and self-esteem has been emphasized throughout this book. Most people can gain benefit from relaxation and tension discharge and many seek these benefits through a variety of activities, from meditation and yoga to games, sports, gardening and playing musical instruments. All such activities are beneficial in a variety of ways and have an important function in individuals' lives, but hypnosis offers a technique that can be used at particular times of stress or when other activities cannot be used.

For example, the business executive can take a few moments to free himself of accumulating inner stresses while seated at his desk, in a train or in a car, and so prevent the progressive building up of stresses throughout the day or week. As we tell our patients, five minutes in hypnosis is as good as an hour's sleep. Such brief periods of self-hypnosis used several times in a day contribute not only to a more relaxed mood but to improvement in poise, confidence and self-esteem, and especially to feelings of mastery and control. It is perhaps most especially in this latter that self-hypnosis can be helpful in everyday life: anxiety is often itself a result of the individual feeling that he is 'losing his grip' or becoming overwhelmed by the situation which provokes the stress.

The experience mediated by hypnosis of exerting direct control over one's own emotional state, level of tension and ability to concentrate increases the experience of being in control of one's life, and so facilitates clarity and purposefulness in work. The increased awareness of bodily processes and sensations and the acquisition of some degree of control over normally autonomous functions restores the individual's experience of and belief in his own autonomy, his ability to 'keep hold of the reins' and to retain control. It may also allow him to become aware of hitherto unrecognized effects in aspects of his lifestyle which are deleterious to him, both physically and psychologically. This increase in awareness may itself, of course, enable him to make changes so that his life becomes more supportive of healthy functioning and less likely to produce dis-ease.

PERFORMANCE PROBLEMS

Stage fright and exam nerves are common problems which interfere with both enjoyment of life and fulfilment of potential. Performing artists commonly employ rituals of some kind before appearing on stage, ranging from superstitious practices to meditational techniques. Sportsmen commonly focus their attention and concentration before beginning play by some ritual of their own devising, and teams of sportsmen may be prepared for the fray by exhortation and rousing encouragement from their trainer or by cheerleaders.

Anticipatory anxiety is readily assuaged by preparatory exercises along the lines of desensitization (described in chapter 9), which need not reduce the degree of arousal requisite for optimal performance. The suggestions made in association with desensitizing exercises in hypnosis should indeed include suggestions of optimal arousal: the subject is encouraged to be well aroused and aware that this is beneficial to his performance, but not anxious or agitated.

Desensitization works extremely well for exam nerves, and this preparatory work can be enhanced by training the subject to enter trance very quickly and briefly and in a very discreet way, which he can then use at the beginning of an examination to clear any residual anxiety from his mind and enable him to feel poised and collected. This can be done by suggesting, while the individual is in hypnosis, that he will be able to enter trance very quickly and briefly any time it would be helpful to him by performing a simple ritual: he is to place a hand momentarily over his eyes, close them, think of a specified 'key word', and thereby instantly go into a light trance. As soon as he feels calm and collected he can open his eyes, remove his hand and become instantaneously fully alert. At the end of the session, the subject is then asked to go through this routine to familiarize himself with the process and to find that he can follow it successfully.

Exercises can also be added to facilitate recall of learned material. For example, the subject can be asked to picture himself in a library representing all the work he has learned in preparation for the examination he is to take. He can pick up any book and read what he needs, since he has free access to all that is in the library. Suggestions linking this image specifically with his own stored memories are encouraging and reassuring to many examination candidates, who may even use the image in a brief period of self-hypnosis while actually sitting an examination to facilitate access to a momentarily 'blocked' item of information.

Script 19.1

[The patient is in hypnosis, and ego-strengthening and any other procedures that are considered necessary have been carried out.]

Let a picture form in your mind of a room in which the walls are lined with bookshelves. It may be a library, or perhaps your own room, or a room such as you would like to have. All around you are books and papers which you know well, the books and papers you have used in your studies. You are sitting in the room, relaxed and comfortable. The room represents your mind, your memory, all that you have learned. All the information and understanding you have acquired during the course you have taken and on which you are shortly going to be examined is stored in the books and files around you. All the information you need is stored here, and you can refer to it without difficulty. It is all there: all you have to do is look it up. Now get up from where you are sitting, take out one of the books or pick up a file and just leaf through it, reading a passage here and there, and notice just how familiar to you is what you are reading.

When you are in the examination room and writing an essay, any time you are stuck for an item of information, just close your eyes, picture that library and yourself looking up what you need to quote, browsing through one or other of the books and papers there until you find what you need. You will find what you need coming into your mind. Then open your eyes again and continue with your work. All that you have studied and learned is stored there and you will be able to let yourself browse in the library of your memory and find what you need.

Another image that has frequently proved its value is that of a jigsaw puzzle. The patient is asked to picture all he knows on the subject of an examination question represented by such a puzzle: the pieces are randomly scattered before him. All he needs for his answer is present and simply needs arranging. By beginning with one or two simple pieces he can see the subject of the puzzle taking shape, and then return out of the trance and translate the puzzle into words.

Hypnosis can be of considerable assistance in focusing attention and eliminating distracting anxiety before sporting or artistic performances. It is now not unusual for sports and athletic teams to be accompanied by their own psychologists, whose function it is to detect and deal with any personal anxieties and weaknesses which may interfere with performance. Hypnosis can be of considerable help in reducing any difficulties of this kind by dissipating inappropriate tensions and eliminating distractions. In addition confidence-building through ego-strengthening can be helpful to a performer.

FORENSIC USES

This is at present a somewhat controversial area in the application of hypnosis. Enhancement of recall – 'hypermnesia' – through age regression to an event that is under investigation in the course of police enquiries has been shown from time to time to be of considerable value in obtaining more detailed information than the witness is able to provide spontaneously. However, detailed questioning in a regressed state in hypnosis tends to carry implicit suggestions. For example, if the subject is repeatedly asked whether he heard a certain noise or saw a specific object, he will tend to perceive a suggestion in the repetition of the question and progressively include the suggested object or sound in his 'memory' of the event. This is the case even when the questioning is performed in as objective and non-directive way as may be possible. The mere fact of asking questions always implies suggestion, and it must be remembered that hypnotized subjects are more suggestible than the same individuals at other times.

In addition, few questioners, especially when an enquiry into criminal matters is in hand, can be totally objective and non-directive. For this reason, some States in the USA have decreed that witnesses who have been questioned in hypnosis cannot subsequently give evidence in court. In assisting police enquiries, hypnosis can be helpful on occasion. We would ourselves advocate that any such interviews should be recorded on videotape and the recording carefully scrutinized to clarify any embedded suggestions and their outcome, such scrutiny being generally more accurate (as well as repeatable) than 'live' observation. Clearly, however, there is considerable, and appropriate, concern about the use to which evidence gained under hypnosis is put in forensic work, and the British Society of Experimental and Clinical Hypnosis has recently issued a statement on its stand over the matter, which includes the suggestion that members of that Society should not agree to carry out such work.

GROUP HYPNOSIS

Hypnosis can be used in group settings as well as individually. Stage hypnotists commonly carry out an induction with the subjects who volunteer for demonstration *en masse*. The usual practice is to select the more susceptible subjects by a simple induction and challenge (such as inability to separate their hands or to remove their hands from the tops of the heads once placed there) and then use only those subjects who respond well to carry out the planned show. This instance is quoted simply to show that hypnotic states can be readily achieved even in public, and with several subjects at a time.

Light hypnotic states are induced in a variety of group situations for therapeutic purposes. These include ante-natal relaxation and preparation classes and anxiety-management and relaxation classes, whilst groups teaching hypnotic and

meditation techniques are increasingly used by business executives and others whose daily lives are conducted under high
pressure and who need to learn to 'switch off' and relax.

A group induction can be as specific as an individual
induction, but on occasion it is easier and more satisfactory to use
a highly permissive approach, which allows individual members
to choose their own imagery. Additional suggestions of systematically described progressive relaxation is the core of such an
induction. Script 3.5 ('Loosening of attention') can be readily
adapted to a group.

Alternatively the creation of a particular image such as a
beach, a river bank or a mountainside can be described,
employing as much detail and sense data as possible: sight,
hearing, touch, and smell.

Script 19.2   Group induction with imagery

*[The group members have been asked to make themselves
physically comfortable, loosening tight clothing, removing
shoes, etc. as they please.]*

You may like now to close your eyes to make it easier for you
to concentrate on what I say. I would like you first simply to
relax as completely as you find yourself able. Let your arms
and legs go limp, let your back and neck relax. Pay especial
attention to your shoulders: let them drop. Now think of your
face. Relax your cheeks and jaws. Let them go slack. Feel the
weight of your cheeks as you relax the muscles in your cheeks
and jaws. Relax the muscles in your forehead; let them stretch
and loosen. Let your forehead go loose and soft. Relax the
muscles around your eyes, so that you can feel your eyelids
resting softly and heavily on your eyes. Relax the muscles
around your mouth; let them go soft and loose. Soft and slack.
Don't worry if your mouth opens ... that is a measure of your
ability to relax ... just let go completely. Relax completely. ...
Relax completely.

Now focus your attention on your breathing. ... Breathe into
your tummy ... right down into your abdomen. As you do so,

over the next two or three minutes, notice that your breathing becomes slower and deeper. Let your breath reach deeper into your body each time you breathe in ... and each time you breathe out, let yourself go a little more and feel your body weigh a little more heavily into the chair. Deeper and deeper ... more and more relaxed. Good.

Imagine now that you are standing at the top of a sandy beach. It stretches away to each side of you, curving round to left and right. At each end of the beach there is a promontory stretching out towards the sea. Notice what you are wearing, and the colours and shapes you can see. ... The blue of the sky, the deep translucent colours of the sea, the little waves creating a dazzling line of foam at the water's edge. The sun is shining, and as you stand here, you can feel its heat on your skin. You can feel the warmth of its rays soaking into your body. Perhaps there is a soft breeze blowing, gently lifting the hair on your forehead. Notice the contrast between the warmth of the sun and the feel of the breeze. Notice too the smell of this beach, that particular combination of sea and salt, and the sounds of this place. ... The soft sounds of the ocean, the seabirds calling. This beach is your own private, personal place. A place where you can come to leave behind the worries of your everyday life and you can enjoy its peaceful warmth and tranquillity.

Now, where you are standing here on the beach, the sand is dry and loose. You might like to take your shoes and socks off so that you can feel the warm sand under your feet, loose and dry. As you do so, feel your feet sinking a little so that you can feel the warm dry sand between your toes. You might like to wriggle your feet around to get the feel of it better. As you look down the beach towards the water, you can see that a little way in front of you is the line that marks the top of the high tide, where there is a little band of bits of driftwood and dry seaweed. Perhaps you would like to walk down towards it, and as you do so, enjoy the sensation of the warm sand on your feet. As you reach that line, notice that the sand is a slightly different colour on the other side, and a different texture, because the sand you are standing on above the high-water line is always dry whilst below it, the sand is washed by the sea twice a day. It is still damp from the receding tide. Still further away is the edge of the sea, with little ripples gently breaking on to the sand.

I would like you now to step over the high-water mark and as you do so, notice how the texture of the sand under your feet changes, and also that it is not as warm as the dry sand on which you stood just now. It is firmer and a little cooler. As you walk on down to the water's edge, notice the sand gets cooler still and firmer, until, when you are close to the water, it becomes wet – and softer again – so that your toes sink into it. Stand there for a moment or two, or, if you would like to, step into the water and feel how refreshing and cool it feels on your feet and ankles. Enjoy the coolness under your feet contrasting with the warmth of the rest of your body, and the soft breeze on your skin. Listen to the sound of the water and the cries of seabirds. Notice the fresh smell of the sea, so that you can almost taste the clean fresh air. Take a deep breath of that lovely clean fresh air. ... Stand there and enjoy all the sensations you are receiving, from your feet, your skin, your nose, your mouth, your ears and eyes. Let the peace and beauty, the warmth and the ease of it all soak into you.

Enjoy the tranquillity of this place and the deep sense of physical well-being you are experiencing. *[Pause]*

Now turn back and walk up the beach again, noticing the change in texture under your feet as you reach the firmer sand near the high water mark. Pause as you step over the high water mark again, and look back at the sea, noticing at the same time the warmth and dryness of the sand under your feet here, perhaps sticking to your feet a little where they are still wet.

As you now enjoy the sensations and feelings connected with your beach, you also know that you will be able to come back to this beach at any time you wish in the future, simply by letting yourself relax, closing your eyes, and letting the picture of the beach build up in your mind, carefully noting what you

see, ... what you feel with your skin and under your feet, ...
the sounds of the sea and the seabirds ... and the smell of
the air.

In a little while, when you come back to the ordinary world
again, bring with you all the good feelings, so that when you
go about your life again, you go on feeling as relaxed and as
peaceful deep inside yourself as you do now.

Now let the picture of the beach fade from your mind. Just let
it fade, knowing that you can come back at any time you
wish. ... In its place, I would like you to picture what you saw
just before you closed your eyes today. Create a picture of the
room in which you are sitting. Remember the size and shape
of the room, the colour of the walls, the furniture *[here add
any appropriate details]*. ... Then, when you have a clear
picture in your mind's eye, let yourself come back to the
ordinary waking state. There is no rush, you can take your
own time ... and when you are ready, and the picture is clear,
you can let your eyes open, and as you do so check out that
the room is exactly as you pictured it would be. So, as the
picture forms, you can feel yourself becoming more and more
alert and awake, but still feeling completely relaxed and at
peace, and become fully awake.

Exercises such as this can be very helpful for general release of
tension, on their own or in conjunction with other tension-
management work. In addition, control of smoking or other habits
can be developed in a group setting in which such a session of
group hypnosis may form an important part.

The uses of hypnosis suggested in this chapter for
essentially non-clinical purposes do not form an exhaustive list.
Possible applications of hypnotic techniques are limited largely by
the imagination and creativity of the therapist and the demands
for his services, and further developments will be pursued by all
those sufficiently interested to explore this very satisfying field.

20

EPILOGUE

TRAINING IN HYPNOTHERAPY

Hypnosis is not a system of therapy but a technique that may be employed to mediate treatment. This has been repeatedly emphasized at different points in this book, and needs perhaps to be further discussed here. Anyone of reasonable intelligence and some sensitivity to his fellow-humans could be taught in a very short space of time to induce an hypnotic state in a willing subject and to evoke many of the hypnotic phenomena discussed. It is less easy, and takes a great deal longer, to train anyone to conduct psychotherapy in a professional and responsible way, and such training is vital if hypnotically mediated therapy is to be undertaken. The same is true of the use of hypnosis in the treatment of physical and psychosomatic disorders: the background of medicine, surgery or other appropriate disciplines is the necessary foundation for treatment.

Furthermore, the fact that hypnosis can be used to mask the symptoms of disease, and that some hypnotic techniques (such as age regression or other ways of precipitating abreaction) can be the trigger by which a fragile or inadequately defended personality can be precipitated into a seriously disintegrated or fragmented state, such as a psychotic episode, can make the use of hypnosis by persons lacking appropriate professional (clinical) qualifications and experience positively dangerous. These considerations make it imperative that proper diagnostic procedures are carried out before any attempt at treatment. Diagnosis can be made only on the basis of prior training and experience in the relevant disciplines, and training in hypnotherapy itself is not such a basis.

At present, hypnosis in Britain is not under any legal control other than that of the 1952 Hypnosis Act, which restricts its use in entertainment. Anyone can set themselves up in private practice as a 'hypnotherapist' and attract patients without any prior training, qualification or experience in medicine, psychology or other appropriate discipline. In addition, anyone may set up a training course, give themselves an impressive title, establish a 'professional association' and endow their trainees with high-sounding qualifications and memberships. This is at present a growth industry, and competition between rival 'colleges' and 'associations' for trainees and clients is growing.

Neither Parliament nor most of the relevant professional bodies express any interest in the regulation of the practice of hypnosis. In this connection, it is sad and disheartening to note that a general dilatoriness and obstructiveness have also bedevilled efforts to establish validated and regulated standards of training and professional ethics throughout the field of psychotherapy.

Naturally, medical practitioners, clinical psychologists and members of other health professions may equally well use hypnotic techniques without any prior training or guidance in their use. To be sure, amongst the older practitioners of these techniques, most are self-trained: since professionally-backed training has developed only in very recent years, no training was available to many of us. Training courses for doctors, dentists and psychologists are now provided by the British Society for Medical and Dental Hypnosis and the British Society of Experimental and Clinical Hypnosis as well as by a few individual psychologists and medical practitioners, including the present authors.

In Britain there are as yet no standards or validation for any of these training forums. The Australian Society of Hypnosis has established both a curriculum and a stringent examination in the principles and practice of hypnotherapy, and admission to membership of the Society involves rigorous training and passing this examination. It is hoped that similar developments will follow in Britain. At present, however, the most numerous and widely advertised training courses are those provided commercially by self-styled institutions, established more often than not by persons without any recognized relevant professional training or qualifications.

It is perfectly possible for any doctor or psychologist to acquire a basic skill in hypnotic techniques from books, and through trial and error with friends and family, and then to apply his pre-existing skills to the use of hypnosis with patients. More formal training, involving especially practice with colleagues under further supervision, is, however, vastly more satisfactory. In particular, confidence, fluency and recognition of the difficulties, pitfalls and limitations of the methods concerned are best acquired in a workshop or other training setting.

THE THERAPEUTIC RELATIONSHIP

The use of hypnosis alters the character and qualities of the patient–therapist relationship in a variety of ways, some subtle and others more obvious. The nature of the relationship which develops in the course of hypnotic work will depend markedly on the attitudes and expectations of the therapist. These may be directive and controlling, so that the patient is regarded as, and feels himself to be, the object for and of treatment. Alternatively, the therapist may present himself explicitly as no more than a guide and teacher, making patent his attitude that the patient himself is in control of the work being done. In this case, the patient and therapist occupy more closely similar relative status positions and may see each other as collaborators rather than as doctor and patient.

There is a marked feeling of intimacy in the contact between therapist and patient when using hypnosis which is rarely experienced in other forms of professional contact. Both the therapist and the patient feel a sense of closeness which seems to be related to the detachment from everyday reality, which is an integral part of the hypnotic state, and which somehow by-passes normal reticences. For example, many patients who would inhibit any impulse to weep, at least at an early stage of the therapeutic relationship, find it easy to give vent to feelings of sadness or grief in this way while in hypnosis. The 'as if' character of the hypnotic experience generally appears to enable many patients to expose emotions more freely than they would otherwise. The therapist is, at the same time, very directly involved with the patient's subjective experience: often more so than he would be in less directive forms of therapy, even when working in a highly permissive way.

This intimacy is a reality which is sometimes exploited by the unscrupulous and unprofessional to facilitate abuse, sexual or otherwise, and cases of such kinds occur from time to time. The patient in hypnosis is more vulnerable to such exploitation than in other forms of therapy, partly because of the intimacy which develops in this kind of work and partly because of the often rapid and ready access to the less overtly conscious parts of the patient's thoughts and feelings. Additionally, the use of imagery and fantasy which can, in the more apt subjects, amount to delusional beliefs and even hallucinations can make the patient more open to abuse.

One patient who had been to see a self-styled 'hypnotist and hypnotherapist' for persistent abdominal pain had been so assaulted. She had permitted the 'therapist' to place his hand on her abdomen while she was in hypnosis. He had suggested that the feeling of warmth from his hand would ease the pain and that gradually she would no longer feel the pain or his hand. After a little while, during which the suggestion he had made worked (that is, she no longer felt either pain or the touch of the hand), she became aware that his hand had moved to her genital area, at which point she came out of the trance in a highly disturbed and confused state.

The use of hypnosis can be improperly attractive to the untrained and non-professional for the same reason: the intimacy inherent in the situation and the intimate contact with the deeper levels of the patient's personality may prove irresistibly seductive, as may the perceived power the therapist can wield in this situation.

To the professional, there is considerable satisfaction in feeling that one is somehow more actively engaged with the patient than in more orthodox forms of psychotherapy. The *collaborative* character of hypnotic work gives the therapist a feeling of being very closely involved with what is happening, and the more equal *status* between therapist and patient may result in a very different relationship from the primarily transferential one of traditional psychodynamic therapy.

The transference is not necessarily avoided through the use of hypnosis. Indeed, transferential processes may become more readily and rapidly patent, but the therapist is as a rule more directly and realistically perceived by the patient when hypnosis is used properly and responsibly. The degree to which transferential characteristics develop in the relationship between patient and therapist depends in large measure upon the nature of the treatment programme. If the therapy undertaken is essentially of a behavioural kind, then patient and therapist are engaged as equals in a co-operative effort, and transference phenomena are likely to be minimal and in any event not the subject of therapy. If hypnotic techniques are employed in the course of a psychodynamic therapy, the transference is likely to be heightened. This can be powerfully utilized to disclose the projective processes involved and thus facilitate their resolution.

Many orthodox psychotherapists and analysts feel anxieties concerning the common belief that hypnosis and hypnotic experiences foster over-dependency and reduce self-determination on the part of the patient. It is hoped that the account given here of the nature and applications of hypnosis has allayed such anxieties. Hypnosis does not present such possibilities to any greater degree than therapy of any other kind. The regression that is a feature of the state is produced by any and all forms of effective therapy. Indeed, the same feature is to be observed in a patient consulting a medical practitioner for a physical ailment. Such regression in analytic therapy is a necessary process which is encouraged in order to work through the complexes and fixations from earlier stages in the patient's psychic development and thereby free him from archaic and over-determined (i.e. neurotic) reactions.

Hypnotic techniques can indeed be employed to establish over-dependency or to abrogate a patient's self-determination and sense of personal responsibility, but the same is equally true of other therapeutic techniques and is so to the same extent.

The potential of hypnotic techniques for *increasing* the ability of the patient to take control of his own functioning and to assume greater responsibility for determining his own reactions and behaviour has been repeatedly emphasized in this book. Properly and ethically used, hypnotic techniques will foster independence and self-reliance, and any use of these techniques that works otherwise will inevitably fail to achieve the proper targets of therapy.

Kroger (1977) offers a wise warning in suggesting that if induction of hypnosis and the evocation of hypnotic phenomena become highly attractive to the therapist, he should stop using the technique: he is then clearly doing it for his enjoyment rather than the benefit of the patient.

At the same time, psychotherapists who are quite accustomed to having their patients leave at the end of a session more distressed than they were when they arrived may find the use of hypnosis properly rewarding. It is decidedly more encouraging to have the patient leave feeling good about himself. In addition, the intensity and speed with which therapy proceeds from time to time brings a reward of considerable significance. Quite properly, hypnotic techniques can give the therapist a feeling of actually having *done* something which is often rather rare, and sometimes very necessary, for the therapist as well as for the patient.

This book is an endeavour to provide a basic introduction to the use of hypnosis in a variety of fields within the provision of health care. As noted in chapter 1, all that has been described has been drawn from the experience of the authors' own clinical practices. For this reason, the account given of hypnotherapeutic techniques may be more limited than in some books, since we have omitted anything of which we do not have first-hand experience, whether in terms of conditions or techniques. We have not listed nearly as many references as are commonly found, but those books that we have quoted are amongst the most useful. In any one of those books are further references, which we take to be subsumed in our bibliography.

We hope that this book will be found of practical use in the context of training and the early days of a practitioner's experience of working with hypnosis, and that it will be superseded as each practitioner's personal experience and increasing skills extend and he develops confidence in creating his own individual style and techniques.

NOTES

1. Turning the eyes upwards in their sockets induces strain and fatigue in the eye muscles more rapidly than in the normal position. In addition, for reasons that have never been clarified, this position of the eyes appears to be a positive aid in inducing trance. It has also been noted that the degree of an individual's hypnotic talent can be assessed by the degree to which the eyes will turn upwards: the more of the pupil and iris which can be turned up under the upper lid, the greater the hypnotizability of the subject.

2. Slow your delivery progressively as you begin to use more repetition.

3. The subject entering hypnosis for the first time has very little idea of what is expected of him or what he should do. It is therefore very important to give 'feedback': to let the patient know he is performing correctly. In addition, as the patient enters trance, so he begins to experience some degree of regression and is reassured, in his regressed state, by receiving explicit approval.

4. Blinking will inevitably occur from time to time. Timing the suggestion so that it immediately precedes or co-incides with blinking will enhance the patient's acceptance of suggestions yet to come. That is to say, when he find himself blinking shortly after the suggestion has been made, he will attribute the blinking to an hypnotic response to the suggestion even if, as often occurs, he did not attribute the sensations of eye fatigue to

suggestion, realizing that it is the natural consequence of maintained fixation. The more one can link suggestions and responses in this way, the stronger will be the patient's 'set', that is, his expectation of automatic response on his part to further suggestions.

5. If the suggestions concerning blinking were well timed, and the patient blinked increasingly, he will now expect his eyes to close 'involuntarily'. It is commonly observed that blinking at this point gradually slows and the lids remain closed for longer and longer periods. Careful timing will enable the therapist to make the suggestion of complete closure at such a point.

6. The phrasing here becomes ambiguous: simultaneously the words employed imply that the patient is *feeling himself* letting go and at the same time they are an *instruction* to 'let go'. Ambiguity of this kind makes suggestions more powerful and more acceptable. Resistance to direct suggestion or instruction, which we all feel on first exposure to an hypnotic induction, is reduced or by-passed by the permissive meaning of the phrasing.

7. The latter passage especially must be adapted to the actions of the patient. The last instruction ('Close your eyes') is occasionally necessary. Some subjects will struggle to re-open their eyes in what looks like (and will be reported as) a dazed and involuntary state and seem to need the instruction or permission to leave their eyes closed. As is pointed out in several contexts, the 'unconscious' is very literal, and it appears that the instruction given earlier ('Keep your eyes on that red disc') remains dominant until countermanded more or less directly.

8. See note 1. Keeping the pen a little above a comfortable forward glance, move it in a circle or ellipse, thus increasing muscular fatigue through the movements of the patient's eyes.

9. The distance from the eyes being less than a normal reading distance means that before long the patient will have increasing difficulty in maintaining binocular vision. The fatigue experienced through this, and the episodes of double vision that will follow, are utilized in inductions of this kind.

10. This instruction contains a contradiction: simultaneous effort and relaxation. The confusion engendered by this (bearing in mind the literal way the 'unconscious' interprets instructions) makes the subject more responsive to the suggestions that follow.

11. If there is delay or resistance in this process, try making the pen move in such an ellipse as to draw the eyes downwards as you say 'closing'. In this way the patient, who should be following the pen with his eyes without moving his head, will of course feel his eyelids moving downwards each time you say 'closing' and, even if he is strongly resistant, is very likely to close his eyes.

12. Remember the patient needs reassurance that all is going well, and that he is co-operating and working successfully.

13. An ordinary metronome run by clockwork can easily be made to flash a light. Remove the base of the metronome and attach to it, by elastic bands or adhesive tape, two small 1.5v batteries. Solder a wire from + on one to − on the other and two short lengths of wire, one to each of the remaining terminals. Connect one of these two short wires by solder to one of the contacts on a lens-tipped 3v bulb. Solder a further length of wire to the other contact on the bulb and solder the other end of this wire to one contact on a small toggle switch mounted on one side, or on the back, of the metronome case. The other terminal on the switch is then connected to the remaining wire from the batteries.

   Tape the bulb to the base of the metronome in front of the batteries so that it points forward. Drill a small hole in the front of the case, positioned so that when the bulb lights it casts its beam through the hole. Glue a small piece of metal foil to the weight at the lower end of the pendulum, cutting it so that it will not obstruct the movement. In this way, the light beam is interrupted by the metal foil as it passes to and fro across the hole. The beam of such a lamp is sufficiently strong to be seen brightly from ten feet or more away.

14.   A very similar induction is described by Barber (1969) using a metronome in this way. The script is, however, flawed in the eyes of many practitioners in its use of the word 'sleep'. Most people prefer to avoid any direct suggestion of the patient entering sleep.

15.   This is said, of course, in time with the metronome itself. All that is said from this point until the metronome is stopped is timed in cadence to the metronome.

16.   Naturally, this is said when the eyes are seen to blink more frequently.

17.   See previous note.

18.   Note the confusion created by contiguous conflicting instructions: on the one hand, to let yourself drift further away; on the other, to let *the world drift away*. Confusion tends to make it easier for the patient to 'let go'.

19.   Even with subjects who can accept the suggestion of inability to perform a normal action, it is as well to avoid using the phrase 'You *cannot open* your eyes', or anything similar. Phrases such as 'They will not open' or 'Your arm will not bend' (instead of 'You *cannot* bend your arm') are preferable.

20.   This tingling sensation follows naturally from a light touch. Its inclusion in the suggestion is an example of the use of natural phenomena to enhance belief in the process and thereby increase the patient's readiness to

accept and produce the suggested phenomena to order.

21. This again is a natural consequence of a very light touch.

22. Note the change from 'your hand' to 'that hand': the intention is that the patient should feel some degree of dissociation from the hand to facilitate the use of such dissociation in later work.

23. It can be helpful if the therapist places his hand firmly but lightly and briefly on the patient's hand to reinforce the suggestion of return to normality.

24. Note the return to 'your arm': the exercise in dissociation is over and it is reassuring to the patient to 're-claim' his arm.

25. Time each *'deeper'* to an inspiration.

26. Once the patient's eyes are closed, and even more so once some level of trance has been achieved, you should *never* touch him without warning or desist from touch without warning. Unheralded physical contact or unexpected loss of contact, as well as unexpected silence, can be very disturbing and can stimulate the patient into immediate arousal from trance, often with anxiety and sometimes anger, which can prejudice trust and co-operation.

27. Note the phrase 'all the rest of you'. The implication from your touch on the raised arm is that that arm will *not* relax and normally, in fact, the raised arm will be felt to become rigid as you *gradually* loosen your hold. It will then remain in position, often totally cataleptic, when you remove your hand. Once the arm is felt to be sufficiently stiff, let go of it for a short while. The patient will experience his arm remaining rigidly in the position into which you moved it, without feeling that he is holding it there himself. In consequence his belief in what is happening to himself is enhanced, and so is his responsiveness to further suggestions.

28.   There is a hidden suggestion embedded in this statement: that the arm had been in an abnormal state, thus again enhancing the patient's commitment to the hypnotic state.

29.   Note here again, as was pointed out in discussion of induction, that one needs to give the subject *warning* of anything unexpected. In addition to this warning aspect there is also the element of determining an expectation, which is especially valuable in forwarding the process involved.

30.   At the cost of being repetitious, the importance of undoing all suggested phenomena, other than things like feeling relaxed, a sense of well-being and so on, cannot be overemphasized. While preparing a patient who was in dread of her forthcoming labour, one of the authors used the image of a block of concrete resting heavily on the patient's foot. On moving to further images, this block was not explicitly removed. At the end of the session, when the patient was about to leave, she remarked that one foot still felt pressed to the floor by a weight. She had to return into trance for the concrete to be removed!

31.   If induction was by eye catalepsy, add: 'You will find that they open perfectly normally when I ask you to open them.'

32.   It is helpful to vary the pace so that after each eye-closure you begin fairly fast, and then slow progressively as the patient sinks deeper.

33.   Here again the pace is varied to emphasize the nature of the experience being sought. As you count back to one, start slowly but increase the pace steadily and progressively; as you count upwards from one again, and the patient is sinking down, begin quite fast and become progressively slower. In the final count, when the patient is clearly descending into a satisfactorily deep trance, allow longer and longer pauses between the last few

numbers. At the same time vary the pitch, intensity and volume of delivery, again emphasizing the *wakening* process as you count back to one, and the descent into quiet, calm and peace as you count upwards again. Thus the words 'wide awake' will be said really briskly, and the 'deep deep down' spoken quietly, slowly and in a deeper voice.

34.   Some patients are anxious that they might not be able to rouse themselves from the trance when on their own, or fear that they will spend too long in the trance before deciding to waken. This is especially the case with, for example, business executives for whom one has recommended regular periods of self-hypnotic relaxation to control blood pressure or other stress-related difficulties, who often jib at spending more than a few minutes in such practices. In these cases it is useful to specify the length of time they will remain in the trance, suggesting that at the end of that period they will rouse automatically and without any difficulty on their part, analogously to the common experience of waking just before the alarm clock rings. At the same time, of course, it is wise to explore the reasons for their difficulty in spending time on themselves.

35.   T.X. Barber and his colleagues devised a series of tests consisting of specific suggestions to produce various phenomena including arm levitation, immobility, etc. These are given verbatim and the patient's responses are quantified. The Scale is quoted in various publications, including Barber (1969).

36.   The Stanford Scale, which contains many of the same items as the Barber Scale, is perhaps more widely used in clinical practice. It will be found in Weitzenhoffer and Hilgard (1959; 1962; 1963).

37.   The Harvard Scales of hypnosis were devised by R.E. Shor and E.C. Orne. They can be found in Shor and Orne (1962).

38.   Naturally, if the patient went into a deep trance very quickly, this particular suggestion can be omitted.

39.   If you pause at this point to give the patient time to go on as you have suggested, make sure that you warn him that you are going to stop talking and that after an interval you will speak to him again. Alternatively, you might like to re-iterate the suggestions more slowly and quietly, leaving short pauses between the repetitions.

40.   Again, if you wish to leave a pause, warn the patient first.

41.   Some patients find it difficult to experience age regression unaided. Some, as previously discussed, cannot identify a good experience to which they may return. The script which follows is designed to facilitate regression to a good experience for such patients by simultaneously providing a focus for attention and a spur to memory.

42.   From this point on, until the patient signals that he has found the right picture, the suggestions are delivered more slowly, with longer pauses and in a quieter voice, simply to offer guidelines in case the patient is experiencing difficulty and to give time for the process to work.

43.   If the patient has not yet signalled, reiterate that he can take his own time leafing through the pages of the album and waiting for a memory to catch his attention.

44.   If the patient agrees, invite him to describe in as much detail as he possibly can the setting and event he is recalling. To enhance the immediacy of the experience, use the present continuous tense yourself, thus encouraging the patient to do the same. Emphasize also all five sensory modalities with suggestions such as: 'There may be a particular smell associated with this place', or 'Notice the feel of the sun/breeze/water on your body and the feel of the bank/bench/sand on which you are lying/sitting/standing.'
    If the patient does not wish to communicate the

content of his image, say: 'That's all right. Just pay especial attention to all that you can feel, see, hear, smell, and maybe even taste. Notice the temperature of the air on your skin and the feel of the surface on which you are standing, sitting or lying.'

It is very rare indeed for patients to report an empty album, even though they may need substantial time to allow an image to materialize. In such cases it will sometimes transpire that the image retrieved has mixed affective associations, such as, for example, a lady whose first response was to use her wedding day was currently suing for divorce. Her present circumstances did not, however, discount the value of using this memory.

45.   At this point, considerable ingenuity may be required of the therapist to identify and emphasize the good and positive affects which the patient indicates. He may, in telling you about the memory, intimate what sort of pleasurable affects he is experiencing, or you may reasonably hazard the feelings from the context, but if you have no idea of the content of the memory or the nature of the experiences he has re-created, much more general comments will be needed. These may be on the following lines: 'Notice how good you feel, how happy, how much you are enjoying yourself, how confident and strong you feel, how good it feels to be inside your own skin.'

46.   Note that the first instance of raising the cigarette is not associated with tension, but its distancing from the mouth is linked with relaxation. It is sometimes wise to repeat the exercise in this form at least once: the link between relaxation and non-performance should be primary, while the link between performance and tension should be secondary and serve also as a reinforcement of relaxation at non-performance. It is important to avoid an aversive emphasis in the whole process.

47.   In such cases, however, there is still a strong probability of resentment, anger and similar feelings directed towards the child concerned, but these are normally very deeply

hidden. It is highly likely that the increasing exhaustion of parents in such a situation stems at least in part from such feelings.

48.   For those not altogether familiar with the terminology of behaviour therapy, the following model will make the terms used here clear. A dog is presented with a plate of meat: he salivates. The meat is the *unconditioned stimulus*, salivation at this point is an *unconditioned response*. A bell is rung as the meat is presented, and the dog salivates. The meat, as before, is the unconditioned stimulus, and the salivation is still an unconditioned response. When this sequence has been repeated a number of times, a new sequence is initiated: the bell is rung, and the dog salivates, without any meat present. The bell is the *conditioned stimulus*, and salivation is now a *conditioned response*.

49.   It may be helpful to suggest that the patient uses a finger or hand, indicating the intensity of his anxiety by the degree to which he lifts the finger or hand, so that the finger rises as the anxiety increases and drops again as it is extinguished.

50.   A detailed account of one such experiment is reported by Eugene L. Bliss (1986, p.103).

51.   At the cost of being repetitious, the importance of giving the patient reassurance, confirmation and feedback about performance must be emphasized. Remember to add a 'Good!' whenever opportunity offers.

52.   Once anaesthesia has developed, the patient will have little or no idea of where his hand is in space and may find it very difficult to move it to a specific target. Therefore take the hand at the wrist, so that your hold is above the limit of anaesthesia. If you hold it distally of that limit, the patient will probably be unaware of your touch, and the absurdity, and perhaps frightening quality, of feeling his arm forcibly moved by an unfelt touch could disrupt the process.

53. This incident provides a useful illustration of an important point. From time to time, patients of any age may appear to make no response at all to an induction. With children this may be especially disconcerting, yet it need not be so. The child in the present illustration responded very well in the dialogue which occurred when it became obvious that there was no response at all to the first induction. This had been in the form of eye-fixation on a coin held by the child.

Therapist:	That didn't work very well, did it?
Child:	[with a giggle] No.
Therapist:	Shall we try a different way to get to fairy-land?
Child:	Yes.
Therapist:	Well, put your magic key down on the chair, there, so you can look at it if you want, but perhaps you should close your eyes, because I would like you to imagine something, and that's easier to do with your eyes closed. Yes, good, like that. Now, imagine that there is a balloon tied to your hand, there...[etc.]

54. The Italian L500 coin is especially apt for this use. It consists of a brown metal coin apparently inserted inside a larger white metal coin, and is both heavy and slippery to the touch. Its noticeable difference from familiar coins is an asset, while its weight and slipperiness help it to slip through the fingers. Another useful object is a small card with three rectangles on it, in strong, almost fluorescent, primary colours. As one stares at such a card, one begins to see patches of the complementary colours. This illusion can be built into the patter.

55. See the previous note concerning suitable coins, etc.

56. If necessary, encourage the child to extend one hand to the appropriate place, even to the extent of gently drawing the hand out.

57.   Again, if necessary, encourage and assist the child to place the hand appropriately.

58.   Show the child by example what is expected.

59.   The therapist continues to bounce his balloon unless or until the child does so freely himself.

60.   If the child does not seem to be able to allow the hand to rise, make further suggestions such as: 'Just try resting your hand on the balloon so that you can feel it being lifted up and floating higher and higher on top of the balloon.'

61.   Time the count to exhalations.

62.   This refers ambiguously or dually to the inner picture or fantasy and to the 'real world' of the consulting room. This involves some degree of confusion, which is helpful, but particularly ties the child's experience of that moment down in verbal form and expresses the therapist's awareness of what the child is experiencing, which is reassuring.

63.   Remember here the importance of using words which are within the vocabulary of the family!

64.   The content of the suggested dream begins with material from a bad dream which the child has described.

65.   The term 'illness behaviour' is used in two quite different senses in different areas of medicine. In paediatrics and child psychiatry it is used in the sense of behaviour that mimics the symptoms of an illness from which the child has suffered after the disorder is relieved. In medical sociology the term is, of course, used in a quite different sense.

66.   Note the use of the present tense. Patients will often be unable initially to immerse themselves in the recovered experience, but the therapist's use of the present tense will

gradually lead the patient into using it himself and going progressively into full involvement with the memory, thus turning it into 're-experience' rather than recall.

67.   Continue to work at gaining an adequate picture of the patient's world at this point, and if necessary make suggestions of getting older or younger to search for the actual event or situation which has been identified as important. The patient's report of his experience will guide the therapist's interventions.

BIBLIOGRAPHY

Barber, T.X.   (1969) *Hypnosis: A Scientific Approach.* New York: Van Nostrand Reinhold.

Beahrs, J.O.   (1982) *Unity and Multiplicity.* New York: Brunner/Mazel.

Berne, E.   (1964) *Games People Play.* Harmondsworth: Penguin.

Bliss, E.L.   (1986) *Multiple Personality, Allied Disorders, and Hypnosis.* London/New York: Oxford University Press.

Burrows, G.D. and Dennerstein, L.
(1980) *Handbook of Hypnosis and Psychosomatic Medicine.* Amsterdam: Elsevier/North-Holland Biomedical Press.

Caplan, G.   (1964) *Principles of Preventive Psychiatry.* New York: Basic.

Chapman, L.F., Goodell, H. and Wolff, H.G.
(1959) 'Changes in tissue vulnerability induced during hypnotic suggestion', *Journal of Psychosomatic Research* 4:99-105.

Collison, D.R.   (1980) 'Hypnosis and respiratory disease', in Burrows, G.D. and Dennerstein, L., *Handbook of Hypnosis and Psychosomatic Medicine.* Amsterdam: Elsevier/North-Holland Biomedical Press.

Crasilneck, H.B. and Hall, J.A.
(1985) *Clinical Hypnosis: Principles and Applications.* New York/London: Grune & Stratton.

Dixon, N.F.   (1981) *Preconscious Processing.* Chichester: Wiley.

DSM-III   (1980) *The Diagnostic and Statistical Manual of*

Mental Disorders. American Psychiatric
Association.

Edelstien, M.G. (1981) *Trauma, Trance, and Transformation.* New
York: Brunner/Mazel.

Erickson, M.H., Hershman, S. and Secter, I.I.
(1981) *The Practical Application of Medical and
Dental Hypnosis.* Chicago: Seminars on Hypnosis
Publishing Company.

Gardner, G.G. and Olness, K.
(1981) *Hypnosis and Hypnotherapy with
Children.* New York: Grune & Stratton.

Gellner, E. (1985) *The Psychoanalytic Movement.* London:
Paladin.

Hartland, J. (1971) *Medical and Dental Hypnosis and its
Clinical Applications.* London: Baillière Tindall.

Hilgard, J.R. and LeBaron, S.
(1984) *Hypnotherapy of Pain in Children with
Cancer.* Los Alto, CA: William Kaufmann.

ICD (1977) *International Classification of Diseases.*
London: HMSO.

Jackson, J.A. and Merrington, H.N.
(1980) 'Hypnosis in family medicine' in
Burrows, G.D. and Dennerstein, L., *Handbook of
Hypnosis and Psychosomatic Medicine.*
Amsterdam:
Elsevier/North-Holland Biomedical Press.

Karle, H.W.A. (1984) 'Hypnosis as an adjunct in analytic
psychotherapy', *Proceedings of 1st Annual
Conference,* British Society of Experimental and
Clinical Hypnosis.
(1985) 'Hypnotherapy in the treatment of
childhood eczema', *Proceedings of 2nd Annual
Conference,* British Society of Experimental and
Clinical Hypnosis (on audiotape only).
(1986) 'Ego state therapy in a case of
childhood sexual abuse', *Proceedings of the 3rd
Annual Conference,* The British Society of
Experimental and Clinical Hypnosis.
(1987a) *Hypnosis and Hypnotherapy: A Patient's
Guide.* London: Thorsons.

(1987b) 'Hypnosis in psychotherapy in the 1980s', *Free Associations* 8:58–80

Kroger, W.S.   (1977) *Clinical and Experimental Hypnosis.* Philadelphia, PA: J.B. Lippincott.

Marks, N., Onisiphorou, C. and Karle, H.W.A.
(1985) 'A controlled trial of hypnotherapy in tinnitus', *Clinical Otolaryngology* 10:43–6.

Mitchell, S.L.   (1914) in B. Sidis, *Symptomatology, Psychognosis and Diagnosis of Psychopathic Diseases.* Boston, MA: Richard G. Badger.

Rimm, D. and Masters, J.
(1979) *Behavior Therapy: Techniques and Empirical Findings.* New York: Academic Press.

Schreiber, F.H. (1974) *Sybil.* Harmondsworth: Penguin.

Sharff, D.E.   (1982) *The Sexual Relationship.* Boston/London: Routledge & Kegan Paul.

Shor, R.E. and Orne, E.C.
(1962) *The Harvard Group Scale of Hypnotic Susceptibility Form A.* Palo Alto, CA: Consulting Psychologists Press.

Watkins, H. and J.
(1979) 'The theory and practice of ego state therapy', in H. Grayson, ed. *Short-term Approaches to Psychotherapy.* New York: National Institute for the Psychotherapies and Human Sciences Press.

Weitzenhoffer, A.M. and Hilgard, E.R.
(1959) *Stanford Hypnotic Susceptibility Scale Forms A and B.* Palo Alto, CA: Consulting Psychologists Press.
(1962) *Stanford Hypnotic Susceptibility Scale Form C.* Palo Alto, CA: Consulting Psychologists Press.
(1963) *Stanford Profile Scale of Hypnotic Susceptibility, Forms I and II.* Palo Alto, CA: Consulting Psychologists Press.

Wolpe, J.   (1958) *Psychotherapy by Reciprocal Inhibition.* Stanford, CA: Stanford University Press.

Wright, E.   (1979) *The New Childbirth.* London: Spar Books.

Index of Scripts

INDUCTION

Script	Page	
3.1	24–6	Preparation of Patient
3.2	31–2	Induction with Stationary Eye-Fixation (red disc) with Relaxation
3.3	32–3	Eye-Fixation with Movement (pen tip) with Relaxation
3.4	33–4	Eye-Fixation with Intermittent Stimulus (metronome) with Relaxation
3.5	34–5	Loosening of Attention with Relaxation
3.6	35–6	Eye-Catalepsy (inhibition of opening)
3.7	36–7	Touch, Tingle, Twitch, and Arm Levitation
3.8	38	Eye-Catalepsy (Eye Roll)
3.9	39	Pacing and Leading with Slowed Breathing
3.10	39–40	Distraction and Confusion (Triple Instruction)
3.11	40–1	Contradiction (Rocking)
	42	Abbreviated ('Instant') Induction

DEEPENING

4.1	46	Relaxation and Suggestion (of deepening)
4.2	47–8	Terrace and Steps
4.3	48	Escalator
4.4	49–50	Arm Levitation
4.5	50–1	Fractionating (opening and closing of eyes)
4.6	51–2	Fractionating (counting up and down)

SELF-HYPNOSIS

5.1	58–9	Training (three breaths and counting)
5.2	60–1	Training (eye roll and exhalation)
5.3	61	Abbreviated Self-Induction with 'Key Word' for Use in
	62–3	Taped Inductions

FIRST INTERVIEW

Script	Page	
6.1	69	Preparation of Patient
6.2	72	Post-Hypnotic Suggestion for Future Induction
6.3	73	Suggestions of Benefit from Self-Hypnosis
6.4	74	Age Regression (known Private Place)
6.5	74	Age Regression (to find Private Place)
6.6	75	Age Regression to Private Place (photograph album)
6.7	76–7	Private Place Constructed by Therapist (woodland scene)
6.8	78 }	
6.9	79 }	Post-Hypnotic Suggestion of Benefit from Trance

TREATMENT STRATEGIES

7.1	88–90	Smoking
7.2	98–9	Insomnia

PHYSICAL AND PSYCHOSOMATIC DISORDERS

8.1	106–8	Private Place (for stress reduction) and Age Progression (to recovery)
8.2	110–11	Hypertension

ANXIETY

9.1	122–5	Anxiety Management with Imagery (garden) and 'Key Word'

PAIN

10.1	137–8	Glove Anaesthesia, Transfer of Anaesthesia
10.2	139	Induction of Anaesthesia by Touch
10.3	142–4	Analgesia (with warmth)

INDUCTIONS WITH CHILDREN

	152 }	
	158 }	Suggestions Incorporating Present Environment
	165 }	
11.1	153	Introducing Fairy-Tale
11.2	155–6	Post-Hypnotic Suggestion for Self-Hypnosis (in eczema)
11.3	158–9	Eye-Fixation ('Magic Key')
11.4	160	Balloon on Water
11.5	162	Magnetic Hands

Script Page
11.6   163   Finger Lowering
11.7   163–4   Secret Door

HABIT AND BEHAVIOUR DISORDERS IN CHILDREN

12.1   169–71 Nail-Biting/Picking
12.2   174–5   Enuresis
12.3   176–7   Bad Dreams

UNCOVERING TECHNIQUES

16.1   227–9   Age Regression to Known Period (clock)
16.2   229–30 Age Regression by Affect Bridge (to unknown period)
16.3   230   Age Regression to Known Event (TV screen)

OTHER USES

19.1   264–5   Information Retrieval (examinations) with Imagery (library)
19.2   267–70 Group Induction (beach)

INDEX

Abbreviated induction 30, 42
Abreaction 20, 55, 210, **225**, 236, 271
Addictions 257
  drink 258
Adolescence 103, 105, 150, **164**, 187
Affect bridge **223-4**, 234, 239
Age progression 103, 106, 170
  technique 107
Age regression 17, 53, 69, 121, 129, 217–18, **223-31**, 234, 237, 239, 241, 265, 271
  techniques 224, **227**, 230
Agoraphobia; *see* Chapter 9
Altered state of consciousness 9
Alternate personality; *see* Multiple personality
Ambivalence
  in feelings 219, 221–2
  to treatment 67, 77
American Medical Association 244
Amnesia 225, 236
  spontaneous 10
  suggested 46
  see also Chapter 18
Anaesthesia 122, 152, 156
  'glove' 133
  induction of 145–51
  precautions 114, 135
'Anchoring' 138
  see also 'Key' word
Anorexia nervosa 99
Anxiety; *see* Chapter 9
  management; *see* Stress

Apprehension about hypnosis 23, 47, 56, 67, 70
Arousal
  heightened (autonomic) 16, 56, 109
  from hypnosis 51, 164
  in physical conditions 110, 184
  reduction of 118, 128
  self-arousal from hypnosis 59, 61–5
Assessment
  for hypnosis 66, 70
  importance of 83
  of susceptibility 150
  of trance 52
  for treatment 67, 68–9, 84, 86, 189
  see also Diagnosis
Asthma 114
  in children 183
  contraindications for hypnosis 114, 183
Australia 6, 187, 272
Autonomic system 13, 15, 104
  imagery for control of 110–11
Aversive techniques 85–6, 91, 93

Babinski reflex 17
Back pain 68, 134, **140–44**
Barber, T.X. 10, 21, 70
Beahrs, J.O. 201, 212, 242, 244, 245
Behaviour disorders (in children): *see* Chapter 12
Behaviour modification

and hypnosis 14
see also Anorexia nervosa,
    Aversive techniques,
    Behaviour disorders,
    Conditioned reflex,
    Conditioned response,
    Desensitization, Enuresis,
    Generalization, Habit
    disorders, Learned behaviour,
    Mass practice, Paradoxical
    intention, Reciprocal
    inhibition
Beliefs, importance of 11–12, 23–4,
    28, 103–5, 212, 233
Birth
    experience of 17, 208–9
Bleeding 16, 109
Bliss E.L. 212, 242, 244, 245, 286
Blood pressure: *see* Hypertension
Borderline personality; *see*
    Contraindications for hypnosis
Bowel control 96
British Society of Experimental and
    Clinical Hypnosis 4, 5, 26,
    266, 272
British Society of Medical and
    Dental Hypnosis 4, 272
Bulimia 100
Burns 16, 41, 109, 181
Burrows, G.D. and Dennerstein, L.
    112, 257
Burrows, Professor G. 254

Co-consciousness 202, 212, 245
Complexes 210, 275
Conditioned response 42, 92, 117,
    126, 286
Conditioned stimulus 118, 286
Confusion: *see* Induction
Contradiction: *see* Induction
Contraindications for hypnosis,
    256, 271
    see also Assessment, Asthma,
    Diagnosis
Conversion states 133, 180–1
Counter-transference 200
Crasilneck, H.B. and Hall, J.A. 41,

83, 91, 145, 257
Cultural differences in
    hypnotizability 19

Dangers, in the use of hypnosis 6,
    120
    see also Asthma
Day-dreaming 13
Deepening; *see* Chapter 4
    35, 42
Defence mechanisms; *see* Ego
    defences
Delivery, techniques of, in hypnosis
    3, 29–31
    see also Pacing
Dentistry, use of hypnosis in 16,
    108–9, 132, 144
Depression 120, 188–9, 190, 208,
    214, 219–20, 222, 250
    anaclitic 238–9
Depth of trance 44–56
Desensitization 14, 105, 117–18,
    127–9, 140, 263
Diagnosis, importance of 8, 120,
    166–7, 171, 176, 188–9, 242,
    259, 271
Difficulties in hypnosis 53–5
Directorate 245
Displacement behaviour 167–8
Dissociation; *see* Chapter 18
Distraction 133
    see also Induction
Dixon, N.F. 212
Dreams, bad 176–8
Drink: *see* Addictions

Eczema; *see* Skin disorders
Edelstien, M.G. 19, 41, 70, 252,
    253
Eeyore; *see* Milne, A.A.
Ego defences 18, 204, 215, 223,
    256
Ego state 14
    therapy 246–56
Ego-strengthening 73, 106, 108,
    146, 164, 176, 227, 229, 260
'Empty chair' 249

'Empty habits' 83–4, 94, 126, 166, 168, 176, 189
'Empty' symptom; *see* Symptoms
Enuresis in adults 95, 97
   in children 166, 171–6, 193
Erickson, M.H. 41, 52
Esdaile, J. 131
Ewin, D.B. 41, 109, 181
Examination 'nerves' 263–5
Expectations, correcting patients' 23
Eye-catalepsy; *see* Induction
Eye-fixation 28
   with children 158–9
   see also Induction

Face-saving, need for 86
Fairy-tales (in inductions with children) 150–1, 159
Fantasy 17
Features of the hypnotic state 12–13
Forensic uses of hypnosis 257, 265
Fractionating 50–2
Free association 20, 204
Freud, Sigmund 17, 19, 20, 200, 201, 202, 204, 209, 210, 212, 225, 245

Gardner, G.G. and Olness, K. 161, 187
Gellner, E. 201
Generalization, in hypnosis 14
Gestalt technique; *see* 'Empty chair'
Gilles de la Tourette syndrome 27
Group hypnosis 266–70

Habit disorders
   in adults; *see* Chapter 7
   in children; *see* Chapter 12
Hair-pulling 94, 166
Hartland, J. 41, 73, 204, 258
Hayfever 27
Headaches 57, 140, 142
   after hypnosis 65
   migraine 57, 140
'Hidden observer' 252

Hilgard, J.R. and LeBaron, S. 131, 140, 184, 187
Hypertension 110–11
Hypnosis Act of 1952 4, 271–2
Hypnotic state 11, 12–15, 22, 23–5, 44, 56
   see also Chapter 2
Hypnotizability 19, 70
   scales of 70, 283

Ideo-motor signalling 135, 226–7, 229
Illness behaviour 180–1, 288
Imagery
   matching to patient 27, 45–6, 77
   see Chapters on Induction, Deepening, Self-hypnosis, Treatment Strategies, Uncovering Techniques
Impotence 38
   see also Psychosexual problems
Incontinence; *see* Enuresis
Induction; *see* Chapter 3
   abbreviated 30, 42
   arm levitation 36
   with children 158–65
   contradiction 40
   distraction and confusion 39
   eye-catalepsy 35, 38
   eye-fixation, stationary 31–2
   eye-fixation with intermittent stimulus (metronome) 33–4
   eye-fixation with movement 32–3
   loosening of attention 34–5
   observation of patient (importance of) 30
   pacing and leading 39
   principles 28
Inhibition, suggestions of 35, 127–8
Insight 202–3, 204–5, 210, 211, 220, 222, 234–5
Insomnia; *see* Sleep
International Congress of Hypnosis and Psychosomatic Medicine 183, 208

International Society for Hypnosis 13, 208
Itching: *see* Skin disorders

Karle, H.W.A. 27, 112, 182, 247, 250
'Key' word 57, 61, 118, 125–8, 263
Kroger, W.S. 41, 54, 70, 85, 91, 145, 258, 275

Labour, hypnosis in 130, 144–5
Language, importance of 150, 192
'Laughing place' 41
Learned behaviour 167, 211, 214, 232–3
Levitation, arm 36, 44, 49–50
Lewis, C.S. 194

'Magic finger' 183
'Magic key' 155, 158
Mass practice 260
Mesmer, A. 255
Metronome, use of in induction 33–4, 279–80
Migraine: *see* Headaches
Milne, A.A. 214
Mitchell, S.L. 20, 204
Mood, disorders of
    in adults: *see* Chapter 9
    in children: *see* Chapter 14
Moro reflex 17
Motivation: *see* Assessment (for treatment), Resistance, Symptoms (meaning of)
Multiple personality: *see* Chapter 18

Nail-biting, in children 166, 169–71
Needle phobia 140
Negative hallucinations 12

Observation, importance of: *see* Induction
Observer phenomenon 18, 248
Obsessive-compulsive anxiety 35

Oculo-motor fatigue 22, 28, 32–5
Orne, M. 243
Over-determination 83, 100, 166–7

Pacing 29, 39
Pain 5–6, 16, 41, 42, 44, 54, 56–7, 59–60, 68, 72, 153–5
    in accidental injuries 11
    in adults: *see* Chapter 10
    in children: *see* Chapter 13
    management of 105–8
    precautions in treatment of 135–6
Panic attacks 72–3, 124–5, 129, 216–18, 229, 233
    see also Anxiety, Chapter 9
Paradoxical intention 260
Parasympathetic system: *see* Autonomic system
Part-personality: *see* Multiple personality
Personality
    changes through treatment 211, 220, 256
    development, normal 205–8, 213–15
    abnormal 222
    in induction 31, 71
    learned 195
    suitability for hypnosis 67–8, 235
    in tinnitus 145
    unsuitability for hypnosis 258, 271
    vulnerability to trauma 102
    see also Chapters 15 and 18
Phobias: *see* Chapter 9
Photograph album 75
Preparation
    of children 149–52, 156
    for hypnosis 66
    for treatment plan 69, 85, 87
    see also Expectations
Primary-process thinking 13
Principles of induction 28–9
Private Place 27, 73–7
    see also Chapters on Treatment Strategies

Psoriasis: see Skin disorders
Psychoanalytic concepts
 definition of 199–213
 in model of personality
  development 205–11
 see also Abreaction, Complexes,
  Counter-transference, Ego
  Defences, Insight, Reality
  testing, Re-cathexis,
  Regression, Transference,
  Unconscious, 'Working
  through'
 see also Chapter 15
 Psychosexual problems: see
  Sexual dysfunction
Psychosomatic: see Chapter 8

Qualifications, professional 4,
 271–3

Reality testing 12, 15, 18, 252
Re-cathexis 238
Reciprocal inhibition 117, 130
Regression
 in hypnosis 13, 20
 hypnotic technique: see Age
  regression
 psychoanalytic 103, 104, 185
Relaxation 16, 27, 31–2, 33–5, 46,
 117–18, 126, 132, 142–3,
 144
Repression 6, 18, 100, 116
 see also Dissociation
 see also Chapters 15 and 16
Resistance
 to hypnosis
  in adults 72
  in children 19, 157; 184–5
 to treatment 67, 84, 85, 88
 see also Ambivalence
Rimm, D. and Masters, J. 260

Secondary-process thinking 12
Self-hypnosis
 in children 161, 173, 175
 precautions in 59, 61, 63
 in treatment programmes 26, 56,
  71, 72–3, 79, 99, 108, 113,

122, 258, 262, 264
 see also Chapter 5
Self-image
 in assessment for treatment 84,
  91, 103
 in children 112
 after surgery 108
Sensorium 16
Sexual dysfunction 220–2, 259–60
Sharff, D.E. 259
Skin disorders
 in adults 16, 112–14
 in children 154, 182–4
Sleep
 in adults 11, 63, 64–5, 83–5,
  97–9
 in children 178
Smoking 83, 88–91, 270
'Split personality': see Chapter 18
Splitting
 of affect 20
 of awareness in hypnosis 12, 14,
  18
 see also Co-consciousness
Stage fright 263
Stress
 management of 28, 71, 107,
  146, 246, 262
 in symptoms 68, 102, 126, 218
Suckling 206–7
Suggestion
 importance of un-doing 37, 282
 post-hypnotic 15
Susceptibility to hypnosis: see
 Hypnotizability
Symptoms
 'empty' 126, 189; see also 'Empty
  habits'
 meaning of 95, 100, 120, 126,
  133, 141, 166–9, 172, 180,
  184, 210, 216, 232–5, 238;
  see also Stress
 removal of 15, 20, 67, 68, 72,
  116, 142, 145, 153, 182,
  211, 260–1

substitution 83

Tape-recorder 2, 58, 62–3
Temper tantrums/outbursts 59,
   153, 191, 192
Terminal illness 187
Therapeutic relationship 273–6
   see also Transference
Tics 261
Tinnitus 145–6
Training: *see* Qualifications
Trance: *see* Hypnotic state
Transactional analysis 208, 244
Transference 13, 20, 199–200,
   211, 214, 221, 231, 234, 274

Unconscious
   affect 55, 97, 218
   beliefs 103–5, 212–13
   communication with 226–7
   conflict 94–5, 259
   determinants of behaviour 126,
      166, 180, 189
   nature of 200–2, 211–12
   resistance 71, 185

Uncovering techniques: *see* Chapter
   16
   in anxiety 116
   precautions 55

Vasoconstriction 16
Vasodilation 16

Watkins, H. and J. 252
Weitzenhoffer, A.M. and Hilgard,
   E.R. 19
Wicks, Graham 13
Withdrawal symptoms 88, 90, 92,
   93
Wolpe, J. 117
'Working through' 204, 239
Wright, F. 144